Dreamseekers

DEWI ANGGRAENI

Dreamseekers
Indonesian Women
as Domestic Workers in Asia

EQUINOX
PUBLISHING
JAKARTA SINGAPORE

first published in Jakarta in 2006 by

PT Equinox Publishing Indonesia
Menara Gracia, 6th floor
Jl. H.R. Rasuna Said Kav. C-17
Jakarta 12940 • Indonesia
www.EquinoxPublishing.com

and

International Labour Organization
Menara Thamrin 22nd floor
Jl. MH. Thamrin Kav. 3
Jakarta 10250 • Indonesia
www.ilo.org

DREAMSEEKERS: Indonesian Women as Domestic Workers in Asia
by Dewi Anggraeni

ISBN 979-3780-28-2

©2006 International Labour Organization

Printed in Indonesia.

10 9 8 7 6 5 4 3 2 1

TABLE OF CONTENTS

ACKNOWLEDGEMENTS

This book is a labour of love and determination, but I alone did not make the book. Without the commitment, participation, and sustained support of many people, the book would remain merely an idea.

First and foremost, I would like to thank the International Labour Organization, Jakarta Office who committed the funds for the research, especially Peter Rademaker, Lotte Kejser and Dorothea Soetiman who have consistently extended all necessary assistance.

In fact, wherever I went in the course of my research, I have always received untiring assistance from close friends, acquaintances, and even strangers.

I would like to thank Widarti Gunawan and Goenawan Mohamad in particular for looking after me and my well-being whenever I was in Indonesia, in many ways impossible to enumerate here. In Australia I am indebted to Ian Fraser for being a patient sounding board, and all my friends who quietly supported me and gave me the encouragement needed.

For my research in Hong Kong, Lestari Dewi accompanied me during most of my first visit for this book, Michael and Janick Vatikiotis kindly assisted by introducing me to their friends who employed domestic helpers from Indonesia. Vivien Wee and Amy Sim enlightened me on many points. Suraya Kamaruzzaman provided me with valuable inputs, and linked me up with Lestari Dewi and Eny Lestari. Muljono Harto helped me to see the situ-

ation from the perspective of local employment agencies. I am also grateful
for the input from Kholifah, Mega Everistianawati, Karsiwulan, Utami, Xu
Xi, and also every single interviewee who asked me not to publish their real
names, and those whose stories provided me with background information. I
greatly appreciate the time given by the Indonesian Consul General, Paiman
Turnip, the Consul on Information Affairs, Dwatmaji Hanomanresi, and the
Consul and Counsellor Enny B Hardjito for the interview and informal chats.
My gratitude also goes to Jenny Fung, Lilian, Elsa Lam, Tony Ng, Ernawaty
Jose, and other employers of Indonesian helpers who told their stories in
informal chats.

In Singapore, I am grateful to Jennifer Lindsay and TWC2's dedicated
workers and networkers, namely Nancy Chng, Braema Mathi, Noorashikin
Abdul Rahman, Constance Singam, and Nai Rui Chng. My thanks also go
to Ming Chrng Chiang and his mother, Helen Tan, Alvin Pang, Amy Fatah,
Lisa I S, Cahyadi Indrananto, Russel Heng, Elizabeth Tan, Hadibah Chew,
Lee Koon, Siti Nuyasaroh, for their generosity in providing inputs and for
linking me up with wider networks. I am indebted to Mohamed Muzammil
Mohamed for helping me to understand the situation from the perspective
of an officer of the court, thus enhancing my understanding of the complex
issue. The Indonesian Embassy's First Secretary (Protocol and Consular)
Fachry Sulaiman obliged me among his very busy schedules, providing me
with valuable inputs and information. My thanks also go to my interviewees
Ninik, Indarti, Yanti, and those who asked not to be identified.

In Malaysia, my thanks go to Meera Samanther, Jessie Ang, Mr and Mrs
Zaman, Dina Zaman, Jeffrey Foo, for opening so many windows in order for
me to broaden my understanding of the situation in Malaysia. Meera painted
a very detailed picture from several angles: legal, social and personal, while
Jessie provided a close knowledge of how the mismatch of expectations occur when the domestic helpers come in contact with the law in this country.
The Indonesian Ambassador, Rusdihardjo, generously shared a great deal of
information and thoughts on the matter, for which I am very grateful. Many
thanks to Zaenab, Sirat, and many others in employment who asked not to
be identified. And without those with whom I had informal chats during my
stay in Malaysia my grasp of the more subtle aspects of the situation would
have been much weaker.

In Indonesia I would like to thank Fikri Jufri and Benny Hoedoro Hoed for their general support, Salma Safitri for providing me with very important angles to the issue, Sinta Nasution and Rusdi Nasution for linking me up with a broader network, Hussein Alaydrus and other executive office holders of APJATI for their valuable thoughts, Wedya Julianti and Juni Djamaloeddin for looking after me in general, Myra M Hanartani and Andi Syahrul Pangerang for shedding light on the government's angles, E A Tamara, Sri Murtiningsih, Sunari Harijono, Tuti Sanarto, Arti, Endah Nuraini, Suprapti, Wellem Liem and Jimmy Liem, for showing me the benevolent and important aspects of the business of recruitment and employment agencies. Lexy Rambadetta kindly shared his visual documentation with me.

All the names mentioned above are by no means exhaustive in terms of the people who have assisted and supported me during my research of this book. And I am grateful to you all.

Last but not least, allow me to express my sincere thanks to Mark Hanusz of Equinox Publishing for his unwavering faith in the manuscript and subsequent determination to co-publish it with ILO.

Dewi Anggraeni
April 2006

OPENING REMARKS
PROVIDING A CONTEXT TO NEWS ITEMS

Over the last two decades we have read about, heard of and seen in the print and electronic media, Indonesian women who come to grief when working overseas as domestic helpers. Since there has not been a sustained coverage of the issue in the media, however, the disconnected nature of the news reporting has not painted a clear overall picture of the situation.

Workers' migration is not a new phenomenon in Southeast Asia. It has been going on since the late 19th century. And labour movement from Java began in earnest when the Dutch colonial government started sending impoverished and landless farmers to Suriname toward the end of 19th century, to work in sugar, coffee and cotton plantations. Then at the beginning of the 20th century, New Caledonia emerged as another destination for more landless Javanese, where they were then indentured to work in coffee plantations.

The workers were all male.

The late 1970s marks a watershed when there was a definite feminization of the migrant labour force. Since then, approximately 70 percent of the workers leaving Indonesia for Saudi Arabia, Malaysia, Singapore, Hong Kong, Korea and for a time, Taiwan, have been women who seek work as domestic helpers.

Sporadic news items then started to appear raising a public awareness that things were not working well for some of the women. Various instances were revealed which should have caused alarm back home. Some women were duped into forced prostitution. Those who were not, and found employment in homes as intended, were not all treated well either. Many were abused in a number of ways.

From time to time there have been cases which triggered anger in the community back home in Indonesia because of the severity of the abuse. After some time, however, they have invariably been forgotten, except by some non-government organizations who specifically concern themselves with women's rights and violence against women.

In the last decade, endeavors to highlight the plight of these women on the part of domestic and international organizations have driven the Indonesian Government to attempt some improvements, though sadly, the situation has nowhere reached a point where those involved can begin to relax.

In the meantime, it is becoming increasingly clear that if the community, including the media, is to pay attention only when there is a serious or sensational incidence of abuse, the situation is not going to improve in any meaningful way.

It is important to gather all the information, and study it. Maybe mentally we could liken the bits of information to pieces of a big jigsaw puzzle, so we could lay them out on a bench, and find the rest of the pieces to form a more comprehensive picture. Then hopefully the appropriate authorities, now confronted with a better knowledge of the lay of the land, will be able to plan and take the appropriate action to improve the situation.

Although I do not claim to be the first person to think of doing this, I would assert nonetheless that I have been very lucky to find a sympathetic ear and a kindred spirit in the Jakarta Office of the International Labour Organization (ILO). It is through the ILO's funding of my research that I have been able to explore a wider field in order to put together a story based on numerous sub-stories, from different angles, all of which are ringing with humanity.

It is easy to lay blame on those who, at first glance, seem to hold the greater power over the powerless. But if we take a closer look, we will see that, while it is true there is a very uneven bargaining position, each party has something to lose. In an ideal situation, if everyone sits down and analyzes how to protect each other's vulnerability, they may simultaneously protect themselves and create a better working system, and everybody will be better off.

Unfortunately, there are parties who draw benefit from the rather loose state of affairs, and who may be unwilling to come out into the open. They are a challenge to the legitimate players in the field and to the government.

The government has a vested interest in the smooth and ongoing operation of the workers' migration, not only because it brings a significant revenue stream to the state, but also because it is a duty of government to maintain a clean national image and to look after the well-being of its people. Indonesian workers are entitled to have the appropriate respect of their employers, and no doubt Indonesians at home would like to know that their compatriots are not treated like cheap commodities overseas.

The ILO and I agreed that I would limit my research to Hong Kong, Singapore and Malaysia, so this book does not pretend to complete the jigsaw puzzle representing the situation of all Indonesian women working as domestic helpers overseas, but hopes to present a significant part of the picture. And this part should be comprehensive enough for the reader to see the complexity of the problems, follow the movement in the continuous power-play, and at the same time, make it easier for the authorities to see the weak points to work on, and the gaps to fill in.

I did not begin my research with any ideological axe to grind, but with an intention to learn about the situation myself, and to share my subsequent acquired knowledge with people who care enough to find out more about it. And I sincerely hope that people – the community and the authorities – become more motivated to help solve the seemingly chronic problems which are the sources of our sisters' suffering overseas.

CHAPTER ONE
HONG KONG

SETTING THE SCENE

In his Labor Day speech at the Government House on 1 May 2004, the then Chief Executive, Mr Tung Chee-hwa, expressed his optimism at the prospect of the Special Administrative Region's economic regrowth following Asia's economic crisis at the end of last century. He was confident that Hong Kong had the wherewithal to keep pace with globalization, a process that had the effect of throwing the balance of supply and demand of human resources into disarray.

Mr Tung pointed to the local economy where consumer spending had increased, property prices stabilized and more jobs created, and predicted a growth rate of six per cent for the year. He then delivered his government's promises on investment in education and improvement in the labor sector.

He concluded his speech by paying tribute to Hong Kong's labor sector which, he admitted, had been the hardest hit during the period of difficult restructuring.

It is not clear, however, whether his tribute extended to a small segment in this sector, the foreign domestic workers, known in Hong Kong as foreign domestic helpers, who had been quietly helping the economy. These workers had enabled those, mostly women, who would otherwise have had to stay at home looking after the family's young children or elderly parents, to become productive members in the economy bent on regrowth.

IN BETHUNE HOUSE SHELTER IN JORDAN

On the same day, Indri Handayani was recovering from the injuries inflicted on her by her former employer a week previously.

Indri, a foreign domestic helper from Central Java, Indonesia, had finally fled in desperation from her employer's apartment in the New Territories, in order to seek help. She came across some police officers and, in her basic Cantonese, told them of her situation, showing them her wounds, scars, and bruises.

The police officers took her to a nearby hospital to be examined and treated, where they also took X-rays of her injuries. From the hospital she was taken to the local police station where she was interviewed with the help of an interpreter.

When the interview was over, the interpreter, knowing that Indri had no money at all on her, gave her enough cash for a fare to go to the Bethune House Shelter in Jordan, and the telephone number of Eny Lestari, the president of the Indonesian Workers' Association in Hong Kong.

In Bethune House, a halfway house owned by a church in Kowloon and run by a Filipino Catholic group, there were ten other domestic helpers from Indonesia, victims of various kinds of abuse.

HONG KONG AS USER OF FOREIGN DOMESTIC HELPERS' SERVICE

Hong Kong was ranked the tenth largest trading entity in the world in 2004. Hong Kong SAR government records put all trade in goods in 2004 at HK$4,130 billion (US$530 billion). This is significantly higher than in 2003, when the total value of its visible trade, which amounted to HK$3,548 billion (US$455 billion) ranked it as eleventh largest.

This is a phenomenal result considering that it has a population of only approximately 6.84 million in mid-2004, living on an area of 1,103 square kilometres.

During the period 1993 to 2003, the Gross Domestic Product grew at an average annual rate of 3.2 per cent in real terms, to HK$1,361 billion (US$175 billion) in 2003. In money terms, the per capita GDP reached HK$179,333 (US$23,030), and in 2004 the nominal per capita GDP was recorded at US$24,080.

The employment of domestic helpers goes back decades, when these helpers were originally local women, or women brought in from mainland China by their Hong Kong relatives, and were known as *amahs*. The arrangement was, however, initially limited to the households of British and other expatriates, as well as affluent local Chinese business people. Towards the mid-1970s, as the Hong Kong economy grew and the number of households who could afford domestic helpers also increased, the culture of amahs gradually died out. Fewer and fewer women were willing to take up the low-paying and low-status jobs, preferring to work in better-paying or at least better-status sectors. To meet the growing needs in the community, the government had to look elsewhere to fill the jobs of domestic helpers.

The first to arrive in large numbers were Filipinos. Indonesians trickled in at first, then the volume picked up around the beginning of the 1990s. According to the Indonesian Consulate General's records, there were then approximately 8,000 Indonesians working as domestic helpers, and by 1995 the number had grown to 16,000. Currently, well over 90,000 domestic helpers from Indonesia are working in Hong Kong.

The Hong Kong Government responded to this development by regulation, to protect the local workers from cheap overseas competition, as well as to protect the overseas workers from exploitation. The law has been regularly reviewed and tightened as the situation evolves.

The current regulation specifies that employers should enter into a standard contract with their foreign domestic helpers. Apart from having a minimum allowable wage (currently HK$3,270 or US$420 per month), the domestic helpers are given the status of workers, hence are entitled to holidays, free medical treatment through the provisions of the Employment Ordinance and the relevant clauses under their standard employment contract. Any disputes between the domestic helpers and their employers can be settled through the Labour Department, the Labour Tribunal and the Minor Employment Claims Adjudication Board.

The regulation is also protective of employers and the Hong Kong labor market in general. The domestic helpers are not allowed to take up part-time or unauthorised work. In cases where a foreign domestic helper's contract is terminated prematurely (currently the contract is for two years), she will only be allowed to remain in Hong Kong for the remainder of her limit of stay or for two weeks, whichever is the shorter. Only under exceptional circumstances may the Director of Immigration allow the change of employer before the contract expires and without requiring the domestic helper to return to her home country first.

To protect the welfare of the domestic helpers, it is also compulsory for employers to take out insurance on behalf of the helpers. In addition, the employers are responsible for the helpers' medical treatment.

To minimise disputes, the current standard contract includes a section titled Schedule of Accommodation and Domestic Duties (see Appendix One). The section specifies that the employer should provide accommodation with reasonable privacy, giving examples of unsuitable accommodation as: the domestic helper having to sleep on made-do beds in the corridor with little privacy, and sharing a room with an adult of opposite sex.

At first glance, and if each party in the employment arrangement abides by the letter of the law, very little can go wrong. But things do go wrong. And when they do, the most disadvantaged party is usually the domestic helper.

A GLANCE AT THE HUMAN SIDE OF THE DOMESTIC HELPERS' SITUATION
In the following stories, when I refer to 'employer' (singular), I mean the person who signs the employment contract. In most cases it is the woman of the household, but there are also cases where the man of the household is the signatory. All names have been changed to protect the identities of the individuals.

Story One
After dropping out of secondary school, Sari felt that her days had become mind-numbingly yet reassuringly monotonous. She wouldn't have minded if it had not been so constricting. There was not much to do outside the day-to-day chores, since anything beyond that would cost money. She had had to leave school so that her younger brothers would be able to continue their education. Her parents, like so many subsistence tenant farmers on the outskirts of Semarang, Central Java, just could not afford paying more than two sets of school fees.

Sari didn't remember when her parents had last bought her new clothes. What she had were not exactly raggedy but they were worn out and shapeless.

She longed to have something new. She was nineteen years old, yet had never ventured beyond the city of Semarang. Even that had been years ago. This longing may have been stirred by Yunisah, one of *Bu* Parman's daughters who had just returned from Hong Kong. Yunisah, as the story went, had worked there as a housekeeper for a rich family who had showered her with beautiful gifts and had paid her huge sums of money every month.

Every morning Yunisah was seen sitting around in front of her parents' hut talking with her mother, apparently planning. The whole village knew that they were going to buy a piece of land adjacent to the village, and eventually, when Yunisah had collected more money from her new employers in Taiwan, they were going to build a house.

'A brick house,' Sari's mother said, taking a break from blowing into their stone stove, kindling the fire.

Sari was silent. She was visualizing the brick house Yunisah was going to have built for her family and was filled with awe tinged with envy. She could not even imagine what it would be like inside, since she had never been inside a brick house.

When Yunisah told Sari she would introduce her to the employment agency in Jakarta who had recruited her, Sari was jubilant. She rushed home to break the news to her mother. But all her mother said was, 'To Jakarta? How are you going to Jakarta? On foot?'

Sari sat down, crestfallen. 'But *Bu*, I'm sure *mbak* Yunisah will lend me some money for the train fare. Besides, she's going there anyway. I'll go with her, she'd like my company.'

'You'd better ask your father,' her mother finally said.

In Jakarta Yunisah left Sari at the agency's office after introducing her to the woman who sat behind the front desk. 'I'll come to pick you up later in the afternoon,' Yunisah had said.

Sari's sense of apprehension never really left her, though she felt less scared after a while. Another woman came over and asked her many, many questions about herself, and told her that she would have to learn many things before she could be sent to work in Hong Kong. 'You'll stay here for several months. You'll learn Cantonese language, and how to look after a house in Hong Kong. You'll also learn how to look after young children, maybe babies, and old people. Many families have...'

Sari's mind had wandered to the other side of her day-to-day reality. She visualized the big house like the one Yunisah had lived in when she was in Hong Kong. But she managed to say 'yes', whenever the woman uttered something which sounded like a question.

That night she stayed with Yunisah at her friend's place not very far from the agency's office. Sari thought it was small and poky. In reality it was no smaller than her parents' hut, but at least her parents' was a lot more airy.

At the agency's training centre, a building behind the office, Sari was taught to speak Cantonese and to carry out home duties. At first the novelty of everything she came across stirred her interest, but after five or six months the routine began to bore her, and she became increasingly impatient to experience the kind of life Yunisah had told her about.

One day Sari and ten other recruits were called to the supervisor's office, who told them that the agency had found jobs for them. Sari was the only one going to Hong Kong. The others were going to Malaysia and Singapore. From that day on, the pace of life accelerated. While she herself did not have to do much, the excitement of having her passport made and waiting for the issuing of her visa, was enough to give her several sleepless nights.

Things were really happening. She was actually going to live and work in a big house in Hong Kong! Who would ever believe that? And she was going to be paid HK$2,000, equivalent to Rp2.5 million per month. That sounded like a king's ransom to her.

The day finally came for her to leave. She met other young women from other agencies who were headed for Hong Kong, and they began chatting. The staff member accompanying her looked a little worried, but she didn't say anything. She saw how Sari looked so relieved when she found the fellow travellers.

They arrived at Hong Kong airport late in the afternoon. After collecting their baggage and clearing customs the women waited to be picked up by their respective agents. Sari's agent was the last to come.

The ride on the Airport Express was fun, Sari felt a little light-headed, maybe from exhaustion, hunger and thirst. Her agent, a woman of about forty who spoke Indonesian to her, took Sari to her own home to stay that night. The house was in a high-rise apartment building. It was much smaller than what she had imagined the house Yunisah had lived in, but it was clean and neat and very tidy. And the furniture and household appliances were similar to those in the agency's training center in Jakarta. She felt somewhat reassured.

She stayed at the agent's house for a week, during which time she was taken to have a medical check-up, briefed about what would be expected of her, shown how to travel by MTR, the Hong Kong underground railway, and had her local ID card made. When that was all completed, one morning the agent told her it was time to meet her employer. During the ride in the MTR, she kept emphasizing to Sari the importance of being polite and courteous, of doing her work diligently, of listening carefully for what her employers wanted her to do. Sari was only vaguely aware of going through at least ten stops before getting off the train, and starting to walk up the stairs following the agent, toward the exit.

They walked several blocks before arriving at another high-rise apartment building. The agent took her to an apartment on the nineteenth floor, stayed for several minutes conversing with Sari's new employer, who eyed her up and down, nodded, then ignored her to return to the conversation with the agent. Sari didn't know whether she was expected to stand around or sit on the floor. She felt awkward.

She was relieved when they called her to sign some papers, then the agent left.

Suddenly Sari felt lost and utterly alone. She looked up and saw her employer's face, her hand gripping the handle of her soft suitcase, looking for the slightest indication that the woman welcomed her into the house, but she found none. Her employer was not unwelcoming. She was just matter-of-fact and businesslike.

When the woman began to speak, Sari felt her palms moisten, and she shifted the suitcase onto the other hand and wiped the free hand on the side of her skirt. The woman had a very different accent and intonation from her Cantonese language instructor in Jakarta. Her employer had to repeat everything two or three times before Sari even had an inkling of what she was saying. Worse still, when Sari finally had enough courage to put a few sentences together, her employer had trouble understanding her.

Sari knew intuitively it was not a good beginning to her relationship with her employer, but she was determined to make it work. It had to work. She wanted to make enough money to help her family back home.

The house was not as big and as grand as what she had imagined the one Yunisah had lived in, but that, at the moment, was the least of her worries. And when she was shown where she was to sleep, in a corner of the family's store-room, she was too pre-occupied to feel anything but grateful.

A month later, Sari thought she had finally managed all the tasks allocated to her, albeit with difficulty. Just as she thought she was getting better at doing them, however, her employer would yell at her, calling her 'brainless', 'stupid', and 'lazy'. And whenever she tried to explain anything, her employer would grab her ear and twist it until it hurt so much she would scream. Sari quickly learned, however, not to scream too loud, because the woman would then pinch her arm or grab her hair and shake her head hard. She would do this frequently when her husband, who only came home at most twice a week, was away, and when the children, seven and twelve, were not in the room.

Every morning Sari had to get up at 5:30 am to prepare breakfast for the family and lunches for the children to take to school, then clean up afterwards. Her employer would leave for work, and Sari had to accompany the children to school. From there she had to go to the grandmother's apartment several blocks away, where she cooked and cleaned, until eleven o'clock. She had to look at the clock all the time, because her employer had told her to note down the time whenever she finished a task. For every five minutes for which she had no explanation, her employer would deduct HK$1.00 off her salary.

From the grandmother's apartment Sari had to rush back home, then begin cleaning the whole house and do the laundry. After picking up the children from school, she had to start cooking.

During the day Sari hardly had time to pause, yet it was still a lot better than the evening, when her employer came home from work. The woman would begin to pick fault even before she took her shoes off. Then as she came further into the house, the yelling and name-calling became worse. She claimed to be tired from work but she had the energy to go through

Sari's time-sheet and would invariably deduct ten to fifteen dollars for various faults.

One day without any warning or explanation she dragged Sari into the bathroom and began cutting her hair short. When her own son asked her why she made Sari look like a boy, she said, 'A maid should not have long hair. It's dirty.'

After two months, the employer became increasingly violent and relentless toward Sari. She would slap Sari's face, bash her about the head, and throw full cans of food at her. Every morning when she had to take the children to school, however, the employer would threaten her, saying that if she didn't cover the bruises she would receive worse treatment.

Sari was forced to sign receipts for her salary each month, but never received a cent. Her employer told her that she was keeping the money for her. 'It's for your own good,' she said, 'I'm doing you a favour.'

Every night as she went to bed Sari wondered whether the following morning she would wake up from this unrelenting nightmare. One day she looked for the piece of paper with the agent's telephone number on it and decided to call her.

When she told her agent about her situation, Sari found the agent's response bewildering and disappointing. 'Maybe you should work harder, better, and listen carefully to what your employer wants you to do,' she said, adding, 'But I'll talk to her to see what is going on.'

The following evening when her employer came home, Sari felt rage rolling almost visibly toward her even before she saw her coming to the kitchen where she was tidying up.

'You animal! You liar!' the woman yelled, punching her in the chest, 'How dare you tell on me? Don't you ever do that again, or you'll regret it for the rest of your life!'

Then she stalked out of the kitchen, leaving Sari winded, cowering and whimpering in a corner, her arms tightly closed against her chest.

After that night she often wondered what happened to all the other young women she had met on the way here, whether they had a better fate than herself. And when nobody was close by, she would let a tear or two drop from her stinging eyes. And she was worried that her mother would find out what was happening to her.

At times Sari would even feel thankful that she had no friends, nobody to talk to, nobody with whom to share her feeling of desperation. At least she knew that her mother would never know of her dreadful situation. And her feeling of being trapped and suffocated increased in intensity as the months crawled on.

Hopeless as it looked, Sari did tick the days in her dog-eared and crumpled calendar she kept in the bottom of her box of clothes, counting the days till she finished her contract. She still believed that her employer would at least hand over her salary then. She was too unsure to think too much beyond that.

The morning of 23 April 2004, as Sari ticked the date in the calendar she noticed that she had worked for the employer for four months and a week. She didn't know then, that it would be a date marking a watershed in her working life in Hong Kong. A mistake in her cooking sent her employer into such a rage that she picked up the wooden soup ladle and began hitting her about the head with it, over, and over, while pushing Sari's arms away from her face and head. Sari thought she would die if her employer didn't stop hitting. She wanted to scream but no sound came out. She was scared out of her mind.

Suddenly the hitting stopped. The woman said something but Sari's head was buzzing, her ears clogged. She pulled her hands away from her face, and just then she felt warm liquid flowing down her neck. She touched it and looked at her fingers. Blood. She touched the area again with another hand. Blood. Blood. Her knees gave way and she fell in a heap on the kitchen floor. She saw her blood trickling onto the floor. When she looked up, she saw her employer's face ten centimetres from her own. The worried look momentarily surprised Sari.

She was worried! Oh my God, it must be bad! Sari began to cry. Even then she couldn't cry out loud. She had been conditioned not to. She whimpered quietly, trying to stem the bleeding with her hands, while her T-shirt and pants were soaking in the red and sticky fluid.

The woman went into a panic. She rushed to the bathroom for a bucket of water, bandages and antiseptic ointment. She knew she had gone too far.

The following morning, the employer came into the storeroom to check on Sari. She told Sari that she would take the children to school, and that Sari should rest this morning, and not to talk to anyone or tell anyone about what had happened.

Sari waited until the front door was closed before she slowly got up and got dressed, nursing her aching head. Miraculously the door was not padlocked from the outside. She got herself down to the street and began walking unsteadily toward the nearest MTR station. She felt sore and dizzy, but she knew there was a police station not far from there.

She had not walked far when two police officers saw her and approached her, asking her if she was all right. She said no. Then she broke into tears, and between sobs she told the police officers what had happened to her.

In the hospital she was given fresh bandages, some pain-killers, and had several X-rays taken. For the first time since the beatings of the previous two months had started, she felt she was able to show the bruises to someone. There was a sense of relief though tinged with apprehension. She didn't know what was going to happen next. Would she be sent back to her employer's home? She tried to explain to the interpreter that she would never go back for fear of being killed. The interpreter nodded understandingly, and gave her a piece of paper with some Chinese characters and a telephone number on it.

'This is the address of a safe house. It is called Bethune House, run by a Catholic Nun from the Philippines. And this is the phone number of Eny Lestari, the president of the Indonesian Workers' Association in Hong Kong. Go to the safe house first, then ring Eny from there. You can take the MTR to Jordan, and it is within walking distance from the station,' the interpreter explained in Indonesian.

When Sari told her she had no money for the fare, the interpreter took out her purse and gave her what she needed.

It was only after she had spoken to Eny Lestari and other people in Bethune House that Sari realized that the minimum allowable wage for foreign domestic helpers like herself was HK$3,270. But that was neither here nor there, since she had never seen even the promised HK$2,000 a month she was supposedly entitled to, despite having signed receipts every month.

With the help of Eny Lestari and other non-government organization workers, Sari was able to obtain a special permit from the immigration authorities to stay, and testify at the Labour Tribunal, where her employer was sentenced to a month and ten days imprisonment. And Sari was hopeful that through Hong Kong Legal Aid, she would be able to claim compensation for the abuse she had suffered.

Story Two

For Rima, her arrival at Hong Kong airport on the afternoon of 24 May 2004 was not her first time out of Indonesia. Neither was the job she was to take up, her first job. Rima had worked in Singapore for two years, and had had short spasmodic stints working as a process worker in factories in Jakarta.

When she returned from Singapore, where she had had a pleasant working experience, she had wanted to live closer to her parents in Solo, Central Java. But within months her depleted savings had only brought marginal improvement to her parents' lives. She knew she had to go back to work.

She met an employment agent, known as a 'sponsor', who promised to help her find work in Taiwan. Rima had heard that the salary for a domestic helper in Taiwan was much higher than the going rate in Singapore. The sponsor brought her back to Jakarta to an employment agency, and Rima was promptly accepted for training.

After five months of improving her Mandarin and her home duties skills, however, Rima was told that the government had banned sending workers to Taiwan. She was asked whether she wanted to go anywhere else. Disappointed, she decided to go back home to Solo and find work closer to home.

Work however, was not easy to find in Solo. So Rima went to visit a relative in Jakarta, who agreed to give her lodgings. She discovered, however, that it was not much easier to find gainful employment in the capital, either. After several months she realized she would never save any money to help her parents, as whatever she earned, she spent on food, transport and lodgings. Again, she returned to Solo.

This time she found a sponsor who promised to help her find work in Hong Kong. She had learned that salaries in Hong Kong were higher than those in Singapore. The sponsor took her to a different employment agency. After four months of training, she was sent to Hong Kong.

Rima waited for hours at the airport. Her local agent finally came at seven o'clock, and took her to a small apartment where there were two other young women staying. They were all waiting to have a medical examination and their local ID cards made for them.

On 6 June 2004, Rima's employer came for her. In the contract Rima and her employer signed, she read that she would be paid HK$3,270 per month.

Rima was told that her employer was a police officer. Since both she and her husband worked, Rima was expected to keep house as well as look after their young son for them.

At first there was nothing unusual about her work regime. Having worked as a domestic helper in Singapore, Rima more or less knew what to do without any major problems. And the son felt at ease with her. She did her housework after taking the boy to school, and often, after he had gone to bed at night.

Rima was nonetheless still feeling her way around her relationship with her employer. She did not remind Rima of her former employer in Singapore at all. Her Singapore employer and her husband, were friendly to her. Her current employer was cold and aloof. So when she wasn't given her weekly rest days, she didn't feel comfortable enough to bring it up. Rima had learned about the weekly rest days from her fellow recruits in the employment agency's training center in Jakarta, and had confirmed that they were one of her entitlements, when she had read the contract.

The first sign of alarm Rima detected was a week or so after she began working with the family. She observed that her employer's husband seemed to work shifts, and was often home during the day when his wife was at work. Though she pretended not to notice, she knew he watched her around the house, not in the manner of an employer wanting to make sure the employee was working properly. She tried to suppress her sense of misgivings, and went on with her chores as if nothing were out of order.

Then he went further. He would come close to her and caress her arm, or touch her shoulder. Rima could only move away quickly. This annoyed the man. He would then yell at her for no apparent reason. He would pick faults at anything she did, and slap her about the face. This really shocked Rima, who had never been physically abused during her time in Singapore.

One afternoon, when the boy was at school, the man called her to the sitting room, where he was slouching on the sofa.

He asked her to massage his feet.

When she started he made a show of closing his eyes. Rima knew, however, that he often opened them and eyed her up and down. Then he tried to engage her in light conversation. He did most of the talking however, while Rima only listened. He told her then that he also was a police officer, watching her reaction. Rima only nodded.

Whenever she asked if it was enough, he replied, 'No, keep going!'

She obeyed, suppressing her fear.

The massage seemed to go on forever. When the man began to grunt Rima felt very uncomfortable. Then he wiggled and pulled down his pants. Rima felt suffocated by a terror which she imagined a trapped animal would experience.

She froze, then looked away. The man suddenly sat up and grabbed her by the arm and pulled her toward him. She fell on his lap and the man quickly got hold of her head and pushed it toward his naked crotch. She wanted to scream and keep her lips tightly pursed all at once.

Half an hour later Rima was still crying from the humiliation. The man, ready to go to work, looked in and said she should never tell anyone what had happened, or he would arrange to put her in jail for years. He would even kill her, and nobody would know better.

'Remember, I am a police officer, and you are only a hussy, a maid! Who do you think people would believe?' he sneered, then walked away.

When he had gone out of the house, Rima rushed to the bathroom and vomited.

From that moment on, Rima's life turned to hell. Each day the man was home the dreadful event was repeated. Many times she thought of telling his wife. After all, the woman was her employer, the person who signed the contract to employ her. She had the responsibility over her welfare.

But she knew intuitively that it would have been futile. How could she expect the woman to protect her when she did not lift a finger seeing her husband hit her in the face?

One morning, as she was preparing the boy for school, he saw the bruises on her face, and asked, 'What happened to you, big sister?'

Rima looked away and said she had fallen from a chair cleaning the kitchen cupboard the night before. Just then the man walked in and said he would take his son to school, and told Rima not to appear outside the house, or she would get worse treatment.

Several times after dropping the boy at school, Rima thought of running away. But where could she go? She only knew the route between the apartment building and the school. She was unfamiliar with her surroundings in Hong Kong's New Territories. Unlike Singapore, everything was so overwhelmingly Chinese here. The characters on the signposts, on shop fronts, everywhere. While she had learned Cantonese at the training center in Jakarta, she was not fluent, and she was unable to spot a sympathetic face among the throng of people she came across every morning. If she ran away, she would surely become lost, then she would really run into trouble. She couldn't go to the police, because the perpetrator of her assaults was a police officer. As the man repeatedly said to her, 'Don't try anything silly. It's your word against mine. And they wouldn't believe you!'

She returned to the apartment, like a lamb to the slaughter.

The man became more daring and more direct. He no longer asked her to massage his feet, but followed her around and grabbed her and touched her up whenever he felt like it.

Then on 29 July 2004, when Rima was cleaning the bathroom, the man grabbed her from behind, tore off her clothes and raped her. When she resisted, he bashed her as well.

That evening she looked at her employer. The woman must have known what had happened, Rima thought. Rima was covered with bruises, her nose was still red from bleeding, and she would break into uncontrollable shaking fits. But the woman didn't say or do anything.

The man, encouraged by the impunity, made it into a regular activity. Rima was frequently raped, vaginally and anally. Her life hung precariously between suicide and numbness. One thing she had difficulty numbing was the feeling of worthlessness, of being only good enough for the scrapheap. She couldn't even entertain the possibility of having a future.

A month after the first penetration, on 29 August, they were on the way back from a Sunday visit to the woman's mother's house, when the woman remembered they had to buy some grocery items. They stopped at a supermarket, and to save the trouble of all filing into the shop, the woman told Rima to go alone with the list.

When Rima walked in, she immediately spotted a woman whose body language reminded her of women in Indonesia. Overcome by desperation, she went up to her and said, '*Mbak*, are you Indonesian?'

The woman was momentarily startled, then smiled, saying, 'Yes, I am. You are too. Do you live around here?'

Rima knew she only had very little time, so without any preamble, she told the Indonesian woman that she was working as a domestic helper, and that her male employer had been abusing her.

The Indonesian woman's face turned serious, and she asked quickly, 'Where are they now?' When told that the whole family was waiting in the car, the Indonesian woman took off her jacket, told Rima to wear it, and pushed her by the elbow toward the exit.

She took Rima to the nearest police station. Encouraged by the Indonesian woman, Rima finally told the police what had happened. When the police officers asked her to come with them to the house to collect evidence, she was nonetheless hesitant. But the police officers said she had nothing to worry about, because even if her employer was a police officer, if he had committed such a crime, he would not be spared the proper punishment.

Rima went with the police officers to the house and collected her own and the man's unwashed clothes, together with other items associated with her physical abuse. The man was there, but Rima was emboldened by the inevitability of the development.

He was taken in for questioning. Rima was particularly stunned by the revelation that the man was not a police officer after all. It was his wife who was in the police force. He himself was a civilian employee in the Police Department. The extent of the deceit and its implications, nearly choked her. If she had had a gun then, she could have happily killed him.

Her case was, at the time of the interview, with the criminal court. She was also waiting for the Labour Tribunal to make her former employer pay her unpaid salary.

When asked if she would go home when all this was over, she said emphatically that home was the last place she wanted to be right then. 'If my poor father and mother didn't die from shock and sadness, they'd eventually wither away, because they wouldn't be able to bear the disgrace. They live in a very tight and conservative community' she said.

'No,' she added after a while, 'I only sent news to them that I was no longer working for that employer, that I was looking for another employer. They don't have to know.'

Story Three

In 2002, in her village on the outskirts of Banyuwangi, East Java, Isma and her family welcomed a friendly, well-presented woman in her late forties, who was not a stranger to the community. She had assisted in the successful recruitment of a number of young women, Isma's older sister included, by an employment agency in Surabaya, which trained and subsequently found them gainful employment in Hong Kong, Singapore and Taiwan.

Isma's older sister Rifah was already working in Hong Kong and regularly sending money home, so Isma's parents felt less apprehensive about allowing their younger daughter to follow her sister's steps.

After several months of training, the manager told her that there was a job in Hong Kong, and she was given the choice of accepting it. Since she had not been trained for very long, however, and she had had no previous experience, she would be unable to ask for the full amount of the minimum allowable wage of HK$3,270, but the employer would be happy to pay her HK$2,000. To Isma, HK$2,000 sounded like an awful lot of money, a lot more than she or anyone working as a domestic helper could ever dream of receiving in the whole province of East Java. Besides she knew that Rifah was not paid much more than that, yet was able to send enough money home to pay for their younger brothers' schooling. So she accepted the job and the terms.

Though, like all her compatriots, she was overwhelmed and disoriented at first in Hong Kong, where the sky was not as obvious as it was in her hometown, Isma was more confident than Rifah had been. Rifah's presence in the same city, reassured her to a degree. Rifah had beaten the path, so to speak, for her younger sister.

The path that Rifah had, beaten however, was not necessarily that which her sister would walk on.

Her employer, an irascible woman of about thirty-five years old, was very impatient and intolerant of mistakes. Whenever she talked to Isma, there was no trace of kindness or acknowledgement of Isma's humanity. This at first distressed Isma, and she related this to Rifah. Rifah said that some of her friends had similar types of employers but they had learned to tune out each time the employers addressed them. Isma, in time, learned to do that too.

Isma was at least grateful of the fact that she was allowed a rest day every two weeks, as she had heard that some Indonesian domestic helpers were only allowed a rest day once a month. On those days she would meet up with Rifah and other domestic helpers in Victoria Park, where they would hang out, have a picnic, and later on go to see a movie, shopping or whatever they felt like doing.

Isma often pondered her situation. The work itself was not too onerous, because she had time to rest in between chores during the day, before she had to collect the employer's two children from school. But as soon as her employer came home, things would go sour. She had to be seen to be busy doing something. It would not take long, however, before the woman found something to lash out at her about. The tablecloth was not laid properly, or had not been washed well; the sunshade had not been lifted fully, the washing was put on her favorite chair; the bathroom floor was not clean enough; the tap was left dripping; her children were still in school uniforms; her children had had too many snacks before dinner; her Cantonese was incomprehensible. Anything would set her off, despite Isma having checked around the house before the time she usually came home.

Fortunately her employer's husband came home not too long after his wife, and the situation was made bearable by the fact that the man was kind to her, and tended to calm his wife when she was angry with her.

One evening Isma steeled herself to say to her employer, 'Ma'am, if you are not happy with my work, please send me back to my agent,' to which the employer replied, 'No way! I paid good money to have you come here! You finish the contract first, then you can go. You're just being lazy!'

Chatting with her friends during their days off together, Isma discovered that her employer had had three previous helpers, the first two from the Philippines, and the third from Indonesia. The Filipino helpers had both left long before the contract had finished, while the Indonesian helper stuck it out till completion of her contract.

One evening, in exasperation, Isma let drop that she knew she was being paid under the legal minimum allowable wage, implying that if she cared to speak up, she could easily implicate her employer.

The woman nearly threw the glass of orange juice she was holding in her hand, at her. But she only fixed Isma with a murderous glare, then dropped the glass on the table and walked out.

Isma didn't know whether what she had done was wise, but she felt somewhat triumphant, having rattled the horrible woman. And deep down, she knew her employer was disconcerted.

After that evening, her employer's attitude toward her was chilling, and occasionally chillingly threatening. She no longer hurled verbal abuses, but would lift her hand to hit her but stop short of actually attacking. Isma found this extremely unsettling, but there was nothing she could do, since she did not actually assault her.

Isma became very careful not to give her employer any reason to fault her, because she knew intuitively that the woman was always on the lookout for something she had done incorrectly. The psychological war eventually wore her down.

One afternoon, after picking up the children from school, then tidying up the house and cleaning everything before the woman came home, she had a serious accident. As usual, she had to use the step-ladder to reach the items on the top kitchen shelf. As she pulled a saucepan toward her, the handle accidentally pushed a big bowl beside it. Down it came, and she didn't have time to catch it.

Isma looked down at the floor, at the pieces of china mingled with coins. She felt fear grow in her chest like a swelling bubble of vacuum. From the other room one of the children was asking if she was all right. Isma replied that there was nothing serious, that she had dropped a dish.

Then she quickly came down, put the step-ladder back in the storeroom, and returned to the kitchen with a broom and a scoop. Breathlessly she squatted down and scooped every piece of the broken porcelain, with the coins included, then tipped them into the garbage bin at the back of the apartment.

When the woman came home, she seemed to know something was out of order, but couldn't tell what it was. Isma tried very hard to act as if nothing had happened and went on her work as usual.

After serving dinner and washing up, Isma brought in the washing of the day, and began ironing. Her employer kept walking in and out of the kitchen, ostensibly to get something, but all the time watching her. Isma was becoming increasingly tense. She was hoping the woman's husband would walk in. But she could hear him in the bathroom showering.

Suddenly the woman stopped. Isma looked up from her ironing and held her breath. The woman was looking at the spot where the china bowl had been.

'Where's my coins bowl?' she suddenly cried out.

Isma didn't answer. She came and grabbed the iron from Isma and looked menacingly at her. 'Answer me!' she barked.

Isma had no choice but to tell her what had happened. But before she finished, the woman had pushed the hot iron on to her arm. For a moment Isma didn't know whether it was extreme cold or extreme heat she was feeling. She gasped.

As if woken up by Isma's gasp, the woman pulled the iron away, and when she saw what she had done, her face turned white.

'I am sorry,' she said quietly.

When Isma had recovered from her shock, she rushed to her room and grabbed a tube of toothpaste, then sploshed the content onto her red, raw, burnt flesh. The pain made her cry. The woman came in with a cup of hot chocolate, and tried to comfort her. Again she said she was sorry.

She came back with a tube of ointment and helped put it on Isma's affected arm, and for the first time since she began working for the family almost two years ago, Isma heard her employer utter gentle words to her, and tell her to rest. Overcome by this unexpected kindness, Isma agreed not to report her, and to work another month till the end of her contract.

The following Sunday was her rest day. As usual she went to Victoria Park to meet up with her sister and their friends. When Isma told them what had happened to her, they all agreed that she should report the assault.

On Monday after taking the children to school, Isma went to the police.

Story Four
Murti was not the first young woman to be recruited by the resident sponsor,

who lived in the same street as her family, in their village on the outskirts of Malang. In fact, it was not the first recruitment for her. Murti had worked as a domestic helper before, in Kuala Lumpur, Malaysia, where her employer and her husband taught her to speak Cantonese.

Having had an agreeable experience in her job, Murti was confident she would be able to take on another job, and further afield this time. She had learned that the salaries in Hong Kong were far higher than those in Malaysia, even Singapore. So she asked her sponsor to take her to an agency who could find her a job in Hong Kong.

Her sponsor took her to an agency not far from Surabaya. She stayed for seven months at the training center, improving her Cantonese and her home duties skills. When the job in Hong Kong came up in May 2004, Murti accepted it, and the agency processed her documents.

She was to keep house for a couple in their thirties, and look after their son. Having had a similar work experience in Kuala Lumpur previously, Murti was fairly confident she was able to do it well. When her employer told her that she was only expected to look after the young son, do the laundry and keep the house clean, Murti did not find it unusual. She was, however, literally not allowed to touch food in the family. The employer did all the cooking, and Murti only received what she gave her.

Apart from not being allowed any breakfast, Murti found that the food the employer gave her was often stale, even bad. She would quietly put it in the rubbish bin and went hungry. One day, however, the woman found out what she had done, and was very angry, telling her she was ungrateful and impudent. Murti was very hurt, but did not dare say anything. Despite her disappointment Murti was hoping that if she showed she could work well her employer would mellow.

The relationship did not improve however. Her employer found most things Murti did unsatisfactory, unhygienic, and unintelligent. Yet when she showed Murti what she wanted her to do, her tone was so rough Murti would often turn off before she finished her sentences. Unfortunately, this meant that Murti only heard part of the instructions. Consequently the situation steadily deteriorated.

Many times Murti was tempted to tell her employer's husband how the woman was treating her, because she noticed that when her husband was around, the employer made a semblance of kindness. The circumstances never arose however, because she never saw him alone without his wife.

After a month of suppressing her own anger, one day when her employer told her off for washing her silk skirt with normal detergent, Murti blurted out that her employer had told her it was all right. 'You change your rules all the time. How was I to know what you think each time?'

The employer slapped her hard and told her never to answer back. When she wanted to defend herself, the woman slapped her again. That was not to be the only time she was physically abused. She was to be hit by various coat hangers about the head. The only witness to the mistreatment was the four year old son, who watched without saying anything.

Murti had nowhere to go for consolation. She was not allowed any days off. The only person with whom she exchanged greetings occasionally was a Filipino domestic helper from the apartment upstairs. One afternoon when she was putting the garbage bag outside, she came across the Filipina. She asked Murti whether she had been hit by her employer, pointing to the bruises on her face. Murti just said yes, and quickly went back to her apartment before she was caught chatting.

The months crawled on, and despite signing receipts for her salary, she never saw a cent, her employer saying that the first four months of her salary went to the agent. Murti had no one to ask if this was normal practice. She kept everything bottled up, which affected her health. She slept fitfully, often from hunger as well.

When four months had passed and she still had not received any money, she braved herself to ask her employer. The woman became so angry, she slapped her and pulled her ear so hard it drew blood.

Murti ran out of the apartment crying, leaving her employer unsure what to do. Murti only knew one person in the whole building: the Filipina who worked upstairs. So she rushed up and knocked on her door.

When the Filipina saw her, she quickly pulled her inside. Murti told her what had happened. The Filipina called her employer, and they both listened when Murti, finally finding sympathetic ears, poured out her grief.

They told her she should report her employer to the police. When Murti agreed, they rang the police. While waiting for the police to come, they asked her if she had any money. Murti told her she had never been paid.

The Filipina went into her room and came out with some cash. And her employer also took out her purse and gave Murti some money. Together they pooled HK$600. When Murti said she didn't know when she could pay them back, they said not to worry. 'Just pay when you can. Now go, the police are here.'

At the end of 2004, Murti was waiting for her case to go to the Labour Tribunal.

Story Five
In 1990 after finishing her secondary school, Kholifah knew she had to do something drastic to help her farming parents pay for her younger brothers and sisters' schooling. In the rural village in Central Java where they lived however, work was not easy to find.

When she met a woman who told her that she could find her a job as a domestic helper in Singapore, Kholifah was not sure whether she liked the idea. She had only known one or two people who had gone overseas to work, neither of them as domestic helpers. The pay however, sounded very attractive, and she hadn't had any success finding any work at all in her hometown. So in the end, she decided to give it a try.

After working four years in Singapore, Kholifah was able to save enough money to help the family's finances. But instead of signing yet another contract, she decided to come home and try again to find work closer to her family.

Her mother was happy to have her around. Several years later, going overseas to work as a domestic helper had become a trend. And one of Kholifah's younger sisters was recruited by a sponsor who took her to an employment agency in Surabaya, where she was taught to speak Cantonese and home duties skills specifically tailored for Hong Kong households.

Her sister was able to send more money home, since she earned a higher salary in Hong Kong than what Kholifah had been earning in Singapore. Kholifah contacted the same agency and expressed her wish to work in Hong Kong also. After several months of training, she landed a job in a household in the New Territories in Hong Kong, where the agency, in cooperation with the local agent, was able to secure a full minimum allowable wage for her, because of the results of her aptitude tests, and her proven skills. On top of that, she would also be entitled to one rest day per week, days off on public holidays, and approved leave in case of contract renewal.

This did not mean, however, that the situation was plain-sailing right from the start.

When she arrived early in 2001, Kholifah told her employer right from the beginning, that she was a Muslim, but she intuitively knew that it would not be wise to tell her then and there that she would pray five times a day. In fact, she did not mention anything about praying.

The work situation went smoothly. Kholifah seemed to please her employer with how she managed the housework in general. She had no issue with her employer's husband, who left everything to his wife. And she looked after the couple's sickly baby well. Whenever the baby had to go to hospital for treatment, Kholifah would stay overnight with him.

For months the employer never noticed that Kholifah would steal away for two minutes five times a day to pray, until one evening when she walked into the bedroom the baby shared with Kholifah. The woman was shocked by what she saw before her. A kneeling Kholifah, covered in a white *mukerna*, a Muslim hooded prayer cape, bowing right in front of her son's cot.

'What are you doing?' the woman cried out, as the sight filled her with fear.

Kholifah completed her prayer, then turned around, and took off her cape. Calmly, she explained that she had been praying.

'Why did you do that in front of my son?' the woman asked.

'Actually I didn't do it intentionally in front of your son. But I have been praying for his health, that his health will improve. And his cot happens to be in the direction of Mecca,' Kholifah said, and explained that wherever a Muslim is, he or she will pray in the direction of Mecca. 'And we do this five times a day,' she added.

The woman thought for a while, still worried by the strangeness of the situation. She said she didn't want Kholifah to pray in the bedroom, because she feared that her son would not get better when there was a collision of two religions in his room, adding that Kholifah's religion was very different from her own.

It was a small apartment, so Kholifah volunteered to pray outside the apartment, on the landing. Her employer reluctantly agreed to that.

Several days later her employer approached her, and said that she had talked to her friends, who told her about Islam. She said, 'You can pray in the kitchen, but please don't wear a white cape. White symbolises grief in our tradition, worn when there has been a death in the family. Can you wear a different color cape?'

From then on, Kholifah observed her prayers in the kitchen, wearing a floral cape. And no more problems arose, until the arrival of Ramadhan, the Muslim fasting month.

Kholifah asked her employer's permission to fast. When the woman learned that Kholifah proposed not to eat from sunrise till sunset, for a whole month, she was incredulous.

'Not eating the whole day, for a month? What if you fall ill? What if you die from starvation? No, I don't want you to!'

Kholifah then told her that she had been doing it for years, and she hadn't fallen seriously ill, let alone die. 'It's much easier fasting inside the house. In my home village, my parents, my brothers and sisters, all fast. And they have to work in the field, under the sun. It's much hotter. People don't die from fasting.'

The employer was adamant. 'No, while you are employed by me, I'm liable if anything happens to you. I can't allow you not to eat for a whole month, regardless of what you said about your family in your home village,' she said.

Kholifah thought for a while, and quietly proposed, that the woman let her try it one day. 'If my work is affected, if I become too weak to do anything, or fall ill, I'll stop it. But if nothing bad happens, please let me continue.'

The woman raised her arms saying, 'OK, OK! If you insist!'

The day went without a hitch, and the woman had to let Kholifah continue with her fast.

A week later, Kholifah had to stay overnight with the baby in the hospital, and when they came home, her employer noticed she was sniffling. She asked Kholifah whether she was feeling all right. Kholifah replied that she suspected she had been affected by the air-conditioned climate in the hospital room. Concerned, the woman took her to see a doctor. Kholifah was given some medication, to be taken half an hour before meals, three times a day. There were no problems taking the morning and evening tablets, but Kholifah skipped the afternoon dose.

When her employer found out what she was doing, she insisted Kholifah follow the doctor's prescription. 'It's not food. It's medicine,' she said.

At being told that she was not to swallow anything, not even her saliva, again the woman raised her hands and gave in.

Later that day something happened which nearly undermined Kholifah's credibility. Her period started. Forced to cancel her fast, Kholifah drank a glass of water. Just then her employer walked in.

'You lied to me!' she said with annoyance, 'You lied to me about all this fasting and religiosity!'

Kholifah explained to her that she was menstruating. The woman looked suspiciously at her, asking, 'So! What has that got to do with your fasting?'

When Kholifah told her that a menstruating woman could not fast, the employer shook her head, saying she had never learned so much in such a short time.

And Kholifah had no more problems praying and fasting.

Story Six

Mega has been working for Lilian and her family for twelve years. And during those years the family has accepted her and regarded her as part of the family.

Mega did not arrive in Hong Kong all primed and prepared. The training she had received in Malang, East Java, was far from adequate. She spoke some English because she had completed secondary school. She spoke hardly any Cantonese. It appeared that she was fortunate because the family who contracted her immediately liked her. At the time, her employer was pregnant. When the baby girl, Candy, was born, Mega developed a close relationship with her, and Lilian gave her the freedom to arrange the order of her chores, provided she gave priority to taking care of Candy.

The tasks were not difficult for Mega, she herself being a mother. The most difficult part of working in Hong Kong for Mega was having to leave her own son behind in Malang, East Java, and communicate with her husband, her son and her own parents, only by telephone and letters. The money she sent home regularly, however, had been able to help the family build a new house, as well as pay for her son's education.

Mega's caring personality won sympathy and respect all round. When five years later another child, Ken, came onto the scene, Mega took everything in her stride. Both children became very attached to her. Ken, now seven, had even learned some East Javanese nursery rhymes.

Mega is paid above the minimum allowable wage, had her weekly rest days, days off on official holidays, as well as the occasional time off to help organise events with the Indonesian Migrant Workers Union. She belongs to a writing club, where they encouraged each other's writing skills, and has published poems and short stories in their quarterly magazine.

Mega writes poetry and paints. Her poetry has been published in hard copy and online. When she told Lilian she was interested in taking painting lessons, they looked for a class in their suburb. The only one they could find was run between 5:00 pm and 6:00 pm in the evening, a very awkward time in terms of her work schedule. Mega didn't think it would be appropriate for her to disappear during that time. Candy, who was also interested in taking the lessons, asked, 'Why not?'

'I have to prepare dinner at that time,' Mega explained.

Lilian, who had been listening, interrupted, 'I can cook dinner on those nights. You and Candy can go.'

That was how she and Candy enrolled in the drama classes. And Mega uses her drama skills directing performances the union organised on Independence Day, Kartini Day, and the occasional protest theatre whenever there is a social issue the group feels strongly about.

One evening, after watching a film on television, Mega, overcome by the story, was missing her family back home. She said wistfully, 'I think I'd better go back home and live close to my family.'

Hearing that, Candy became very upset and said, 'But we are your family. Please don't leave us. If you leave us, I'll kill myself. I'll jump out the window like the girl in the film!'

Candy's words shocked her into sobriety. She hugged Candy and comforted her, saying, 'I won't leave,' and quietly to herself, 'not for a while, yet.'

Story Seven

In 1977, when Wulan, short for Karsiwulan, was only fifteen years old, her parents forced her to marry a man she didn't know. In the East Javanese village where they lived, that was not unusual, and most girls accepted the situation.

Not Wulan. While she did not openly rebel, she did not acquiesce fully. The wedding night was such a shock to her that she refused to talk to, or to have anything to do with, her husband after that. The pressure of returning to the matrimonial bed finally hardened her determination. She ran away, and went to stay with relatives. It lasted a week. She wasn't sure if her relatives had alerted the family, or that being in a village it was not hard to trace someone.

Nevertheless, she refused to return to her husband. So it was agreed that she go to her grandmother's home. Despite her mother's and grandmother's cajoling, Wulan still wouldn't go back to her husband. Finally they left her alone.

Suddenly left to her own devices, Wulan was not sure what to do next. Her mother made use of her sense of uncertainty. She visited her often, making Wulan feel special. Every day the mother and grandmother prepared something for her to drink. Wulan only knew it was fragrant water.

Wulan would drink it when her mother or grandmother were around. As soon as nobody was looking, she threw the liquid away. Some ten days later, her body began to feel strange; sometimes feverish, but only momentarily. She felt heady most times.

A week passed, and her condition had not changed. She thought she had the flu, and suspected the water she had been drinking may have been unboiled, so she stopped drinking it altogether, regardless of whether anyone was watching.

Just when she began to feel better, her husband came to see her. The passage of time seemed to have eroded her revulsion toward him, because she was somewhat happy to see him. And when he asked her to come home, she went without much protest.

They were still to face a rocky road ahead. Wulan's husband liked to gamble. And he would not hesitate to spend the money allocated for housekeeping. Heated arguments would follow if Wulan criticized his gambling habit. That was when her revulsion of him returned. And when she could not stand the situation any longer, Wulan would pack her things and go home to her parents. This happened several times, until she became pregnant, and felt obliged to stay with him.

In 1980 she gave birth to a son. Her husband's gambling habit was compounded by his inability to hold down any job. He didn't feel driven to work, since his parents were able to support him and his new family. With him gambling away any money his parents gave him, however, Wulan often ended up with nothing, and had to ask her own parents for loans.

Eventually she was so fed up, she took her 2 1/2 year old son and went to live with her parents. To lure her back to her husband, her parents-in-law built them a house on the block adjacent to their own. This arrangement worked for a time, but everything soon turned sour. Having built the house, and having to support them as well, her parents-in-law felt they had the right to meddle in their affairs any time and in any manner. Again, Wulan took the son and went back to her parents.

Seeing that Wulan would not be persuaded to come back home, her husband finally moved in with her. He brought his gambling habit with him, however, and they continued to have heated arguments.

Despairing, Wulan walked out on her husband and left her son with her parents. Without saying goodbye to the man, she went to Jakarta.

She quickly found a job in a small garment factory, and lodgings at her boss' home. For the first time in many years, Wulan felt in control of her life, and she actually had money she earned herself. After a year, she began to contact her parents, and sent some money home for her son. Unfortunately, as soon as the family discovered where she was, her parents sent her older brother to bring her back home. She was told not to disgrace the family. Her independence was short-lived.

Her revulsion of her husband increased when they got together again. She bided her time, but she was determined to find independence, yet again.

When her son turned ten, she began to hear about people going to work in Saudi Arabia. Wulan was tempted, but Saudi Arabia was a long way away and she had no friends there.

Just when her home situation became unbearable toward the end of 1992, a friend told her to try an employment recruitment agency in Malang.

When she presented herself at the company, they found her suitable for training. She agreed to accept the offer of training. After a relatively short training period, which included being taught basic Cantonese by an Indonesian woman, she was sent to work, said to be an apprenticeship, at one of the company's staff members' house. They then found her a job in Hong Kong. She gave the agency a one-off payment of Rp350,000, leaving no debt owing to them.

Wulan arrived in Hong Kong on 30 January 1993, thinking she was prepared for everything. She knew how to keep house; she knew how to look after children, she knew how to look after elderly parents; she knew how to say basic things in Cantonese.

But she was far from being prepared.

The real spoken Cantonese with its genuine variants of intonation, the landscape of Hong Kong where one had to look vertically upward to see the sky, the signposts with foreign names and characters, tossed her into complete disorientation.

She was taken by a local agent to a house, where she was told to start work then and there. The choice being sink or swim, Wulan had no choice but to comply. There didn't seem to be any problems. She would start work at dawn, and finish after 11:00 at night. She didn't know when she would get paid. She worked like an automaton, having no time to pause to think.

A week passed, and nobody mentioned anything about payment, rest days, or whether she was doing things correctly or incorrectly. Then suddenly early one morning, she was woken up and told to go back to her local agent. When she asked what she had done, her employer said that she didn't want a thief in the house.

Wulan protested, but the woman showed Wulan the purse she had found in Wulan's room, with several hundred dollars in it. She said that she recognised the serial numbers of the notes when she brought them home from the bank.

Wulan was really shaken. She didn't know how the notes had got into her purse. She usually had her purse in her room, and her room was never locked. Anyone could come in and take it – just like the way her employer had done – and planted the money there. They took her to the agent's, who was not amused at being bothered early in the morning. He told the employer to leave Wulan with him. Once alone, he interrogated her rigorously, and was finally satisfied that she was telling the truth.

The agent called the employer and persuaded her to take Wulan back. After that event, Wulan made sure she hid her purse.

One morning she noticed that her employer's youngest son opened the washing machine before the cycle was completed, so she stopped him, and told him how dangerous it was, what he was doing. He scuttled off without saying anything. That afternoon, taking the washing out of the dryer, Wulan noticed that there was something bulky in the youngest son's jacket. When she checked, she found a wad of banknotes in the pocket. She promptly called one of the elder sons and showed him what she had discovered.

The boy said that his mother mentioned having lost some money. When they fronted up to the mother that evening with the afternoon's discovery, instead of receiving an apology for the false accusation she had received, Wulan was still reprimanded for making an issue of something which had nothing to do with her. Wulan felt the blatant unfairness of the situation, but didn't dare say anything.

When payday came, she was given HK$1,200. She knew that the minimum allowable wage then was HK$3,200 (US$410), so she asked her employer to clarify the situation, mentioning also the rest days to which she knew she was entitled. Again she received a tongue lashing, this time for being impudent.

Her employer said she could have one rest day per month, but deducted HK$100 from her already reduced pay. Wulan tried to ask her agent to rectify the situation, but all he said was that she had to be grateful for having a job at all, and that she could never get that amount anywhere in Indonesia.

There was nowhere Wulan could go for help, hardly any advocacy groups having been set up at the time.

Something, however, made her snap. The couple's second son was caught taking drugs. His father grounded him, to the extent of not allowing him to leave his room. And to make sure he did not, Wulan was tasked with policing him, while everyone was at work or at school. Wulan had no experience with drug addicts. She just knew that when desperate, they could become violent. After a nerve-wracking couple of days, when the employer and the children were home for the day, she told them she wanted to go to buy cigarettes, and did not come back.

Wulan headed for the police station, but as she was waiting her turn to speak to the officer-in-charge, she fell into conversation with an Indonesian man, Jee Liang, and told him her predicament. Jee Liang, who happened to be an employment agent, asked her what she wanted to do. Wulan said that she had tolerated the humiliation from her employer long enough, and that she wanted some justice done. The man said she could stay at his agency's half-way house.

No longer living in the employer's house, Wulan felt she had a better bargaining position. Jee Liang helped her negotiate with her own agent, who passed on her employer's offer to pay her HK$5,000.00 provided she withdraw her statement to the police and leave Hong Kong to return to Indonesia immediately. Wulan refused.

The case went to the Labour Court, where her employer was found guilty and fined HK$40,000.00. Wulan received a month's wage as compensation, and an air ticket to return to Indonesia. But she told Jee Liang that she didn't want to go home.

Jee Liang took over her employment file, and found her another employer. Wulan was able to cash in her ticket.

Her new employer paid her HK$2,500.00. The first month was gruelling because she had to make a lot of readjustments to comply with the family's requirements. As she entered the second month, Wulan again found herself being accused of theft.

Just when she was ready to go to bed after a long day's work, her employer burst in and accused her of stealing her mother-in-law's money. Wulan was incredulous. How could she be so unfortunate? At the moment, all she wanted was to shut out everything and have a long sleep. Just when she felt that she was beginning to take control of her life again, she would lose it.

Suddenly she remembered Jee Liang. He was not like her earlier agent. He seemed to care. So she asked her employer to call him. True enough, Jee Liang arrived soon after. When he heard Wulan's story, he turned to her employer and demanded how she could tell that the money Wulan had in her purse, was the grandmother's. Fortunately by then Wulan had learned to note down the serial numbers of the banknotes she received as her salary. She proved to them that the money was hers, part of the salary of the previous month.

Jee Liang was livid. He told the employer that he would not allow any of his clients to be subjected to such humiliation, and that he would report the mistreatment to the Labour Tribunal. Wulan again went to stay at Jee Liang's halfway house, together with other domestic helpers who had encountered problems.

Wulan eventually found an employer who treated her like a decent human being, and has been working for her family for nearly five years, looking after two children and keeping house. Her employer, a secondary school teacher, left it to her to decide how to structure her time and work. She was paid well above the minimum allowable wage. During the day, after taking the five year old to school, she sometimes put the 2 year old in a stroller and took a walk to the nearby park, or had a cup of coffee at the nearby coffee shop.

The money she sent home had helped build a house where her son and his wife lived. She had divorced her husband, and was enjoying her relative independence.

⟞⟨◊⟩⟝

The above stories have been selected not because they are better than the others in my collection, but because of their representative nature. It is hoped that they opened a broader window to the world which had been shrunk, even distorted, by myths of stereotypes. These stereotypes were reinforced by the tendency of people, some media included, to paint only sensational pictures of this world.

WHY EMPLOY AN INDONESIAN DOMESTIC HELPER? THE EMPLOYERS' POINTS OF VIEW
The following stories are based on selected interviews with some employers, most of whom are the women of their households. I came across very few employment situations where the signatory of the employment contract was the man of the household.

Story One
Jenny, a senior public servant, needed a domestic helper to look after her two children, and to keep house. She had been employing foreign domestic helpers for ten years.

Her first two helpers were Filipinas. They were good and efficient workers, and Jenny had few complaints about the way they carried out their tasks. The only drawback about them she remembered was the bills she had received after each of them had left her employment, their contracts completed. She realized they had borrowed money from some financial institutions, and had not given the institutions any forwarding addresses despite the fact that they had not finished paying back their loans. After being left twice with the same unpleasant after-taste, Jenny decided to try employing a helper from Indonesia. She didn't make the decision based on the consideration of costs, because she was prepared to pay at least the minimum allowable wage.

Jenny felt the difference almost immediately. Yati spoke Cantonese, which meant that she was able to communicate properly with Jenny's non-English speaking relatives. And to her delight, Yati also knew how to correctly address all her employer's relatives according to Chinese tradition, instead of just using 'Sir' and 'Ma'am'. Yati was courteous, happy to oblige her beyond the call of duty, and worked as well and as efficiently as her previous helpers.

At first, Jenny had expected to treat Yati in the same manner as her former Filipino helpers. Every month she gave Yati her salary directly. Initially the young woman was surprised, because she had expected Jenny to keep it until the end of the contract.

Jenny gathered from Yati that she had allowed her agent to keep all her documents, including her passport. She owed the agent a sum of money equivalent to seven months' salary. Jenny told her that the arrangement was between her and the agent, and insisted that she handle her own money. When toward the end of the contract the agent returned the passport to her, Yati handed it to Jenny, for safe-keeping.

At this stage Jenny learned something else about employing Indonesian helpers. Having had the experience of renewing contracts with her Filipina helpers independent of agents, Jenny had expected to be able to do the same with Yati. But it was not to be.

The agent told her that contract renewals had to be done through an agent. So she had no choice but to comply, paying the agent a HK$2,000 handling fee, while Yati also had to pay the same amount. In fact, the agent said it did not matter who was paying what amount, provided the total amount the agent received was HK$4,000. On top of that Jenny had to pay HK$400 to the Indonesian Consulate to renew Yati's work visa.

Between contracts, Yati went home to Indonesia to get married. When she returned to Hong Kong she was very upset and told Jenny her unpleasant experiences at the hands of Indonesian authorities.

Yati had been told not to carry too much cash with her, so she had sent most of the salary she had saved to her parents through the bank. On her way back to Hong Kong, however, she was stopped at the immigration checkpoint in Jakarta airport. The immigration officer told her she could not leave the country because her passport had not been stamped when she had arrived. Yati told him that she had not been aware of the fact. The immigration officer said that was not an excuse, and as a result she would not be able to leave. Yati pleaded with him to let her go, because she had a contract to meet. Finally, the immigration officer said he would fix her passport for her if she paid him HK$3,000. Yati said she didn't have that much money with her. The man asked her to show him how much she had in her purse, several hundred dollars.

'Alright, just give me all you have,' he said. And Yati was too despairing to argue. She paid up.

Only after talking with fellow domestic helpers in the same situation did she realize that it was a set up, because many of them had received the same treatment. Yati was convinced that the first immigration officer had deliberately not stamped their passports in order for his colleague to collect their extortion money later on, when the workers were on the way out for another term of contract.

Jenny was amazed that these people would do such a thing to their own compatriots.

She continued learning when she employed her second Indonesian helper. After completing her second contract, Yati decided to go back home to her husband, and start a family of their own.

The second and current Indonesian helper, Hani is approximately the same age as Yati. Apart from wanting to help her family back home, she has dreams of improving her own life.

Jenny often finds Hani in a depressed mood. She asked her once if there were any problems with her work, but Hani told her it was not her work. It was her family back home.

Hani had been sending a portion of her salary to the family and keeping some for her own savings. Her savings were continuously being depleted, however, because everyone back home asked her for financial help. She had been helping them buy cellular phones, new appliances, new clothes, even a motorbike. Each demand effectively cleaned out her savings, and she saw her own dreams fading away.

Jenny feels very sorry for her, but is only able to suggest that she stop telling her family how much she has saved up.

Like Yati, Hani also speaks Cantonese, and is able to fit into Jenny's family's living environment and culture. The whole family is very happy with her working for them.

Story Two

Lilian was pregnant with her first child, and she intended to continue working after the baby was born. To maintain the family's lifestyle, they needed her income. So the family agreed to look at the possibility of employing a full-time helper.

Lilian, a senior nurse, contacted an employment agency. She and her mother-in-law went to their office and were shown the photographs of a number of prospective helpers from the Philippines, Indonesia and Thailand. Her mother-in-law chose a young woman from East Java. Her intuition told her the young woman would work well in their family. Arrangements were made, and Lilian signed the employment contract.

When Mega arrived, she was able to communicate in English with Lilian and her husband fairly effectively, but not with Lilian's mother-in-law. With the mother-in-law teaching her every day, however, she quickly learned to speak Cantonese. In no time Mega and the mother-in-law were able to have friendly chats.

Lilian taught Mega how to cook Chinese food and how to do housework according to their standard. She also knew Mega was Muslim, and did not eat pork. They worked out a *modus operandi* which did not compromise her religious observance. Eventually, they also worked out a relationship balance which included Mega working on official rest days where needed and taking time off on ordinary days. And as the arrangement evolved with changes in each family member's needs, it avoided complications thanks to the thoughtfulness of each party.

Now twelve years and several contract renewals later, the relationship between the family and Mega eventually extended beyond a mere employment relationship, because Mega fits so seamlessly into the family life. Lilian is happy that Mega was so good and close to the children, because it was indeed her primary reason for employing a helper in the first place.

Lilian knows about Mega's family back in East Java, as she tells her stories about them. She knows that eventually Mega would like to return to live close to her family, now that she has helped them build a house, and pay for her son's schooling. She knows that Mega would like to be a writer. She is just hoping that Mega won't mind working a little longer until her daughter Candy, eleven, and son Ken, seven, are independent enough to look after each other and themselves during the times she is at work.

Lilian is not sure she wants to employ another helper, of Indonesian or any other nationality, when Mega returns to Indonesia.

Story Three

Tony and Elsa decided to employ a domestic helper eight years ago when their son was barely six years old, because Elsa wanted to resume her career in nursing. They contacted an employment agency, and selected Angelita, a Filipina who had had several years' experience as a domestic helper in Hong Kong.

They were happy with their choice, because Angelita was good at housework, had a good standard of hygiene, and was familiar with Hong Kong. Within a short time, Elsa had trusted her with grocery shopping and picking their son up from school. That year he still went to school for only half a day, so having Angelita was a boon, since it was not easy for Elsa to negotiate her shifts at the hospital in order to pick him up from school in the middle of the day.

The following year her son went to school all day, so he did not have to be picked up in the middle of the day. Whenever Elsa worked nightshifts however, she would notify Angelita so she knew she would need to take him to school.

Things began to go wrong after Elsa and Tony renewed the employment contract with Angelita.

When Angelita went out on her weekly rest days, she would stay out all night. While Elsa did not feel comfortable with this new behavior, she was reluctant to say anything, because, after all, Angelita was older than herself, knew Hong Kong well, and hence should be able to look after herself. Angelita would, however, sometimes disappear for two nights in a row, for instance, leaving the house on Friday and returning on Sunday evening after 11:30.

Elsa began to be really concerned when she was told by her son's school that during the weeks Angelita took their son to school, he was always late. Elsa was naturally not very happy. She asked her son what happened the mornings Angelita took him to school. Her son told her that they did not go directly to school, but would go to places, where Angelita delivered some packets. And when they eventually went to his school, it was always late.

Elsa confronted Angelita and asked her to rearrange her priorities. She paid Angelita a wage well above the minimum allowable amount, and expected her to focus on her work.

Tony worked out that Angelita had begun a pyramid-selling business from their home during the days when she had the run of the house all day, while Tony and Elsa were at work, and their son at school. She even stored the merchandise in their store-room as well as her own bedroom. He would have tolerated the situation if Angelita had given priority to the work for which they had employed her.

Tony had had to intervene, because Angelita said Elsa was not her employer, because she was not the signatory of their employment contract, Tony was.

The improvement was, however, only short-lived. Elsa began to wonder why her grocery bills were swelling out of proportion. When she checked the bills, she found that all the usual cleaning products, such as laundry detergent, floor cleaner, window-cleaning fluid and dishwashing detergent, had been replaced by the brand that Angelita was selling. Unfortunately, they were up to three times more expensive than the usual brands they had been using. When confronted, Angelita argued that her brand was much better, cleaning better. Elsa demanded that she return to the brands they had used before.

The relationship between Elsa and Angelita became so tense and difficult that Elsa felt the futility of having a helper. Angelita demanded that if Tony's mother wanted to come to visit, she (Angelita) had to be notified two days beforehand. And if she wanted to stay overnight, she (Angelita) would want to know three days beforehand. And she always delivered these demands to Elsa, when Tony was not around.

Both Elsa and Tony thought Angelita's demands were unreasonable, and told her so. Angelita refused to cook or clean up when Tony's mother was visiting, unless they met her terms.

When the second contract had nearly expired, Elsa and Tony decided not to continue employing her by renewing the contract. To their dismay, they found out that Hong Kong regulations specified that after two contracts or four years' employment, employees were entitled to a contract renewal and a long-term service levy. If the employer decided not to renew the contract, the employee could take them to the Labour Tribunal and make the employer pay severance pay.

Elsa and Tony decided to cut their losses and pay Angelita compensation for not renewing the contract.

After Angelita left, Elsa realised how stressed she had been the last two years. So she resigned her position at the hospital and re-acquainted herself with housework and housekeeping.

Elsa had heard from her friends about domestic helpers from Indonesia, that they worked well, but needed to be trained to the employer's standard. Now that she was not working outside the home, she felt she was able to spend time training a new helper.

The agent she contacted offered several candidates, and Elsa chose Yuni. She chose Yuni partly because Yuni had never worked for anyone else, so she hoped it would be easier to train her up to her own standard.

At first Elsa had to send her back to the agent to be retrained, because she knew almost nothing about housework, such as how to use appliances and what they were, and how to structure her day. Another Indonesian domestic helper took her on as an apprentice. After a month, Elsa was able to continue where Yuni's instructor had left off.

Yuni is a slow-learner. Elsa is teaching her Cantonese, and she learns a word a day. Sometimes she even forgets the words from several days previously. Elsa likes her, however, because she is a very pleasant person. Elsa teaches her by doing everything slowly and letting Yuni watch. Where necessary she will repeat certain tasks over and over again, until Yuni remembers.

After teaching her for some time, Elsa realised that Yuni's 'yes' when asked if she had understood how to carry out certain tasks, did not always mean that she did understand.

Yuni is also scared of being left alone at home. So at first, when they all went out, Tony's mother had to come and stay with her. Then they got themselves a dog, and Yuni is now happier being left at home with the dog.

After two years in her employment, Elsa felt that while Yuni had not quite mastered everything to her satisfaction, she could be trusted with basic housework if Elsa returned to work. They renewed her contract, and Elsa resumed work part-time at the hospital.

Yuni has a caring personality. When Elsa comes home from work, she makes sure Elsa has a rest and does not have to do much. She also takes care of their son like an older sister toward a younger brother. And Elsa is impressed at her care at not wasting resources.

Elsa feels more comfortable now that Yuni is much happier because one of her sisters also now works in Hong Kong. Yuni and her sister often go out together on their rest days and other holidays.

While it took sometime for Elsa to get to know Yuni, and she is still teaching Yuni some things, she is happy with her.

Elsa could not help observing how complicated it was to renew the employment contract with an Indonesian helper. And it was a lot more expensive compared to renewing an employment contract with a Filipino helper.

'A Filipino helper will go to the immigration department, obtain the contract form, take it to the employer and the consulate for signing, then obtain a visa extension. There is no agent fee,' she observed.

As for renewing the contract with Yuni, to begin with, her Indonesian helper's passport was kept by the agent. Elsa and Tony had to renew Yuni's contract through the agent. They had to pay the agent's commission fee, reimburse the administration fee charged by the consulate, reimburse the passport fee and the visa fee.

They also inadvertently discovered that the agent would charge a much higher commission fee if the helper was paid under the legal minimum allowable wage. When they were arranging the contract renewal with Yuni, the agent at first was going to charge them a fee they knew was much higher than the standard amount. When they questioned it, the agent asked them how much they were paying Yuni. When Elsa and Tony told her, she apologized, and reset the amount to the standard HK$4,000 (theoretically HK$2,000 from the employer and HK$2,000 from the helper).

Like many people who employ foreign domestic helpers, Elsa and Tony are aware that many Indonesian helpers are paid below the minimum allowable wage, however they prefer to stay within the law. This may be due in part to their law-abiding nature as well as with Tony's work as a government auditor.

Story Four

Being Indonesian herself, Erna made a conscious decision to employ an Indonesian domestic helper. Her English husband Kevin went along with her, especially when he was not a stranger to Indonesia himself, having lived a number of years in the country.

When they first arrived in Hong Kong, Erna and Kevin went to the Indonesian Consulate to find out how to find important places and places of interest. Erna became friendly with one of the staff, whom she consulted on various issues. When Erna asked her where she could find an Indonesian domestic helper, her friend gave her the name of an agency.

Erna, who was soon to give birth, then specified for the agent what she wanted. Primarily she wanted someone good at looking after a newborn baby. She also wanted her to be able to cook, clean and do general housework. The agency suggested Tariyah.

Having a child herself at home in East Java, and having worked for another Hong Kong family for four years previously, Tariyah had no problem looking after Erna and Kevin's baby. And cooking Indonesian food came naturally to her too.

They paid Tariyah above the minimum allowable wage, and gave her the occasional gift. Having no communication problems, Erna had been able to negotiate with Tariyah what she and Kevin preferred in terms of priorities, and how certain things should be done.

Erna had had to teach Tariyah to be more imaginative and to take more initiative, and not to wait for her instructions for every little task. Now they had reached a working arrangement satisfactory to both parties.

After the first contract was nearly completed, Erna asked Tariyah whether she wanted to move on, because if that was the case Erna had to begin looking for another helper, since she was by then carrying her second child. Tariyah said she would be happy to stay in their employment. The second contract was followed by a third.

Erna and Kevin never demanded the impossible from Tariyah. Provided the children were well looked after, if the house was less than spotless, they did not complain, or if Tariyah was too busy to cook, they would dine out.

Tariyah was responsive to her employers' flexibility. If Erna and Kevin wanted to go out on a weekend, she was happy to stay to look after the children, and take her rest day on another day.

Erna and Kevin have employed Tariyah for six years now, and if, at the end of the current contract, Tariyah wanted to move on, Erna knew she would employ another Indonesian helper.

SOCIAL ASPECTS WHICH MAY CONTRIBUTE TO ABUSE OF DOMESTIC HELPERS
I was not able to interview employers who abuse their Indonesian domestic helpers, since they understandably refused to speak to strangers, especially a stranger who is going to record their behavior in a book. I was, however, able to have informal chats with residents who, on the face of it, had very little to do with employing Indonesian domestic helpers, as well as those who had been observing the situation closely. From various conversations with them, several issues came to the surface. I shall discuss the salient and persistent points which seem to contribute to abusive behaviour toward foreign domestic helpers, particularly those from Indonesia.

A conscious or unconscious expectation of impunity
The myth that only employers who are ignorant and uneducated abuse their foreign domestic helpers has not been proven true. Many of these are individuals who obviously know they are committing despicable crimes, who know that nothing could save them from prosecution if they were caught. Rima's abuser for instance, was holding a civil service position somewhere in the low to medium ranks, who was undoubtedly aware of the law in Hong Kong.

It appears that these abusers allow their basest and ugliest instincts to overwhelm their healthier mental state, because they believe that they will not get caught so their outwardly respectable-selves will remain intact.

No doubt there is a psychological side to this behavior, which may point to causes such as a deep resentment on the part of the abusers of their real status vis-à-vis their desired status, but this issue is beyond the scope of this book.

Even in their own family situations, the abusers usually try to hide their abusive actions, or at least most of their abusive actions, from their own spouses, and in the case of older offspring, from them as well.

They are relying on the vulnerability of the domestic helpers, believing that the helpers will not reveal the true situation to anyone. They know, or hope rather, that the helpers know that it would jeopardize their own situation if they told anyone. And just in case these helpers cannot help themselves, the abusers usually forbid their victims to go out of the house, depriving them of their legitimate rest days and other holidays.

These individuals are not ignorant. They know that the helpers fear being sent back without having been paid the money they hope to earn. And in many cases, they also know that their agents would not take the helpers' side in a situation of conflict, because these agents are also implicated in that they knowingly set up an employment arrangement where the employer is going to underpay the employee. So despite the law being in place to protect the helpers by recognizing them as workers, these abusers have an expectation that they can avoid prosecution by avoiding being caught.

The lack of bargaining power on the part of the helpers
Before I began my research in earnest into the situation of the Indonesian women who work as domestic helpers in Hong Kong, Singapore and Malaysia, I was repeatedly told by various people, in government as well as in the private sector, that most of these workers were well off, had been able to amass an awful lot of money, and had been able to build fairly big and beautiful houses when they returned to their home towns or home villages.

My first private reaction to that suggestion was that, good luck to them, and good luck to their families. Indeed, many have also been able to start their own businesses from their savings at the end of their working time overseas. And no doubt they deserve this success.

What should be of concern, however, is that incidents of abuse have not stopped. In fact, they have increased. This is particularly significant in Hong Kong, where the foreign domestic helpers are regarded as formal workers who enjoy the protection of the country's Labour Law.

It is worth mentioning that while incidents of abuse of domestic helpers from the Philippines have also occurred, they rarely go on for an extended period of time before the crimes are reported and the perpetrators taken to court and prosecuted. Abuse of Indonesian domestic helpers usually goes on for weeks, even months, before the victims will come out and approach the authorities. And it is never known how many abuse situations are still occurring, unreported. In many cases, the victims collaborate in hiding the fact.

It is interesting to note also, that those who are abused by their employers are usually paid below the minimum allowable wage, though not all of those who are paid below the minimum allowable wage, are abused.

Employers are also humans. And it is human nature to stretch the possibility of obtaining something cheap to the limit, without being necessarily evil.

A number of the helpers, who are initially underpaid, gradually work up the ladder and end up receiving salaries well above the minimum allowable amount. This is usually achieved by a combination of factors.

The helpers, who start work with skills below the standard generally acceptable in the eyes of most employers, learn over time and eventually become so competent in their work that they gain enough self-confidence to negotiate in an acceptable manner with their employers for higher salaries. And their employers have become so reliant on the helpers, knowing that the helpers can be trusted, that they do not mind paying them more. The situation would not be possible, however, if the type of employers involved were people who regard their domestic helpers as quasi-slaves, over whom they could exercise their power. In other words, without the necessary level of skills to begin with, the helpers do not come to the working arrangement with any bargaining power; their fate depends very much on the goodness of the employers' heart. If they are sent to good employers, they are lucky. If they are sent to bad employers, they are doomed, or at least potentially doomed.

Prevailing patronizing attitudes in the community

During my research in Hong Kong, whenever I fell into conversation with strangers, I usually said I was from Australia. When the topic of foreign domestic helpers came up, what I heard often saddened me. It was common to hear comments like, 'Indonesian maids are like children. They can't do anything by themselves. You have to tell them everything,' or 'Indonesian maids are cheap, but you really have to watch over them. They steal, they don't understand hygiene, and they bring their boyfriends home when you're not there.'

The preconceptions may very well have been based on some real experiences of some employers or former employers, however they have been blown into mythical proportions. And these preconceptions often govern the mindset of an employer who employs an Indonesian domestic helper for the first time. Here, unless the helper comes with the necessary working skills, communication skills and self-confidence, as shown by Kholifah (Story Five, *Where Working Arrangements are Positive*), the myth will undoubtedly perpetuate itself until the helper is pushed into a tight corner.

The manifestation of these preconceptions is felt not only by the helpers in their working environment, but also in their day-to-day life outside the working environment. Even other Indonesians experience this prejudice by proxy.

The following were incidents experienced by an Indonesian friend, Suraya Kamaruzzaman, who was then doing her Ph.D. program at a university in Hong Kong.

Incident One

On 13 July 2004, Suraya went to a major bank in Hong Kong where she had an account, accompanied by a foreign friend who, like Suraya, was residing in Hong Kong temporarily. When they walked in, Suraya saw Ani, an Indonesian domestic worker friend of hers, who seemed to be waiting for something. Another young woman was with her. When Suraya asked Ani what she was doing, she related something rather disturbing.

Ani and her friend had come to the bank to open an account. In an apparent attempt to confirm her occupation, the teller who served them asked Ani if she was a domestic helper. When she said yes, the teller told her that the bank policy did not allow domestic helpers to open accounts. Ani explained that it was to be a joint account with her friend, who was not a domestic helper. The teller then asked them to wait, while she apparently went to consult her superiors.

When the teller reappeared, Suraya and her friend joined Ani and her friend to find out what the problem was. The teller said then that it was all right for Ani and her friend to open the account. She was very courteous and friendly to Suraya and her friend, detailing all the advantages of having accounts in this particular bank. Suraya's friend was taken by the sales pitch, and decided to open an account there.

Just then the teller asked about their nationalities, then walked away, presumably to consult her superiors again. When she returned, she said to Ani and her friend, 'I'm terribly sorry, we don't accept accounts from Indonesian citizens.'

Suraya was taken aback. She had thought it had all been sorted out. But apparently while her friend who was not an Indonesian citizen, was welcome to open an account, her Indonesian friends were not. She confirmed that it was Indonesian citizens who were barred. When she asked how long the bank had had this policy, the teller replied, 'Since two or three years ago.'

Suraya then produced her bank book and showed it to the teller, at the same time revealing her Indonesian nationality and adding that she had had the account for less than two years. It was clear to her the teller or her superiors had made up the rule on the spot.

They didn't seem to get anywhere arguing with the teller, so Suraya went back to her office at the university and wrote a letter to the newspapers.

Incident Two

On 20 July 2004, Suraya accompanied a domestic helper friend to the Civil Registry Office, to register her oncoming marriage with her Hong Kong boyfriend. When it was their turn to come up to see the official, he asked, 'So which one of you is a domestic helper?'

Suraya was surprised that it was an issue. Her friend painted a bigger picture for her later. The experiences of her friends indicated a practice inherently patronizing and prejudiced.

When an Indonesian domestic helper was going to marry a local man, they would immediately be interviewed separately. Very intrusive questions were asked, such as, 'What color knickers does your girlfriend wear most often?', 'How many times a week do you have sex?', and 'Where do you usually have sex?'

Suraya was very cross that her friend also had to undergo such an intrusive and humiliating interrogation simply because she was going to marry a local man.

Incident Three
Toward the end of 2003, Suraya had to go to the Immigration Department on Lamma Island. Leaving the building, her mind was wandering because she was thinking of various things which she had to do before the new year.

Suddenly she was jolted by an incident unravelling before her. A little boy of about four years of age had been riding his bicycle when the end of his handlebar inadvertently touched the hand of a middle-aged Caucasian woman walking past. The little boy got off his bike and apologized to the woman, 'I am so sorry, Madam.'

Suraya was so impressed by such good manners shown by someone so young that she stopped walking and looked. Imagine her surprize when the woman suddenly turned to her and said gruffly, 'Next time don't daydream and do your job properly!'

Just then a woman who obviously was the domestic helper of the boy's family rushed to him and thinking he had been hurt, asked what had happened.

The Caucasian woman then realized her mistake, but she didn't say anything, let alone apologize. Obviously to her, Suraya was just one of the women from the country where 'unreliable' and 'incompetent' domestic helpers come from.

EMPLOYMENT AGENCIES HAVE TO RUN A VIABLE BUSINESS: THE AGENT'S POINT OF VIEW
According to the record held by APPIH, the Indonesian acronym for the Association of Agencies for Indonesian Workers in Hong Kong, in November 2004 there were 168 agencies accredited by the Indonesian Consulate General to arrange employment of workers from Indonesia. These agencies need two layers of accreditation, one from the Hong Kong Department of

Manpower and another from the Indonesian Consulate General.

These Hong Kong employment agencies have established business agreements with employment agencies in Indonesia, known by their collective Indonesian acronym PJTKI (*Perusahaan Jasa Tenaga Kerja Indonesia* or Administering Agency for Placement and Protection of Indonesian Workers Overseas). Each of the Hong Kong agencies usually keeps a list of names of Indonesian domestic helpers, complete with their particulars, sourced from its PJTKI partner(s) who supposedly have trained, or are training, these candidates. An interested employer who seeks an agency's service will be shown such a list.

When the interested party makes his/her selection, the agency will contact the PJTKI that handles the particular candidate, with a job order. The PTJKI will notify the candidate. If the candidate agrees to accept the job offer, the PJTKI will process her documents, her contract, and arrange for her pre-departure orientation program. When the domestic helper arrives in Hong Kong, the agency dealing with the employer will take care of her. In most cases, the domestic helper will be accommodated by the agency in its half-way house while the agency arranges for her local ID to be made. In some cases, however, the employer collects the domestic helper himself or herself. There may be flexibility in the agreement between the agency and the employer.

There are two important requirements for an employment agency to meet before it is accredited by the Indonesian Consulate General. Firstly, it must have a proper office, and secondly, an appropriate half-way house that can function as accommodation for newly arrived domestic helper candidates as well as a shelter for the domestic helpers who are having problems with their employers.

The Hong Kong Special Administrative Regional Government recognizes domestic helpers as formal workers. Consequently they are entitled to the same legal protection that other workers receive in Hong Kong.

I interviewed the director of one of the agencies mentioned by a number of Indonesian domestic helpers as having a caring attitude toward helpers. Muljono Harto is also a former president of APPIH.

I asked Muljono to explain why some agents or their agencies kept the Indonesian domestic helpers' passports.

He replied, 'It is illegal not to allow the helpers to keep their own passports. If a helper reports this to the Indonesian Consulate General, the consulate will call her agent and request the agent to return the passport to its legal owner, that is, the domestic helper.

'There has been some confusion, however, in that, often when helpers claim at some stage that their passports are held by their agents, when confronted, the agents say that the helpers asked them to keep these documents for safe-keeping. So to avoid further unnecessary confusion, many agencies now have a prepared letter, in Indonesian language, for the helpers to sign if they want the agencies to keep their passports.'

A number of employers reportedly prefer that the helpers not have their passports with them. They have had unpleasant experiences of being the victims of stalking by 'heavies' of some loan sharks from whom their former helpers borrowed money and did not complete the repayment. When a helper 'disappears' from the address, the loan shark to whom she owes money, descends on the former employer who is still at the address, and pressures him/her with stalking and threatening phone calls - often saying that they know where the children go to school, until the employer either pays off or contacts the police defying the threats. It transpired that many loan sharks only need the borrowers' passport details and addresses to lend money.

Some of these employers therefore, may take their helpers' passports and keep them themselves. This situation, however, can be potentially problematic for the agencies.

'According to Provision 104 of Indonesian Department of Law Regulation, the domestic helpers are the responsibility of their respective PJTKI, from the moment they are recruited until the moment they return to their home village or home town. And the agencies in Hong Kong have the obligation to liaise with their PJTKI partners, and update them on any changes and developments with their clients,' Muljono explained. Apparently, despite briefings and orientations given to Indonesian domestic helpers, most of them do not appear to have an inherent or well-developed legal awareness of their situations. As Muljono said, 'There have been cases where the employers who keep their helpers' passports, take them overseas. Innocuous as this may sound, the situation lends itself to a potential legal problem. If something happens to the helpers, they are not covered by insurance, because the coverage of the compulsory insurance policy that the employers have to take out for them, is not valid outside Hong Kong.'

In relation to those helpers who keep their own passports or whose employers keep them, some unscrupulous employers have even been known to send their helpers home, without notifying the helpers' agencies. So neither the Hong Kong agencies, nor the PJTKI legally responsible for the particular helpers, know where the helpers are, unless the helpers themselves notify their PJTKI.

If all parties abide by the law, the following should happen. the helper keeps her own passport and a copy of the employment contract, while her employer, their agency, the Indonesian Consulate General, and Hong Kong Immigration Department each keeps a copy.

WHEN CONFLICT OCCURS BETWEEN DOMESTIC HELPERS AND EMPLOYERS

In Hong Kong, there is a legal recourse when conflict occurs between a domestic helper and her employer. If a helper is abused by her employer, she can report it to the police. If it is a quarrel about the salary or working conditions, she can report it to the Department of Labour. And depending on the nature of the case, it may be settled privately, in the Labour Court, the Civil Court or the Criminal Court.

The law governing the relationship between employers and foreign domestic helpers has been translated into the Indonesian language, and published in a booklet. Each domestic helper arriving from Indonesia is, and should be, given a copy.

Many domestic helpers from Indonesia nonetheless, still request, and expect, assistance from their respective agencies, in conflict situations. Strictly speaking, the agencies have no obligation to give assistance, but some good ones do offer counselling and mediation services. And all of them, based on the terms of accreditation from the Indonesian Consulate General, have a half-way house to accommodate them, in the case where, pending the settlement of conflict, the helpers have nowhere to go.

APPIH, according to Muljono, regularly writes to local papers and Indonesian community papers, encouraging domestic helpers with problems to come and seek their counselling service. The organization has handled a number of potential suicides.

SERVICES BEYOND LEGAL REQUIREMENTS

Many agencies do not extend their services beyond the legal requirements of facilitating employment agreements, either the initial setting up or renewal of existing contract at its expiry. There are also agencies, however, which perceive and accommodate the need to offer services beyond the legal requirements. Apart from a counselling and mediation service, some agencies from time to time give financial assistance to domestic helpers in trouble.

On a number of occasions agencies have found helpers, whose employment arrangements they facilitated, have left their employers' homes and are thus no longer employed. The employers, having tracked them down, are suing them for compensation.

The helpers come to the agencies for help, because if they have only just started working, they may not have the money to compensate the employer. They claim that the employers kicked them out, but the employers counter-claim that it was the helpers who ran away, thus defaulting on their contract.

Being generally legally unaware, the helpers have not collected any evidence that the employers actually kicked them out, so they often have difficulty proving their claims. They are therefore liable to pay compensation to the aggrieved employers. Some agencies help, others do not.

Muljono's staff usually ask the domestic helpers they place to contact the agency first if they feel like leaving. And when a helper does contact them and tells them she does not want to go on working with her current employer, the staff will counsel them. They will try to find out what the source of the problem is. If it is possible to solve, then it should be solved without the helper walking out, because her walking out will cost her money she may not have.

If it is the employer who chases the helper out of his/her house, then he/she is liable to pay compensation to the helper. Either way, the claims have to be proven.

SOURCES OF AGENCIES' REVENUES

Principally speaking, employment agencies in Hong Kong receive agency fees from employers who use their service. This fee has, however, shrunk from HK$3,000 per helper, to approximately HK$670 or HK$680, because of fierce competition. So from their point of view, it is in their interest to provide the best and highly competitive service to their clients.

The agencies' lists of clients begin with the PJTKI in Indonesia. Without the PJTKI they will not get the domestic helpers. They have to prove to these clients that they are able to do good business by finding good and viable jobs for the domestic helpers, because bad feedback about particular agencies spreads fast, and PJTKI quickly learn to avoid doing business with them.

PJTKI also realise that agency fees can no longer be relied on to provide adequate revenues to the agencies in Hong Kong, so to help those agencies about whom they receive good feedback, the PJTKI will give them 'promotional' fees, since the agencies are not allowed by law to receive commission fees from the PJTKI.

Agencies also charge contract renewal fees of HK$2,000 each to the employer and the domestic helper when they renew their employment agreement contract.

DOMESTIC HELPERS WHO ARE PAID BELOW THE MINIMUM ALLOWABLE WAGE

Muljono believes that most domestic helpers from Indonesia being paid below the minimum allowable wage in Hong Kong, knowingly accept the arrangement. As far as he knows, this is how it usually happens:

Some domestic helper candidates have still not acquired the level of skills employers usually require, even after being trained for the required number of hours. Many of these continue training, while just as many also, become bored and effectively stop learning. There are limits to what a training center can offer.

In the meantime, some would-be employers who find the minimum allowable wage too expensive, try to find out if they can get some 'discounts'. So an understanding is reached. These employers can pay lower salaries but they need to allow the helpers to learn on the job. This arrangement is regarded as the helpers' apprenticeship.

Implicitly, the helpers understand that if they demand the minimum allowable wage, with their skill level, they will most likely be sent home after a brief time, since they cannot match the expectations.

The number of helpers being paid below the minimum allowable wage may have a lot to do with its relatively high amount, currently HK$3,270.00, which is a lot more than the going rate in Singapore, S$300.00 which is equivalent to HK$1,500. So even if a helper is paid HK$2,000, she is still being paid above the Singapore standard wage, Singapore being an appropriate yardstick for comparison.

WHY MANY DOMESTIC HELPERS HAVE TO WAIT FOR SIX OR SEVEN MONTHS BEFORE RECEIVING THEIR SALARIES

Ideally, when domestic helpers start work in Hong Kong, they can look forward to receiving their salaries after the first month. Most of these people have to wait six or seven months, however, before actually receiving any money for their work. This is because they have to repay their PJTKI for the costs incurred for their airfares to Hong Kong and other expenses barring the costs of processing their documents, which are legally payable by the employer. And since it is a repayment in instalments, they are charged interest as well. The calculated costs amount to HK18,000.

The agencies in Hong Kong usually collect the instalments from the helpers and pass them on to their PJTKI partners in Indonesia.

HOW UNETHICAL AGENCIES ARE REGARDED BY OTHER AGENCIES

Each time an unscrupulous agency does something unethical vis-à-vis its clients, be they the helpers or the employers, the said agency collectively taints the whole employment agency community. The employment agencies run a business, where trust and reputation are crucial. Barring the fly-by-night enterprizes, most of them want to maintain a viable and profitable business, which rely very much on clients' feedback.

Unfortunately, agencies are often in situations where the interest of one type of clients – the employers, is not necessarily the same as that of another type of clients – the helpers, the agencies often have to make a moral decision and this may not please all parties.

THE ROLE OF THE OFFICE OF INDONESIAN CONSULATE GENERAL

The Indonesian Consulate General plays an important role in laying down the rules for employment agencies which seek to establish business partnerships with PJTKI in Indonesia. These agencies are, at least in principle, unable to put these partnerships into operation without consulate accreditation, because all legal job orders for the counterpart PJTKI have to be endorsed by the consulate.

From my conversations with the domestic helpers in Hong Kong, as well as those who have left their employment in Australia and Indonesia where they now live, the consulate's presence does not loom large in their day-to-day experience. The only occasions they come in contact with the consulate office are when they want to renew their employment contracts, their visas, or their passports. And the other occasions, sadly, are when they run away from their employers after serious clashes or after being abused, and their agents are unresponsive.

The consulate has an emergency shelter for such an occasion.

To seek the views of the Office of the Consulate General, I requested an interview with the Consul General, Paiman Turnip, which he kindly granted. We conducted the interview on 22 November 2004, in his office in Causeway Bay. Present also were the Consul on Information Affairs, Dwatmaji Hanomanresi, and the Consul and Counsellor Enny B Hardjito. Here is the edited version of the interview:

How do you see the evolution of the Consulate General's role in the situation of the domestic helpers working here, since the end of 1970s?

At the time there were only a handful of PJTKI who recruited domestic helpers for Hong Kong. Similarly, there were only a couple of employment agencies in Hong Kong that handled the placement of these helpers. So it was easy to monitor the cases. The number of domestic helpers arriving from Indonesia increased gradually. In 1992, it had reached around 8,000. A steep increase followed then. By 1995, there were over 16,000 domestic helpers from Indonesia working here, with around twenty local employment agencies handling their placement.

Problems began to surface. The Consulate General's brief remains the same. We have the obligation of serving and protecting our citizens wherever they work.

That core brief is the same for every diplomatic mission. Of course in practice there are variants in each locality.

What kinds of problems did the office of Consulate General encounter early in the 1990s?

We came across problems such as early termination of contracts. They were relatively easy to handle. This may be because the employers in Hong Kong were generally from the upper middle-class who were used to employing domestic helpers. Later on the number of households where both husband and wife have to work continued to increase. Many of these employers, who are workers themselves, are probably more demanding. They probably think that they are paying the helpers a significant proportion of their own salaries, so are terribly unhappy when the work of the helpers is not up to their standard.

In the meantime, our domestic helpers are becoming more assertive. They argue. Here we have a situation where neither party concedes being at fault. The conflict may lead to the helper leaving the house. The employer goes to the police saying that the helper ran away, the helper goes to the police saying the employer kicked her out, or that the employer abused her.

If it is the helper who runs away from the employer's house, then seeks protection from the Consulate General, will the consulate encounter legal problems with the authorities?

No. If any of our helpers comes to us, claiming she has been abused, we will report the case to the police. And the police will arrest her employer, and set a legal proceeding in motion. If the claim is proven, the perpetrator goes to jail. This is what I like about Hong Kong. The law is enforced.

Do people who come here as domestic helpers know that is the case?

They should. The Hong Kong Government has produced information brochures and booklets specifically for foreign domestic helpers, translated into appropriate languages, which, inter alia, tell the helpers not to sign blank documents, to expect being compensated financially if not given a weekly rest day, and just as importantly, how to sue abusive employers.

Can the consulate in any way monitor the working conditions of the domestic helpers?

We have no mechanism for that. What we are able to do is to hear out complaints from the domestic helpers who come to us, then respond appropriately. The consulate has a twenty-four hour access line for all Indonesian domestic helpers working in Hong Kong. Each section head has a cellular phone for the specific purpose of receiving complaints from the helpers. Their numbers are regularly broadcast on the radio, and are given individually to helpers who come in contact with us.

Are diplomatic and official relations between the Indonesian Consulate General and the Hong Kong SAR government very good?

Yes, very good indeed. Whenever we report anything to any government department, it is acted on immediately.

How do you describe the role of Indonesian Consulate General in relation to the working arrangement of the domestic helpers?

We have an agreement with the Immigration Department here that all employment contracts have to be endorsed by our office. Those which are not, will not be passed by the Immigration Department. So we can demand all employment agencies who handle placement of domestic helpers from Indonesia to have our accreditation. One of the conditions for the accreditation is, they each have to have a shelter for helpers who run into problems with their employers.

The shelters are relatively small, but each accredited agency has one. And on top of that, the consulate has an emergency shelter, too.

Have there been agencies who have their accreditation cancelled?

Yes, whenever we discover that an agency has breached their obligations, we cancel its accreditation. In the seven months since I took up my post, there have been four cancellations. Added to that, a number of agencies have been suspended for a period of time.

Many domestic helpers as well as employers have been unhappy about the new regulation regarding renewing contracts independent of agencies. The helpers are required to produce documents that are difficult to obtain in the time allowed. The documents in question are statements from parents or guardians at home stating that they do not object to the helpers renewing employment contracts independent of agencies, and a copy of family cards endorsed by their village heads or regional heads. These things take time to obtain in Indonesia. Why is it so difficult to renew contracts without agencies?

All domestic helpers know when their contracts expire. If they think obtaining the documents will take a long time, they should allow the time necessary to obtain the documents if they intend to renew the contracts independent of agents.

But why is it necessary to have those documents to renew a contract without agents?

When a helper renews her contract independent of agents, she is on her own, in charge of her own welfare. If something happens to her, however, it is our responsibility to give her assistance. That is fine and good. But if she falls seriously ill and needs repatriation, it is our responsibility to make sure she is appropriately repatriated, or if she dies, to send her remains to her family. That would be fine if she had a clear and proper address. You know addresses in rural areas in Indonesia can be very complicated. So we need at least the information concerning her family, substantiated by the village head. It is all to ensure that we would be able to find the right address if the worst scenarios happened.

If she is still using an agent, who is accountable to the PJTKI which sent her in the first place, if something happens to her, we can hold them accountable for her welfare, such as her proper address, and so forth.

In fact, there have been a number of occasions where remains were sent to a wrong address, simply because the consulate was given inaccurate information.

Why is it necessary for them to have a letter of permission from spouses, parents or guardians? If they are grown up enough to work overseas, aren't they grown up enough to renew their contracts?

When recruiting a domestic helper, a PJTKI requires a letter of statement from her parents or spouse. So there is a direct contact between the PJTKI and the recruit's parents. If something happens to the person in Hong Kong, the parents or spouse can be immediately notified. Now if the PJTKI is out of the picture, supposing the person commits a crime and is imprisoned, goes missing or dies, the consulate is responsible for notifying the parents or spouse. How are we to do that if we don't have the contact details? We also want to make sure that the parents or spouse know that the person is no longer with an agent or PJTKI.

Do you know that in 2004 alone, thirteen domestic helpers died. Seven from illness, and six from suicide. So we know what can go wrong, and we have to be very careful.

Why do some agents keep the domestic helpers' documents?

There is nothing in the law which specifies that the agents should keep the domestic helpers' documents. In fact, legally the domestic helpers should keep their own passports. If they don't report this to the consulate, however, we cannot take any action.

I can only speculate why this arrangement takes place. Firstly, the domestic helpers, and probably the agents as well, are afraid that the documents might get lost, secondly, in case the helpers run away from their employers, they cannot leave Hong Kong, thirdly, the agents don't want them to go to another agency.

There have also been many cases where those who have their passports with them, are persuaded to be witnesses for their friends who borrow money from some dubious financial institutions, then find themselves in trouble when the friends disappear with the money.

Does the consulate send regular reports about problems in Hong Kong concerning the situation of the domestic helpers to the Department of Manpower in Indonesia?

Every week. However, in terms of the cases of domestic helpers who fall victims to loan sharks, there is not much the Department of Manpower in Indonesia can legally do.

How do you see the situation in Hong Kong?

It is complex. The people who come here to work as domestic helpers come for different reasons. Some come because they have seen the success their friends had, some urgently want to help their struggling families in their home towns, some want to get away from their families, and some are driven by their sense of adventure. We have to study them in order to be able to assess how to prepare ourselves to face the problems which arise out of the increasing complexity of the situation.

Regarding unscrupulous agents and PJTKI, as soon as I find out about them I report them to the Department of Manpower.

It is more difficult to assess the situations in relation to employers. We can only surmise. Take a recent case, where one night an employer flew into a rage and beat up her helper. The helper left the house and came to the consulate. A security guard received her. The guard reported it to the police, and was subsequently able to testify that he had seen fresh bruises on the helper's face and arms when she had come to the consulate. So what actually started the incident we don't know for sure, but we know for sure that the helper was physically abused. And as I said before, the authorities here take immediate action.

What proportion of your time is taken up with handling the domestic helpers' situation?

Our main brief here is handling trade and economic relations with Hong Kong, since political issues are handled from Beijing. So it is our task to exhort Hong Kong business people to invest in Indonesia and to buy Indonesian products. It is our task to beat the path for Hong Kong residents to come and visit Indonesia. And it is also our task to make sure that Indonesian workers have a good ambience to work in. All those things have to be done proportionally.

Since the problems relating to the domestic helpers are more urgent and have the potential to cause human suffering, they take up many more of our working hours.

Are you and non-governmental organizations who are concerned with the domestic helpers' issue doing the same work in this case?

The same goal, which is to seek justice for the aggrieved party. The non-governmental organizations, however, usually have one advantage over us. When the court cannot prove the guilt of a perpetrator of cases of abuse of a domestic helper, we cannot go further. These organizations can. They have certain mechanisms to do that.

THE ROLE OF NGOS IN THE REGARD TO INDONESIAN DOMESTIC HELPERS

There are now several non-governmental organizations related to Indonesian domestic helpers in Hong Kong. They are not all actively engaged on advocacy programs, but each has an important role to play in the support, be it of a moral, emotional or legal nature, of the Indonesian domestic helpers working in Hong Kong.

Of the advocacy type organizations, the Indonesian Migrant Workers' Union (IMWU) has links to other workers unions in the region, and has access to wider workers' networks as well as media network.

Of the more mutual support type organizations are *Annisa*, *Majelis Ta'lim*, *Himpunan Sosial Aktivis Sholehah Indonesia di Hong Kong Halaqoh* and *Forum Komunikasi Mukminat Peduli Umat* (FKMPU) which have varying degrees of Muslim emphasis; Jogja Club which has an ethnic Central Javanese emphasis; *Sanggar Budaya* and *Forum Lingkar Pena Hong Kong* (FLKHK) which have a creativity emphasis; *Asosiasi Masyarakat dan Mantan Tenaga Kerja Wanita Indonesia di Hong Kong* (AMANAH) which has a social fellowship emphasis.

And embracing almost all these emphases is the Coalition of Indonesian Migrant Workers in Hong Kong (*Koalisi Organisasi Tenaga Kerja Indonesia di Hong Kong* – KOTKIHO) which encompasses IMWU, FKMPU, AMANAH, *Jogja Club*, *Majelis Ta'lim* and *Sanggar Budaya*.

The most prominent of these organizations, especially in the media, is IMWU. It is through IMWU that many people outside Hong Kong learned about the situation of the Indonesian domestic workers in this special administrative region. This is in addition to articles about the domestic helpers in various user-countries that are published from time to time in the Indonesian media. The dissemination of information no doubt has an effect in pressuring the Hong Kong Government to make legislative improvements in the area of foreign domestic helpers' employment.

This certainly does not mean that the more mutual support type organizations are of secondary importance, because they provide a comfort zone – albeit mainly moral support to many helpers -, a sense of not being alone, friendless and hopeless to those toiling away in other people's homes, their places of work.

Unique to Hong Kong, is the presence of *Sanggar Budaya* or Cultural Workshop, and *Forum Lingkar Pena Hong Kong or* Hong Kong Forum of Pen Circle, where those who have various degrees of artistic and creative drive can develop and build their talent and provide mutual support. They have had a number of performances which drew praise and positive reviews in local community newspapers.

Just as important, is the role of non-governmental organizations such as Hong Kong's Mission for Filipino Migrant Workers, a legal aid center which has extended assistance to many Indonesian domestic helpers by taking up their cases, thus obtaining special permits for them to stay in Hong Kong beyond the usual fourteen day limit while waiting for the hearing at the appropriate courts.

And since the women need food and shelter, there are also shelters run by various non-profit bodies, which depend mainly on donations. One example is Bethune House, a halfway house and shelter owned by a church in Kowloon and run by a Filipino Catholic nun, who also extends generous helping hands to Indonesian domestic helpers in trouble.

CHAPTER TWO
SINGAPORE

SETTING THE SCENE

Relations between Singapore and Indonesia are expected to strengthen, if signals at the ministerial level are to be believed. On 8 November 2004, Singapore Prime Minister, Mr. Lee Hsien Loong made his introductory visit to Indonesia. Mr. Lee, then fifty-two, the third prime minister of Southeast Asia's most technologically and economically developed country, met with Mr. Susilo Bambang Yudhoyono, the sixth president of the region's largest though not its strongest, economy. During the meeting, the two leaders agreed to resolve bilateral issues rationally and avoid the "megaphone" diplomacy of the media.

Answering reporters' questions after the meeting, Mr. Lee said negotiations between the countries should be rational and constructive so that the result is a 'win-win' outcome. Several issues remain to be resolved, however, such as extradition, trade transparency, smuggling and, last but hardly least, the approach to terror and security in the region.

Trade is also a focus. On 7 December 2004, almost immediately after her appointment as Trade Minister in Indonesia's new government under Yudhoyono, Ms. Mari Elka Pangestu, visited Singapore at the invitation of Singapore's Minister for Trade and Industry, Mr. Lim Hng Kiang. The two ministers discussed issues relating to closer economic cooperation, the on-going negotiations on the Singapore-Indonesia Investment Guarantee Agreement, and plans for a Singapore-Indonesia joint tourism mission to China.

Singapore was Indonesia's fifth-largest investor in 2003, buying up considerable assets of former conglomerates and state enterprises, such as banks and telecommunications.

On the humanitarian front, two days after the 26 December 2004 tsunami disaster, Singapore's Ministry of Manpower urged all employers of foreign workers from affected countries to show compassion and patience, and to assist their workers whose families may have been affected by the catastrophe, the most devastated of these being Indonesia.

AT GROUND LEVEL

On 20 December 2004, newspaper reports in Singapore told of an Indonesian domestic helper who jumped to her death from the twenty-third floor on an apartment building after dropping the baby she had been meant to look after.

'She stood on a wooden stool and climbed out onto the window ledge, where she sat with the crying baby balanced precariously on her lap for at least five minutes before letting go of the boy,' reported DPA.

An eyewitness, John Chua, was quoted, 'She was sitting there... and kept turning her head back as if she was talking to someone inside the room. Suddenly, she just extended her arms out and let the baby slip from her hands. A while later, she pushed herself off the ledge with her hands.'

She had been working for the family for less than a year.

Two months previously, on 22 October 2004, a newspaper item told of an employer of an Indonesian domestic helper, who was prosecuted for not paying the helper for almost two years.

She was fined S$12,075 (US$7,144), the equivalent of two years and eleven months' foreign domestic helpers' levy, for illegal employment, and S$3,000 (US$1,775) for failing to pay the helper. She was also ordered to pay S$3,580 (US$2,118) to the helper.

Helen Tan, then president of the Association of Employment Agencies, was quoted as saying that the court order sent a very strong, good signal so employers would realize that it was their basic responsibility to pay their foreign domestic helpers their salaries.

SINGAPORE AS USER OF FOREIGN DOMESTIC HELPERS' SERVICE

Neighbor with a stronger economy

World Bank's statistics put Singapore's 2004 per capita income at US$24,220, and updated Bloomberg's data on the country's unemployment rate put it at 3.7 per cent. Indonesia's 2004 per capita income has been put at US$1,140 with an updated unemployment rate of 10.3 per cent. This may be rendered even more stark when complemented by a reality check.

Even ignoring the hidden unemployment or underemployment in Indonesia, and taking the figure 10.3 per cent at face value, 10.3 per cent of Indonesia's working population of 120 million, is over 12.36 million. So the actual number of officially unemployed people in Indonesia is 12.36 million; two and a half times the entire population of Singapore of under 4.5 million.

Added to the above reality are two major contributing factors which drive the need of Singapore households to employ domestic helpers. The first is the continuously increasing education levels of Singaporeans with more and more women aspiring to their own career paths. The second is the Singapore 'Dream', much aired on electronic as well as print media in the region, of the five 'C's: cash, car, condo, credit card, and country club membership, which has to be supported by two incomes.

With both husband and wife in the workforce, the existing childcare service is not an ideal solution, since what needs to be done at home is a lot more than just looking after the children. There are chores like cleaning, washing, general tidying-up, even cooking to do. And if there are elderly parents living in the household, they need looking after too.

Market forces come into play, with a little help from the government. The neighboring countries, Indonesia, the Philippines, India, Bangladesh and Thailand have a surplus of inexpensive human resources, eager to take whatever work is on offer. And for Singaporeans, employing a live-in domestic helper means being able to concentrate more on the job in their own places of work.

Government laying out the legal infrastructure, and laying down the law

The authorities are very much aware of the spatial limitations of the city-state, and that at the same time the lure of living in a comparatively healthy economy is felt by those in the less wealthy neighboring countries in the region. The combination of the need for the inexpensive service of foreign domestic helpers, and the caution not to open the door too wide, is reflected very clearly in the Ministry of Manpower's regulation on bringing in foreign domestic workers/helpers.

According to the government's Foreign Domestic Worker Scheme, a Singapore citizen can apply directly for a foreign domestic helper to the Work Permit Department in the Ministry of Manpower, or through a domestic helpers' agency. To guard against foreigners flooding in to Singapore with the hidden intention of becoming domestic helpers, the regulation speci-fies that the person to be hired should not be in Singapore at the time the work permit application is submitted. She (or he, for that matter) can enter Singapore only after the employer has been given an in-principle approval letter from the Work Permit Department, and the employer has paid a se-curity deposit of S$5,000 (US$2,958).

The S$5,000 security deposit (known as 'security bond'), is to ensure that the employer repatriates the helper at the end of the two-year contract. Failing to do so will cost the employer the deposit. In the day-to-day life, this policy effectively recruits the employer as an unofficial monitor on the helper's well-being, behavior, and often, their whereabouts.

The employer is responsible for the helper's observance of the compulsory initial and subsequent six-monthly medical examinations, and for making sure that the helper does not fall pregnant during the duration of the two-year contract. This responsibility may cause some employers to be reluctant to allow the helper too much freedom of movement.

In the meantime, before the Ministry of Manpower can issue a work per-mit to the helper, she has to promise to abide by a list of conditions, which include among others, not to go through any form of marriage or apply to marry under any law, religion, custom or usage, with a Singapore Citizen or Permanent Resident in or outside Singapore, without the prior approval of the Controller of Work Permits, while holding a work permit, and also after cancellation of her work permit. If she breaches this condition, she will be expelled and prohibited from re-entering Singapore.

If there are any loopholes in terms of the helper forming any relationship with a Singapore citizen or resident, they are closed by the clause where the helper has to promise not to co-habit with any of the above.

In fact, to make sure no children are born of foreign domestic helpers, the conditions also include a promise from the helper not to become pregnant or deliver any child in Singapore during the validity of the helper's work permit or visit pass, and not to engage in any relationship with a Singapore resident that will result in the birth of a child.

At least all the above are clear-cut and easy to prove. One clause however, is so ambiguous that it must cause concern to those who read the conditions carefully and ponder the possible implications: a promise not to indulge or be involved in any illegal, immoral or undesirable activities including breaking up families in Singapore.

No minimum allowable wage; no standard contract

Singapore Law does not recognize foreign domestic helpers as formal workers, so they do not have legally protected rights such as rest days, annual leave, or leave of absence. As informal workers they do not have a standard contract, but the government encourages their employers to have an individual contract, specifying the working arrangements. They do not have a minimum allowable wage, and interestingly, neither do formal workers in Singapore. Market forces play an important role, because both employers and employees have the continuum of the going rates as their bargaining parameter.

In the case of foreign domestic helpers, the only definite amounts payable by the employer in the employment arrangement are to the government: the S$5,000 security deposit, and the monthly levy of S$250 or US$148 (reduced on 25 August 2004 from S$345 or US$204). The helper's salary is negotiable. Indonesian domestic helpers usually receive between S$150 (US$89) and S$250 (US$148).

Another cost incurred by the employer is a personal accident insurance for the helper. The employer can shop around for the best insurance cover provided the minimum payout is S$10,000 (US$5,917).

With no standard contract, the terms of employment are potentially very flexible. The government advises employers to draw up an employment contract with the helpers specifying terms and conditions of work such as salary, rest days, medical benefits, and scope of duties, but stops short of making it compulsory.

Employers are also exhorted to develop good relationships with their helpers, and warned not to mete out physical or other punishment themselves in instances of conflict.

Employers found abusing their helpers are threatened with prosecution in court and punished according to the law. What is more, the Penal Code has been amended so that employers found guilty of committing an offence against their helpers face heavier penalties. Here are some examples:

- For voluntarily causing hurt: up to one-year imprisonment or up to S$1,500 (US$887.50) fine, or both.
- For voluntarily causing hurt by dangerous weapons or means: up to five-years imprisonment or fine or caning or any two such punishments.
- For voluntarily causing grievous hurt: imprisonment of up to seven years, and shall also be liable to fine or to caning.
- For wrongful confinement: up to one-year imprisonment or up to S$1,000 (US$592) fine or both.

Abuse, nonetheless, occurs. And on some occasions, abuse leads to retaliation against the abusers. And when all this happens, the immediate victims are not only the foreign domestic helpers or the employers, because in the big picture, everyone who is in anyway related to those involved, is affected. The violence detrimentally affects the lives of both parties and their families and those close to them.

HOW LIVES ARE AFFECTED: A SAMPLE OF THREE HIGH-PROFILE CASES REPORTED IN THE REGIONAL MEDIA

Story One

Juminem, nineteen, and Siti Aminah, sixteen, both domestic helpers from Indonesia, were arrested by Singapore Police on 2 March 2004, charged with murdering Juminem's employer, Esther Ang Imm Suan, a forty-seven year old procurement specialist in an oil company. Ang was found strangled on her bed with bruises on her neck, hands and legs. Juminem had worked for Ang for approximately six months before the murder, while Siti Aminah had worked five months for Ang's second former husband.

This story has been selected because it was the first time the state assigned two senior counsels, Jimmy Yim and Alvin Yeo, to defend foreign domestic helpers. I have reconstructed the story from informal interviews with various sources and reportage of the following media: *The Straits Times, Cyberita, Channel News Asia, Media Indonesia, Kompas, The Jakarta Post, Koran Tempo, Jurnal Perempuan, Jurnal Depnakertrans* and *Waspada*. At the time of writing, the trial was still continuing in a Singapore court.

Who is Juminem?

The now twenty year old woman is the youngest child of subsistence farmers Kadiman (seventy-two years) and Sukiyem (sixty-eight years) in a village in Lampung, South Sumatra. She is the only secondary school graduate among the children of Kadiman and Sukiyem, and the only one still unmarried.

In mid-2003, Juminem was approached by a 'sponsor', a person who recruits young women to work overseas as domestic helpers. The sponsor told her of the wonderful prospects of working in Singapore, which no one in her position would normally dream of having. She would get proper training beforehand at a training centre belonging to an employment and recruitment agency or PJTKI, be matched with a suitable employer, and have her documents processed. The then barely nineteen year old woman was understandably interested, especially when she thought of how she could help the finances of her family.

Finally she told her parents about her extraordinary luck at finding the opportunity to improve the family's lot. Her parents were at first apprehensive, but knowing that Juminem was their brightest and most educated child, they relented and gave her their blessings. Juminem left her village in July 2003, to receive training in Jakarta.

On 2 September 2003 Juminem began working for Esther Ang Imm Suan in Singapore.

Who is Siti Aminah?

Siti Aminah is the only child of Sumini and Sabik, residents of the village of Kraton, in the region of Jember, East Java. Upon finishing junior secondary school (Year Nine), she was approached by a sponsor in the same village, and asked if she wanted to follow the example of many young women before her, who had been recruited to work overseas as domestic helpers. Aminah did not need much persuasion. In fact, of the 3,500 families in Kraton, only a handful of families had never had any of their daughters working as domestic helpers in Saudi Arabia, Hong Kong, Singapore and Taiwan. Most of these women returned after a successful time working and earning money abroad, enough to build new brick houses or remodel their bamboo houses into permanent brick houses.

Aminah was subsequently trained by a PJTKI and sent to Singapore. She was employed by Jack Boon, where she met and made friends with Juminem, the domestic helper employed by Boon's former wife Esther Ang. Juminem, although employed by Esther was told to clean Boon's house twice a week.

The friendship could have proven to be detrimental to Siti Aminah's future as domestic helper in Singapore, or anywhere else, because she became the co-accused in the murder case of Esther Ang, a crime punishable by a death sentence.

Juminem's working experience
Juminem began working for Ang on 2 September 2003. The young woman reportedly noted in her diary that it did not take Ang long before she started abusing her verbally. Ang, according to Juminem, would call her 'a pig' and 'a dog', and often 'a stupid pig' and 'a stupid dog', both animals being respectively *haram*, non-kosher, and najis, unclean, in Islam, Juminem's religion.

Later on, Ang would progress to physically abusing her, by pinching her, pushing her, and when she was down, kicking her in the chest.

Juminem was forced to work in three homes: Ang's own, Ang's sister Irene's, and Ang's former husband Jack Boon Ching Chung's. She worked from dawn until near-midnight, and when she was too tired and made mistakes, Ang would abuse her and 'fine' her S$10 for each mistake.

The diary entries tell of Juminem's anger and feeling of humiliation, and her pleading to God to make her employer realize what she was doing to her.

The assault on Ang
On 2 March 2004, Jack Boon, Ang's former husband, contacted Singapore Police after Juminem and his own domestic helper, Siti Aminah, reported

to him that there had been a robbery in Ang's house and Ang was fatally wounded.

Police found Ang's body on her bed. She had been strangled, and there were bruises on her neck, hands and legs. Police also found Juminem injured. She had cuts and bruises on her forehead, consistent with having been hit with a hard object.

Suspicious circumstances and subsequent confessions

Police found discarded receipts and a cheque for S$25,000 made out to Siti Aminah, all bearing what looked like Ang's signatures. Further investigation and questioning brought out confessions from Juminem and Siti Aminah, that Juminem, with Siti Aminah's help, had murdered Ang. They had allegedly confessed and each signed a written statement without even asking for a lawyer.

Juminem wrote that her employer Esther Ang had ill-treated her, and that she had been subjected to verbal and physical abuse such as beating and clawing by Ang. She also stated that she had been forced to work at three different homes, and for the two other homes she had to clean twice a week, she was paid $10 extra per month. She killed her employer Esther Ang by using a pillow to cover Ang's head when she was asleep. When Ang struggled, Juminem sat on her and strangled her.

Siti Aminah in her written confession stated that she had worked for the victim's former husband for five months. Her father had to lie that she was nineteen because Singapore had a minimum age requirement for foreign domestic workers, then eighteen (which was raised to twenty-three at the beginning of 2005). Siti Aminah also made a written statement, saying that she and Juminem had discussed how to kill Ang. She said she had tried to persuade Juminem to change employer instead, but eventually agreed to help her. Siti Aminah wrote that she watched Juminem kill Ang, then tied up Ang's legs.

What the trial uncovered

Apart from recording in her diary her anger at the constant humiliation she received from Ang, Juminem confided in Siti Aminah. She told her fellow worker that Ang was not only abusing her everyday and fining her S$10 each time she made mistakes, the woman also withheld some of her salary. She then expressed a desire to kill Ang.

Siti Aminah suggested that Juminem take the money owing to her and change employer, without having to kill the woman. But Juminem was determined.

How Siti Aminah eventually took part in the act was a source of disagreement between Deputy Public Prosecutor David Khoo and Juminem herself. DPP Khoo suggested that it was Juminem who had persuaded Siti Aminah to take part. Juminem, on the other hand, said that Siti Aminah had disliked Ang very much, and had indeed been a willing participant.

After Ang died, Juminem took Ang's keys from her bag, opened a drawer in Ang's wardrobe, took money from it and gave it to Siti Aminah. She then practised forging Ang's signature on receipts, before actually forging it on a cheque payable to Siti Aminah. When she felt it was still not good enough a forgery, she discarded it and wrote another one, payable to herself. She knew Ang's signature because she had seen Ang sign documents. Juminem also asked Siti Aminah to hit her on the head with a bottle to make it look like a robbery had taken place.

The prosecution used the fact that Juminem had discussed the attack with Siti Aminah a week previously to put to the court that the murder had been premeditated. The prosecution also submitted that the premeditated murder had been motivated by an intention to rob Ang of her possessions, giving as proof the fact that Juminem had forged a cheque, taken cash as well as nine credit cards belonging to Ang.

Dr Douglas Kong, a psychiatrist who examined Juminem, however, had the view that the young woman had acted in a lapse of self-control brought on by severe provocation by Ang. Refuting the prosecution's suggestion that the ability to formulate a plan showed that Juminem was capable of logical thought at the time, Dr Kong explained that people could carry out many seemingly complicated activities in a state of numbness and incoherence. He added that only people under great emotional duress could hurt themselves without thought of pain, as Juminem eventually had done in having a bottle smashed against her own forehead.

Following Dr Kong's argument, the defence argued that Juminem's taking of the nine credit cards belonging to Ang had not been premeditated. It could not have been part of her natural thinking, since she had never owned a credit card, nor had she ever learned to use one before.

Juminem's lawyer, Jimmy Yim, said Juminem had been suffering from 'reactive depression', and that she had finally snapped after a long stretch of provocation, and had lost her self-control.

In seven months, Juminem's weight had gone down from fifty kilograms to 46.4 kilograms.

Esther Ang was described by Juminem, directly as well as in her reading of entries in her diary in court, as an abusive person who enjoyed hurting her domestic helper. This was to an extent supported by Ang's own younger siblings who testified in court.

Ang's younger brother and younger sister both admitted that Esther Ang had been quick and short-tempered. The sister, Irene Ang, said that she had seen the victim screaming at Juminem on one or two occasions.

Ang's former second husband, Jack Boon, testified that Ang had been a fastidious woman who would look under the table for dust, and that she had had gambling problems. He also claimed having heard Ang threaten to fine her domestic helpers if they had been lazy or if they had broken a glass.

It was interesting to note, however, that Boon said he had not been aware of Ang ill-treating her helpers. He did not regard making the helpers work every day from 6:00 am to 11:00 pm without a single rest day, or verbally abusing them regularly, as a form of ill-treatment.

Sentenced to prison terms

Both Juminem and Siti Aminah escaped the death sentence. On 5 September 2005, Justice Choo Han Teck sentenced Juminem to life imprisonment and Siti Aminah to ten years imprisonment for culpable homicide. Justice Choo was satisfied that they were suffering from 'abnormalities of mind' at the time of the offence, and hence stood down the murder charge proposed by the prosecution.

Story Two

In late July 2002, Singapore went through a week to ten days of shock, after learning about the case described as 'the worst maid abuse case in Singapore'.

A freelance tour guide, Ng Hua Chye, was tried for heinously abusing his family's domestic helper for nine months, culminating in a severe beating which led to her death on 2 December the previous year (2001).

I have chosen this story, because the case has shocked so many people in Singapore that a civil consciousness group, TWC2, was formed almost immediately after the story appeared in the media. For at least a week, Singapore society was in an intense shock at the extent of inhumanity existent among them. The case was widely reported in the media, including Singapore's *Business Times, Straits Times, Electric New Paper,* Hong Kong's *Asian Wall Street Journal,* Indonesia's *Koran Tempo, Kompas, Suara Merdeka,* and *The Age* in Australia.

Nineteen year old Muawanatul Chasanah started working for Singapore couple Ng Hua Chye and Tan Chai Hong at the beginning of 2001. Nine months later, on 2 December, she was dead. Her body was a horrific sight, covered in cuts and other injuries. *The Straits Times* reported that her left ear had been battered into a 'cauliflower', that post mortem reports recorded the rotan marks crisscrossing her buttocks and limbs, and sores, some yet to be healed, which dotted her back, the result of jabs with a hammer's handle. Her back and neck were discolored, reported the newspaper, evidence of scalding. 'Her final indignity: She was found with vomit on her T-shirt with a distended stomach that could barely fit into the blue jeans which were being held up by a string', wrote Karen Ho and Elena Chong of *The Straits Times*.

What the trial uncovers
For nine months Muawanatul Chasanah was regularly starved and subjected to violent physical abuse by Ng Hua Chye. She worked in two apartments, one in Chai Chee belonging to Ng, and another in Bedok Reservoir, belonging to Ng's sister, where the young woman was found dead.

She was only given a packet of instant noodles for her lunch and dinner, despite having to work hard day in day out, looking after the house and looking after the children. Each time she did something which displeased Ng, she would be kicked, punched, slapped, whipped, jabbed with sharp objects or scalded with hot water by her employer.

When she first came to Singapore, she was a healthy nineteen year old weighing fifty kilograms. At her death, she weighed only thirty-six kilograms with more than 200 injuries on her body.

Some journalists found it hard to believe that the abuse could be taking place for nine months without anyone in the apartment buildings knowing about it. They finally found a sixty-nine year old neighbor in Chai Chee who remembered seeing a young woman, 'She would peer through the flat's window shutters, saying that she was hungry. She was given only a few packets of Maggi *mee* to eat. She said she couldn't stomach it, so she would ask me if I could buy her some bread.' The neighbor said he had bought bread for the young woman seven or eight times. He also revealed that over the past year or so since Ng and his family came to live in the building, they had had four domestic helpers before Muawanatul, and each had only stayed for a couple of months.

Ng, according to the Chai Chee neighbor, had always been scolding the domestic helper, however he then said, 'but I don't know what he (Ng) was saying.'

In the Bedok Reservoir neighborhood, only one neighbor remembered the young woman. The thirty-one year old neighbor said the family had kept very much to themselves. And the domestic helper had seldom left the flat. 'I saw her only a few times in the mornings or in the evenings watering plants outside the flat. She was very thin, and always looked tired and unhappy,' he recalled, adding, 'She was nineteen but she looked like she was in her forties.'

Asked if he would have reported the abuse to the police if he had known about it, the neighbor reportedly said, 'Even if I knew, I wouldn't have called the police, it's not my business. He can do what he wants. That's his problem. And anyway, God can see.'

On that fateful day, accused of stealing leftover porridge from Ng's infant daughter, Muawanatul was kicked so severely that her stomach ruptured. She died several days later of peritonitis, lying in a vomit-stained T-shirt before police arrived too late to save her.

On 26 July 2002, Ng was sentenced to a total of eighteen years and six months' imprisonment and twelve strokes of the cane for what the prosecution described as the worst case of abuse of a domestic worker in Singapore.

On 21 February 2003, Ng's wife, Tan Chai Hong, also a freelance tour guide, was sentenced to nine months' imprisonment for her part in the abuse of their domestic helper. Tan had known what her husband had been doing to the young woman but had failed to report the abuse. She had even inflicted pain on Muawanatul herself, by grabbing the young woman's breasts and squeezing them hard, when she caught her bathing one of her children incorrectly.

Story Three

This story will be presented roughly in the order the case was unravelled in the media, and how the public in Singapore, Indonesia and other countries in the region heard about it, then followed it. It is treated this way so that we can imagine how the public, especially in Singapore, formed an impression of the behavior of Indonesian domestic helpers.

On 29 May 2002, news broke out that there was a suspicious fire at an office block in Bukit Merah Central the previous night. The bodies of a woman and a young girl believed to be those of thirty-four year old Ms Angie Ng Wee Peng and her three year old daughter Crystal, were found inside one of the units. Ng's Indonesian domestic helper, Sundarti Supriyanto, then twenty-two years old, was found alive but hurt, on the floor in a corridor outside the unit, holding Ng's one year old baby.

The domestic helper identified herself to the police, but because she appeared in pain, she was taken to Singapore General Hospital. Later, in the hospital, when asked by Nurse Aidah Mohamad Kassim who attended to her, about what had happened, Sundarti told her, that she had been with her employer Ng and her two children in the office at Bukit Merah at about 9:00 pm when eleven people had come into the office wearing masks that covered their faces. The light had then gone out, and suddenly a fire had broken out. When Nurse Aidah asked her about the bite marks found on her body, Sundarti replied that a woman had bitten her.

Assistant Superintendent of Police Michael Sim then interviewed Sundarti in the hospital ward. She told him then that three women had come into the Bukit Timah units, then the light had gone out and the fire had started. Apart from the three women, there had been nine men who had also stormed in. They were all wearing masks or stockings over their faces.

Sundarti was repeatedly interviewed by police officers, nurses, and a social worker. Initially she told them she had only a vague memory of the whole event. She remembered that she had been carried and one of the women had bitten her before leaving her in a dark and smoky room. To the social worker Sundarti said that she had had no problems working for Ng.

She later changed her story several times during separate interviews, however, making the police increasingly suspicious that she was not telling the truth.

In the meantime, the bodies of Ng and Crystal were taken to Alexandra Hospital. A subsequent autopsy revealed that the injuries sustained by them indicated that Ng had been murdered before the fire. The victim sustained numerous deep and gaping wounds. The fatal one according to Dr Gilbert Lau, the senior pathologist who performed the autopsy, was a deep cut in the neck, which resulted in extensive, severe and acute haemorrhage. Crystal's death was reportedly caused by stab wounds in her chest.

Eventually Sundarti admitted that she had had a fight with Ng, but denied that she had murdered Ng and Crystal. The injuries on Ng, according to Sundarti, were self-inflicted. She also told of continuous abuse she had received from Ng during her employment; how she had often been deprived of food for days, and had always been blamed for everything that had happened in the family, as well as being the subject of various instances of humiliation.

The following are portions of Sundarti's written statement to the police, copied from the court transcript of 'Public Prosecutor v Sundarti Supriyanto [2004] SGHC 212':

'Mom [the deceased] ill-treated me. At home, I was made to eat the 2 children's faeces on 3 occasions. Whatever Mom held she would throw at me. When I was holding a knife, mom would take it and throw it at me. When I was preparing milk, mom would take the milk and throw it at me. There was a vegetable container in the fridge at home. Sometimes, mom forgot to close the container but she would throw the container at me and told me to close it properly. Sometimes, mom also punished me by telling me to kneel down for 2 hours as punishment and at the same time, I had to pull my ears. These were when mom scolded me for cooking too much porridge for the baby or for [sic] the porridge was no tasty enough. If I did not pull my ears, mom would cut $10 from my pay. If I did not clean up the faeces of the children in the office and mom thought that I did not clean it thoroughly, mom would throw the wet tissue used to clean up the faeces at my face. In the office, the children urinated on the carpets with the words 'A', 'B', 'C' and so on. Sir would scold mom because there was a urine smell in the office, which was air-conditioned. Mom would scold me for not cleaning up the carpets. I had already cleaned them but there was a smell because mom did not allow me to use soap. There was no soap in the office. When the porridge fell on the baby's clothes, I would take a tissue to take out the porridge from the clothes but mom would scold me for wasting the tissue, asking me if the tissue belonged to me or my mother, as if it was my own place. When mom's daughter cried, Sir would scold mom and mom would beat the daughter and she would scold [me] for not knowing how to take care of the children. I could not bear to see mom use the cane on her daughter. This is enough, I am pleading guilty to the offence. I am remorseful. I hope the Judge would take into consideration what I have said about mom and give me a fair sentence. There is more I want to say. There are seven staff in the office and whenever Sir was not happy with the performance of the staff, he would show it to mom. Both of them would argue in the car on the way home and the daughter would be frightened and she would be crying. Sir would also tell mom the maid, meaning me, was not capable of looking after the children. There is one staff by the name of Esther. She likes to give foodstuff to the children. I did not tell mom about this. However, mom knew about this, mom scolded me for allowing Esther to give foodstuff to the children, saying that the children would fall sick. When the son got wind in the stomach, mom also blamed me. The son always fell sick and mom would blame me. I also felt pressurized because of what mom did to the previous maids. I am responsible for causing the office to be burnt. I am responsible for causing mom to die. I am responsible for causing mom's daughter to die. I am angry with mom for pouring hot water on my hands and my left leg, mom also hit me and pulled my hair. Mom also threw telephones at me. Mom tried to kill me with a knife but the knife accidentally struck her daughter twice on the chest. The daughter bled badly. Mom took the knife as if she was in a trance and she was very fierce. I ran towards the kitchen. I took a knife and told mom to stop, otherwise I would use the knife on the son. Stop, I would kill her son. Mom was trying to strike me with her knife and I was trying to strike her with mine. Mom's knife is a chopper and mine is a vegetable knife. Mom's knife did not strike me and my knife did not strike mom. Mom's knife cut mom on her own hand. Mom and I struggled in the toilet until the door broke. I managed to escape but mom pursued me. I told mom I was going to count until three and she must kill herself and if she did not, I would kill myself and her son. Before I escaped, mom actually took a kettle in the kitchen and splashed hot water at me. The hot water touched me and also mom. In fact, when I threatened mom that I would kill her son, I was chasing after her son and mom was chasing after me. Mom had some magical power, which nobody could win her. There is a playroom in the office. Mom entered the playroom. Mom poked a knife against her throat and her chest and she was bleeding. I then pulled mom and her daughter to the kitchen. I washed all the knives that had blood. There were 3 knives. I put my shorts that had blood in a pail and put soap and water. I also put my T-shirt in the oven to dry. I then went to mom's office and took money, 2 cards, 2 handphones and went to buy petrol. I took a taxi to the nearby petrol kiosk. After obtaining the petrol, I returned to the office. I poured the petrol in the office at several locations. I lighted a flame. Then, I went to the playroom. The fire became big. I took mom's son but as I did not have the strength, the baby managed to escape. The baby ran towards the door of the playroom. There was fire there. I saved the baby by carrying him and used a chair to break the glass door to come out of the unit. I sat outside the office, I had no strength as I was injured badly. Many people came and saved us. When I was in the hospital, the police took away my clothings. Inside my shorts, there were the money, 2 cards and 2 handphones.'

On 10 June 2002, Sundarti was officially arrested, and on 11 June, Singapore Police sent a letter to the Indonesian Embassy notifying the Embassy of Sundarti's arrest. She was charged with six offences: murdering her female employer; murdering her employer's daughter, Crystal; setting the office at #06-3661/3663 at Block 165 Bukit Merah Central on fire; stealing her employer's properties in the flat; stealing her employer's properties in the office; stealing her employer's money by using her employer's ATM cards.

The first trial opened in September 2002. During this, and subsequent trials, the picture unravelled further, revealing events which have thrown light on Sundarti's working conditions leading up to the violent, unfortunate incident of 28 May 2002.

Sundarti Supriyanto is the eldest of a family of three children in the village of Mengge, Regency Magetan, East Java. She wanted to help the family's finances, so she agreed to be recruited by a PJTKI to work as a domestic helper overseas. She was then sent to a training center in Jakarta, where she was taught English, cooking and housekeeping. An offer came from Singapore, to work with a Chinese family with three children. She accepted it and arrived in Singapore in April 1999.

After two years working in the city-state Sundarti returned home, and not long after that, in September 2001, her father died. Wanting to help again, Sundarti received further training in order to find a better-paying job. Returning to Singapore in April 2002, she met Ng, and after an interview, Ng decided to hire Sundarti on a trial basis.

When she was brought to Ng's office premises at the Bukit Merah Central block, Sundarti saw two other helpers whose names she discovered later were Jami and Aminah. She also discovered that Jami was leaving and she was supposed to replace her.

In the few days that followed, Sundarti recounted that she had seen Ng abuse Aminah by pulling her hair, pinching and kicking her. She had also seen Ng throwing Aminah out of the house for some mistakes the helper had allegedly made. It was a big enough occasion for someone to call the police. The following day Aminah was sent back to her employment agency.

Sundarti also told the court she had seen Ng abuse Jami by slapping her and pushing her head. This story was corroborated by Jami who gave evidence at the trial. Jami told the court that during the time she had been employed by Ng, she had been continuously scolded, frequently slapped, poked and kicked, and that Ng had always found faults in her work. A form of punishment Jami described, which interestingly corroborated a segment of Sundarti's official statement to the police, was being forced to hold her ears while kneeling.

Sundarti told the court that, after seeing how Ng treated Aminah and Jami during the first few days, she had become scared and had asked Ng to send her back to her agency, but Ng had refused.

She had continued to work for Ng, where her tasks had been mainly preparing food and taking care of the children at the family home and office premises. For her main meals, she had had to eat leftovers from the meals she had prepared at home for Ng's husband, or bread when there was some at home. For breakfast, she had usually eaten two plain slices of bread and nothing else. During the first few days when Jami and Aminah had been told to prepare lunch in the office, Sundarti had had something to eat. After the two helpers had left, Sundarti had nothing to eat for lunch, except for the times one of Ng's staff members, Fiona Ong, Esther Hong, Margaret Low or Nancy Ee, offered her bread and snacks.

According to Ng's staff members and Sundarti herself, however, Ng would become agitated whenever she had found out about the helper receiving food from her staff members, and would scold the helper later. The practice had continued surreptitiously however, because Sundarti had needed some sustenance to keep on working.

The court also heard that Sundarti had often gone without dinner when Ng's husband was away overseas, because Ng would forbid her from cooking. Three weeks before the violent incident of 28 May 2002, Ng would not allow Sundarti to cook at home, resulting in her not receiving her rations of leftovers.

On 26 May 2002, Ng's husband had left for overseas for business. Sundarti had had a slice of bread for breakfast, and had been forbidden from having anything else. In the afternoon she had gone with Ng and the children to Ng's parents-in-law's home. The mother-in-law had cooked some rice-vermicelli and had told Sundarti to feed a bowl to the baby, but had not given Sundarti anything to eat, barring some warm water. When they had returned home, Ng had forbidden her from cooking, since the husband had not been home. So Sundarti had gone to bed hungry.

On 27 May 2002, there had been no bread at home and Ng would not allow her to cook at home, so she had had nothing to eat all day, barring some warm water.

On two occasions when Sundarti had complained of hunger, Ng had told her to eat the children's faeces. On one of the occasions, Ng had told her that if the children would not eat their porridge, the porridge should be thrown away, and if the helper wanted any food, she could eat Crystal's faeces. Sundarti said she had put the faeces in her mouth to show Ng that she would rather eat the faeces of the baby she loved, than the food provided by Ng.

While the veracity of the evidence regarding Ng telling Sundarti to eat her children's faeces was not given any credibility by the prosecutor, the fact that Sundarti was regularly deprived of food was corroborated by some of the witnesses provided by the prosecution itself.

On the day of the incident, 28 May 2002, Ng's staff members, Esther Hong, Margaret Low, and Nancy Ee were having food at the reception area in the office. Ng came to them and complained that Sundarti had eaten her son's food. Then when the helper appeared, Ng scolded her in front of them. Later on in the afternoon, Esther Hong and Margaret Low met Ng, Sundarti, the baby, and Crystal at a handphone shop at Block 166 Bukit Merah Central. Margaret Low offered some fruit to the baby. Ng stopped her, saying that her son was unwell. Low then offered the fruit to Sundarti, but Ng stopped her from doing so.

Another prosecution witness, Rose Ang, the cleaning lady, testified that Sundarti had told her of being very hungry and had not eaten for a few days. Rose Ang had then given her three biscuits which Sundarti had quickly eaten. Rose Ang also mentioned that Ng had had a total of eight domestic helpers coming and going from her employment over a period of one year or so.

The prosecutor also refuted the veracity of Sundarti's statement that she and Ng had been involved in a fight, saying that Sundarti had murdered Ng and Crystal relatively unprovoked.

One of the prosecution's own witnesses again corroborated Sundarti's story. Joseph Lefort, who worked in the building, testified that on 28 May 2002 at about 8.46pm, while he had been in the toilet of Block 165 Bukit Merah Central #07-3661, he had heard a woman calling out the words 'Jangan, jangan!'. The voice, according to Lefort, sounded like a desperate plea for help, and that it was very distressful. Immediately after that, he had heard a young child scream.

Events leading up to the fateful evening

On 28 May 2002, Sundarti woke up at 5:30 in the morning and proceeded to do the household chores. At 8:30am, she fed the baby its porridge and Ng fed Crystal. Sundarti didn't have any of the porridge, because it contained pork. She had not had anything to eat since the morning of 26 May 2002, so she was understandably extremely hungry. When she asked Ng if she could have anything to eat, Ng grudgingly gave her two packets of instant noodles. When she went to get a cooking pot to cook the noodles, Ng stopped her and told her to eat the noodles raw.

Sundarti took out a plastic container, filled it with hot water and placed one packet of instant noodles in it, together with the sauces. She then sat on a chair in the kitchen and was about to eat the noodles when Ng came in and told her not to sit on the chair. Sundarti got up, then Ng told her to eat in the toilet. Sundarti went and sat on the toilet, and started eating. But she had only taken two spoonfuls when Ng called out to her to leave for the office. Sundarti left the rest of the noodles in the plastic container as well as the unopened packet, in the toilet. Police would later find these items exactly in the positions described by Sundarti when they were conducting their investigation.

They did not leave until 11:30am, however. At the office, Sundarti took the children to the playroom and stayed with them, and Ng went to do her work. She came to the playroom at about 2:30pm and gave Sundarti a thermos flask containing noodles to feed the baby, and proceeded to feed Crystal.

While Sundarti fed the baby, some of the noodles spilled on his shirt. She quickly used tissue paper to wipe them off the shirt, but Ng had already seen it. She was angry with Sundarti for using too much tissue paper, yelling, 'You think this belongs to your parents?'

Sundarti went on feeding the baby, blowing at the food to cool it before feeding it to the child. Ng saw it and was going to yell at her when the baby then urinated on the carpet. Ng turned to him, took a cane, hit him, then turned to Sundarti and hit her on the buttocks, accusing the helper of eating the baby's food.

Esther Hong, Margaret Low and Nancy Ee, who were at the office at the time, heard the commotion in the playroom.

When the children were fed, Sundarti went to the kitchen to wash the dishes. She came across Rose Ang, the cleaning lady, and told Ang that she was hungry and that she had not been given food since the morning of two days previously. Rose Ang gave her three biscuits, which Sundarti ate quickly. This was to be corroborated by Rose Ang in her testimony.

Sundarti then began preparing the foodstuff to make dinner.

At about 6:00pm Ng told her to come with her and the children to go shopping. At a shop where Ng was buying a cellphone, they came across Esther Hong and Margaret Low. Low offered some fresh fruit to the baby, but Ng stopped her, saying that her son had a cough. Low then offered the fruit to Sundarti, but Ng stopped her, saying, 'Don't give her.' Sundarti was very disappointed, and felt humiliated.

After shopping, Ng, Sundarti and the children returned to the office, where Ng spoke to Fiona Ong for some time before going to the kitchen to make sure the food was ready for the two children.

Fiona Ong left the office at 8:00pm, when Sundarti and Ng were feeding the two children in the playroom. Sundarti fed the baby while Ng fed Crystal. The children were unsettled and moving around, making it very difficult to feed them. Ng became angry and yelled at Sundarti, saying she was lazy, and that she only came to the office to sit and eat while the children ran wild. She then picked up a feeding spoon and poked it in Sundarti's ear. It hurt her, but she did not bleed.

The baby then had to go to the toilet. Sundarti took a potty for the baby to use. When he had finished, Sundarti began to clean him with wet tissue. Ng yelled at her saying she was too slow, grabbed the soiled wet tissue and threw it at her face. Sundarti cleaned her face and continued cleaning the baby with clean wet tissue, but Ng repeated her action, and one more time after that.

Sundarti was feeling nauseous yet hungry, so she drank some warm water. Ng continued yelling at her to keep feeding the baby. Sundarti told her she was hungry. Ng told her to eat the baby's faeces. She did, to spite Ng. Then she threw the spoon on to the floor and took the potty to the toilet. She washed her face and went into the kitchen to get a drink of water. She didn't realize that Ng was standing behind her. Ng then pulled her by the back of her shirt-collar and dragged her into the playroom and threw her down on the floor with a thud. Ng then told her to finish feeding the baby.

While being fed, the baby kept moving around, then grabbed a computer mouse and played with it. He cried when Ng took the mouse away from him. Ng picked up the cane and hit the baby with it.

Ng then told Sundarti to pack up and leave for home. The helper asked Ng whether she wanted Crystal to be dressed in her pyjamas. Ng's response was to angrily pull the red backpack Sundarti was holding. Sundarti lost her balance and fell on Crystal who was behind her. Crystal started to cry and Ng tried to pacify her.

In the middle of this, the baby took the computer mouse again. Sundarti took it away from him, and he cried in protest. She was going to give it back to him to stop him crying but Ng grabbed it from her. Again she lost her balance and this time fell on the baby. Ng then threw the computer mouse at the helper, but missed.

By this time, Sundarti could hardly contain her annoyance any longer. She stood up and said, 'Ma'am, why you do to me everyday like that. I very pain [sic].' Ng's response was to yell and scratch the helper's face. The scratches were superficial enough not to leave marks, but they hurt. And what is more, they inflamed Sundarti further. She grabbed Ng by the dress, and a physical fight broke out.

Sundarti tried to punch Ng several times, but Ng was able to ward off the blows. She then grabbed a cable from under the table and tried to tie her employer's hands, but Ng was able to wrench the cable off her hand. She ran to the kitchen to look for something to replace the cable. When she could not find anything, she kept looking. In the toilet she found a rope and returned with it to the playroom. All she wanted to do was to stop her employer attacking her. But again, she did not succeed because she could not pin her employer down long enough to tie her hands. The fight continued. She used the rope against her employer's neck choking her. By that time, Sundarti was overcome with rage.

Ng became limp. Sundarti threw the rope away and went to the two crying children, trying to pacify them. She picked them up and hugged them, Crystal on her left, and the baby on her right. Crystal pushed her away, however, and might have bitten her on the shoulder. She could not remember because she didn't feel any pain then.

Suddenly Ng got up and kicked Sundarti from behind. The fight started again. Ng managed to grab the helper's hair and banged her head against the wall. Sundarti eventually was able to break free, then ran toward the kitchen to look for something to fight her employer with. Ng came behind her and pushed her, and she fell to the ground. Just then Ng grabbed a kettle and tried to throw it down at the helper, but the helper kicked Ng's leg, and she fell into the toilet still holding the kettle. Hot water splashed from the kettle on to Sundarti's arms and legs. The fight continued in the toilet, causing the toilet door to dislodge and fall on Sundarti.

Sundarti managed to break free again and ran toward the glass door of unit #6-3663. As she was running away, she noticed that Ng was chasing her with a small knife. Sundarti reached the glass door but was unable to open it. By this time Ng was right beside her threatening to thrust the knife at her. Sundarti shouted, 'Jangan, jangan!' (Don't, don't!), dodged the attacks and ran back to the playroom.

In the playroom she saw Crystal and the baby. She picked them up, Crystal on the left and the baby on the right, intending to use them as shields. But Ng continued to attack her with the knife. Sundarti, exhausted with the load, dropped the baby on to the floor and held on to Crystal.

She positioned Crystal in front of her as a shield against Ng's knife attacks, but Ng did not stop. The knife stabbed Crystal once in the chest, but even then Ng did not stop attacking her. Sundarti was able to back out of the playroom, dropped Crystal on to the floor and ran to the kitchen to find something to fight Ng with.

She found a knife, took it and ran back to the playroom with it. In the common office area outside the playroom, she saw Ng rushing toward her. She side-stepped Ng, who ran into the kitchen and re-emerged carrying a knife in each hand.

From this point on, Sundarti's account became too extravagant for ready acceptance:

Ng tried to stab Sundarti with the knives but slipped, hitting a computer and a table in the office area instead, and accidentally cut her own hand. Sundarti then ran to the office common area and picked up the baby. Ng followed her. Sundarti held the baby and placed a knife at his neck. She told Ng that she would kill the child unless Ng cut her own hand. Presumably she wanted to disable Ng. She repeated the threats when Ng did not respond.

Ng then sat down and sliced her left hand downward with the big knife. Then she got up and began to run toward the helper again. Sundarti ran away from her and Ng kept chasing. At Margaret Low's desk, Ng dropped the big knife and threw books, stationery and telephones at the helper, still holding the small knife in her right hand. None of these caused Sundarti to let go of the baby. She was still holding the baby with a knife at his neck.

Ng seemed to have run out of steam and went to the playroom. When Sundarti went toward the playroom she heard Ng saying, 'I die.' There were no more sounds after that. Sundarti went in and saw her employer lying on the floor with her right hand holding the small knife which was embedded in her neck. She was covered with blood.

Sundarti slowly approached Ng's body, used her leg to check if she was still alive. There was no response.

She pulled the knife out of Ng's neck, collected all three knives, took off Ng's watch which was covered with blood, and took them all to the toilet to wash. There she also applied some toothpaste to the scalded parts of her arms and legs, where hot water had been splashed from the kettle earlier in the fight.

Sundarti then dragged Ng's body into the kitchen and left it there. She then picked up Crystal and placed her on Ng's body. Then she went to the playroom, and it occurred to her to get rid of the blood with fire. Something she had learned from telenovellas.

She took a set of keys found on the playroom floor to open Ng's room. She took the contents of Ng's wallet – about US$350 and about S$100, and other valuables from the room. She was going to buy petrol to burn the office, but suddenly noticed she had blood on her shirt. She washed her shirt and dried it in the microwave oven before going out of the office, taking a container to carry the petrol in.

Leaving the baby in the office she carried the container to buy petrol by taxi. She returned to the office and poured petrol around, then ignited the fire. She placed the baby beside her and lay on the floor. She wanted to kill herself, because she knew she had no future. But the baby got up and walked toward the fire. Seeing his hand and hair catching fire Sundarti got up, grabbed the baby and used her hands to put out the fire on him. Tucking him under her shirt, she rolled on the floor until she reached the glass door entrance and broke it with a chair. She put the baby down when it was safe and was going to return to the fire. But she heard the baby crying for her, so she went back to him.

She picked him up and sat in the corridor nursing him. That was how they were found.

On 24 September 2004 High Court Judge Rubin J, taking into account mitigating circumstances presented by Defence Counsel Mohamed Muzammil bin Mohamed, sentenced Sundarti to life imprisonment.

A SAMPLE OF FIRST-HAND STORIES: FROM THE DOMESTIC HELPER'S POINT OF VIEW
Not all domestic helpers' stories are full of abuse and violence, many are easily overlooked for their ordinariness revealed by the following accounts, which are based on personal interviews with the related sources. They are remarkable by their humanity rather than anything sensational. The sources are identified by their actual first names, unless specified.

Story One: She was inexperienced, but her employers were understanding
When she graduated from secondary school in a small subdistrict of Solo, Indarti (now twenty-two) knew what she wanted to do. She wanted to work overseas. She had made acquaintances with a sponsor during her last year in school. The sponsor had told her about the fantastic prospects of working overseas as a domestic helper, earning in foreign currency, and being able to save up to help the family's finances back home.

Her parents worked hard as subsistence farmers to feed and clothe their children, and were far-sighted enough to make sure they sent them to school as well. They were a close family.

Indarti had thought about her dream for months, so when she finally told her sponsor acquaintance that she wanted to find work in Singapore, she knew she meant it. She had chosen Singapore because she had learned that in Singapore Malay was spoken by a fair number of the population. Not being very good at English, and having no knowledge of Chinese languages, Indarti was hoping she would be able to communicate with her employers in Malay.

With her parents' blessings, she went to Jakarta with the sponsor, who took her to a PJTKI. She had to falsify her age to twenty in her passport, because she was not quite eighteen years at the time. After one and a half months in the recruiting agency's training center, where she was taught some English, Indarti was told they had found her a job in Singapore.

Indarti began working in Singapore in 2000, for a Chinese couple and their two young children. The second child was less than two months old then. Her employers were aware that it was Indarti's first job, so they were not too demanding.

Indarti remembers how scared she was of making her employers angry, because she simply didn't know how to do the housework. She had been shown how to operate a washing machine and a vacuum cleaner, but there were so many appliances even in the kitchen alone. She wasn't sure whether she should admit not having seen, let alone used, half of these appliances, but her female employer figured it out immediately. She started by showing Indarti how to use a few – the most commonly used, such as the juicer and pulverizer, the rice-cooker, and the electric fry-pan. The next step was to know how to structure her day. There seemed so much to do in a day that she didn't know where to start. Again, her employer walked her through it. Indarti was quickly accepted by the older child, and had no problems taking care of her. As for the baby, however, Indarti found him very cute, but she was too scared to handle him. So her employer didn't ask her to pick him up straight away. She allowed Indarti several days to become familiar with the baby's routine and gradually encouraged her to begin handling him.

The family also taught her Mandarin. Indarti made notes of everything she was taught. Within several months she had mastered all the chores, and a year and a half later she was fluent enough to communicate in Mandarin.

Indarti liked her employers. They treated her well. And she was paid the going rate. They paid her directly, and Indarti then paid off her debt to the recruiting agency within seven months.

She also remembers when they asked her how often she wanted a rest day. 'I was quite happy staying on working. What would I do on rest days? I didn't know places, I didn't know anybody. I knew how to go to the elder child's school and back. That was about all,' she reminisced with amusement, 'So I told them I didn't need any rest days.'

Indarti realized that her employers were not sure whether she was being polite or whether there was another reason for her refusal to take rest days. Or maybe it was her way of saying that she wanted them to decide.

Her employers insisted she should take a rest day at least once every two weeks. Indarti didn't say anything. A month later, on a Sunday, her female employer said, 'Indarti, why don't you take today off? We'll take the children out.'

Indarti didn't say anything. They told her to get dressed and go out, and when Indarti looked reluctant, they took her by the hand and made her take her purse from her room, and took her to the front door. Indarti walked slowly out, and they closed the door.

Half an hour later, the whole family were walking out of the apartment on their way to the car park, and were amazed to see Indarti still standing there.

'Why are you still here?' her female employer asked.

The young woman explained she didn't know where to go.

Finally they took Indarti with them. After that, they made it a habit to go for a drive together regularly.

At the end of her two-year contract, Indarti decided to go home to be close to her family again. She left with a pleasant memory of her former employers and of Singapore.

Story Two: Not driven by economic necessities, so she demanded fair treatment

Yanti (now thirty-six years) was born in Jakarta, but grew up in Semarang, Central Java. She doesn't come from a struggling family. They are not rich, but neither are they poor. What brought her to Singapore was not pure economic necessity.

When Yanti was twenty-eight she felt that her life was not going anywhere, so when she heard about people working overseas, she was very interested in trying it herself. After talking to a sponsor, she knew that despite having completed secondary school, she was not qualified to do any other job but domestic work. She decided to give it a go.

The sponsor took her to Jakarta to a PJTKI, where she received some training. Yanti didn't recall a training center as such. It was more a matter of finding a room where an English lesson would be taught, or an ad-hoc briefing about the lifestyles in the destination countries. She recalled being treated well, nonetheless.

Her first job in Singapore was a disaster. Her employers were the type known among domestic helpers as *Cina Bukit*, or Hillbilly Chinese. They watched over her like hawks, criticized her for everything she did. In fact, nothing she did pleased them, so she was continuously told of her own incompetence. Yanti was not allowed to leave the apartment, in case she spoke to people in the neighborhood. She had to pray surreptitiously. She was so stressed that her weight dropped from fifty-four kilograms to thirty-seven kilograms in two weeks. So she decided to practice the strategy the agents had taught her as a last resort: go slow. Fortunately for her, it worked. The employers sent her back to her Singapore agency.

The following employers were a mixed couple, Indian husband and Chinese wife. They had young children. They were very particular about what they liked, but treated her fairly. They allowed her to observe her prayer times. She worked hard every day, but whenever she needed to go out, she was able to. Unfortunately, the job only lasted several months, because the employers had to go to Australia for further studies.

Yanti then found another job with another mixed couple: Chinese husband and Malay wife. By this time Yanti had quickly accumulated useful work experience. She had learned how to do housework according to Singapore standard, as well as how to look after and relate to young children the way Singapore families expected her to.

By the end of 2004 Yanti would have worked for these employers for seven years. When she started they had two children, at the time of this interview, they had three. Yanti was now thinking of returning to Indonesia after finishing the current contract. She had saved up a fair amount of money, and wanted to start a restaurant business in Jakarta. Throughout the years she had collected various cookery books, so she intended to use them for her business.

Having been back to Jakarta three times, between contract renewals, Yanti also managed to learn various lurks of not being 'charged unofficial fees' at Cengkareng airport in Jakarta, where returning domestic workers have had to go through a special terminal, known as Terminal Three. She still found herself with something some officials pounced on, nonetheless.

She described her relationship with her current employers as good and workable. Despite the long hours, she was able to take time off regularly and socialize with her friends. She was able to take short courses offered at Darul Arqam, and have religious discussions there as well.

Yanti was aware of the problems some domestic workers encountered. The way she saw the situation was that, having paid the levy, the salary, the insurance premium, as well as the security bond, employers tended to squeeze the last drop out of the domestic helper to get their money's worth. But she quickly added that many, mercifully, do not have that kind of attitude, including her current employers.

'But I am quite tired now of working. I look forward to going back home at the end of this contract, and rebuild my life there,' she said, smiling.

Story Three: Landed on her feet

Ninik, twenty-four years, was born in Wonosobo, East Java. Despite her youth, Ninik came across as someone who knew what she wanted in life.

She left formal education after finishing Year Nine, the end of junior secondary school in Indonesia, and went to find work in Jakarta, where one of her married elder sisters lived. She worked as a shop assistant, for various employers.

Three years later she had to go home to Wonosobo, because her father fell ill. When he recovered, Ninik began to think of making new plans. Some sponsors from different PJTKI were around, trying to recruit young women to work overseas. Ninik was approached too, but she was not interested then.

It so happened that her sister in Jakarta gave birth, and asked her to come and stay, for company and moral support. Several months later, when her sister seemed to be handling the home situation better, Ninik returned to Wonosobo.

She quickly became restless and looked for something definite to do. The issue of working overseas came up again when a relative suggested she consider working in Singapore. A friend of hers offered to introduce her to the local agent of a PJTKI in Jakarta. It did not take long for the agent to decide that she would be suitable for working in Singapore, and signed her up then and there. Two days after that she was taken to Jakarta for training.

After three weeks of English language lessons at the training center, she left for Singapore. She only had three days of training in cooking, laundry, and how to use electrical and electronic appliances.

When she arrived in Singapore, Ninik discovered that there were discrepancies between what she had learned during training and what she was expected to do. She had not been prepared for the real work.

She felt very awkward having to do housework, especially as she was unfamiliar with the way Singaporeans lived. Her employers had two children, one in Singapore and another in Australia. Both employers worked outside the home. Ninik was unable to cook the food they liked, and they did not have time to teach her. Her English was too rudimentary to explain her difficulties. The employers did not become impatient and abusive, however, and fortunately the husband spoke some Indonesian. They just gradually told her how they liked certain things done and showed her how to prepare the dishes they liked.

In the meantime, the employers gave her a language book, and Ninik learned from it herself, and thus improved her English. She and the employers practised a lot, and they communicated better over time.

Ninik was paid the going rate. During the first four months, however, she only received ten dollars per month, because the rest was paid to the agent to pay off her debt. After that she always received full salary, paid directly into her bank account. Her documents were kept by her employers and she was happy with this arrangement.

Both parties eventually reached a working arrangement comfortable for each of them. At first, when she told them she had to pray five times a day, her employers were not terribly happy. So Ninik limited her prayer times to the evenings only.

She had told her Singapore agent that she would like to go to religious discussions and prayers at Darul Arqam once a month, and her agent had suggested that she compromise by wearing her Muslim scarf after leaving the house. Gradually she made it known to her employers, and found that her employers did not object.

She had a minor problem when, during her second contract, the employer's son from Australia came home. He brought his dog with him. This initially disturbed Ninik, being a Muslim, however she tried to see the situation in a rational way. So far, she had always cooked what her employers liked, but for herself she cooked halal food. The presence of the dog should not alarm her, because she did not have to have the dog in her room. She was feeling more comfortable after that.

Ninik learned a lot during the time she worked for these employers. They were very particular about the structure of their day, and she had learned to work herself into it. On top of that, because they did not necessarily have the same tastes in food or fashion, she learned how to please each of them in her cooking and laundry management.

Before the two-year contract was over, however, Ninik's employers migrated to Australia. Fortunately, her agent found her another job almost immediately.

Comparatively speaking, her current employers were very easy to please. They did not mind her praying five times a day. During the middle of the day, when their young daughter was asleep, she had some time to herself and she had some freedom to structure her own day.

Each morning Ninik went to the office with her female employer and the daughter. She usually brought her ironing to do there during the time the daughter had her nap. That way she had plenty of time to herself in the evening. Her employers did not worry when she did her work, provided it was done well.

Ninik's plan for the future included trying to find work further afield, such as Canada, if her current employers decided not to renew her contract after the current one expired.

She wanted to go back home and use her savings to do further studies, so that she could apply for work in Canada, where the requirements were too high for her just now.

FROM THE EMPLOYERS' POINT OF VIEW

Story One
Selina needed domestic help because she worked full-time, and her husband was often away. Her two teenage children were busy with school work. Selina had been employing domestic helpers for ten years, since her younger child was only four.

She started with a domestic helper from the Philippines. She had problems with her. While her work was of a relatively high standard, it was not high enough for Selina to leave the whole rein to her, which the domestic helper demanded. She also demanded weekly rest days. What Selina disliked most was that she made telephone calls to the Philippines from Selina's phone without asking her permission first.

Selina then tried domestic helpers from Indonesia. While the salaries were lower, Selina had to train them again, because their skills were way below standard, despite the local employment agencies' claim that they had been trained. Since she was paying the going rate for Indonesian helpers – admittedly lower than the going rate for Filipina helpers, she had at first expected a better standard.

She had now employed five domestic helpers from Indonesia, none of whom were up to her standard. Each time she employed a new helper, she had to train her from the beginning again. Asked why she had not renewed the contract with those she had trained, she replied that the helper had wanted to move on.

Indonesian helpers, according to Selina, were slow learners, had no sense of hygiene, and had dubious morals. When asked to elaborate, Selina gave examples.

The first one she employed, spoke so little English Selina had to speak Malay to her. Selina taught her how to clean the house, detailing the implements to clean different things. After a week, however, Selina still caught her cleaning the kitchen bench with the mop for the floor. And Selina caught her stealing sweetmeats from her sweetmeat box. But when she was reprimanded, she said she was checking whether to clean the box.

The second one had body odor. Selina told her over and over again, to have a good wash before preparing food and serving the family meals, but she still smelled, putting the family off their food. She had to return that helper to the agency.

The third one was a fairly good cook, had a cheerful personality, but had a habit of lying. Selina had told her not to use the phone to chat with her friends, but she discovered from her telephone bills that the phone had been used many times during the day, when she was at work and her children were at school. When confronted, the helper denied the allegation. She also lied about where she went on the occasions she had asked to take a day off to do something important in relation to family matters. Selina discovered that she had only gone off to see her friends, whom Selina was sure were a bad influence on her. After seeing her friends, the helper was invariably more impudent toward her, like answering her back, or questioning Selina's criticism of the work she had done.

The fourth and the current one also often lied, but Selina had learned to tolerate that. She just knew how to interpret the truth from what they told her. And they also had a poor sense of hygiene. Selina often caught them putting clean washing on something inappropriate, such as the top of the dirty laundry basket, or her son's schoolbag.

'I'm beginning to wonder if it's worth employing a maid at all. They have never been a good influence on the family. We often quarrel over nothing, because my own children often take the maid's side,' she said, adding that it was also a burden on her mind, because if the helper got into trouble with the bad company she kept, she would lose the S$5,000 security bond, while the insurance, which was compulsory, did not cover everything.

Story Two

Lee Koon needed domestic help because she and her husband had just started a business. Both her mother and his mother were unable to come and look after her baby daughter, and Lee Koon could not bear to leave her baby with anyone the whole day, so day-care was not an option.

Lee Koon stayed home until her baby was three and a half months old, then began taking her to the office. At first she was able to do that with few problems, because normally she was alone in the office, mainly receiving phone calls, her husband working outside. So Lee Koon was able to feed the baby, bathe her and play with her. It also helped that the baby slept a lot.

Problems arose when Lee Koon began to give her daughter solids. The baby would not eat, and became clingy instead, requiring more attention.

She needed help, so she went to an employment agency. At that moment, she learnt that a domestic helper would soon become available because her current employers were no longer in a position to employ her. After interviewing her, Lee Koon and her husband found her suitable.

They had never employed a domestic helper before, so they had no prejudice or preconception about what it was going to be like, but they knew they liked Ninik.

Their priority was for Ninik to look after the baby, and she seemed good with her, so they employed her.

Ninik came to the office with Lee Koon and the baby in the morning, helped look after the baby, especially during the time the baby was being weaned. Since they were in a small office at the time and there was nowhere to cook, they ate packaged food. Then in 2002 they leased a bigger office and put in an electric stove. Ninik was able to cook dinner and they would eat before going home in the evening.

Now the daughter was three and a half years old and went to school for three hours every day. Every morning Lee Koon took her to school, Ninik stayed home then picked her up at noon, they both came to the office and stayed until after dinner. Then they would go home together.

On weekends they stayed home, and once a month Ninik went to Darul Arqam for short courses and religious discussions. On her second rest day of the month, Ninik would go out and meet with friends.

Lee Koon and her husband's employment arrangement with Ninik was clear-cut. They paid the agency fee of over S$700, which was the standard rate for a domestic helper transferring from an unfinished contract, a new one being approximately S$400. Like other employers, on top of the helper's salary, they also paid a S$5,000 security bond, an insurance premium for Ninik, and a monthly levy of S$250 to the government. Lee Koon and her husband had been happy with Ninik, and with the agency's delivery of service. After Ninik started, the agency called several times to make sure everything was to their satisfaction.

Lee Koon and her husband understood that they were responsible for Ninik's welfare and well-being. They believed that if they communicated effectively, they should have no problems. Ninik was free to observe her religious obligations. Whenever there was anything they did not like, they would tell Ninik, and Ninik would do the same. Lee Koon and her husband believe that almost anything could be solved by effective communication and maturity all round.

Lee Koon had seen advertisements in the newspapers placed by agencies offering the opportunity to would-be employers to change domestic helpers without charge as often as they liked. She passionately disagreed with the idea. She didn't think domestic helpers were commodities to be changed like merchandise.

When Ninik's contract expired in August 2005, Lee Koon planned to look after her daughter herself. 'By then she'll go to school longer, and will be able to stay in day-care until I can collect her,' she said.

Story Three

Kalsom began employing domestic helpers in 1991. She had just started a family and wanted to keep a part-time job. She had been working full-time, so the thought of having to clean the house, cook and tidy up after her husband, her mother-in-law and herself seemed daunting at the time.

Her first domestic helper came from Purwokerto, Central Java. The employment agency she had contacted told her that Pari was nineteen years old. One look at her, however, told Kalsom that the young woman was nowhere near nineteen. She discovered later that Pari was in reality only sixteen.

Before Pari began, Kalsom gave her a briefing for an hour. She told Pari that she demanded honesty and cleanliness in all her work, which she then detailed for her. And knowing that Pari was very young, Kalsom also warned Pari to be careful when socializing.

Though Pari was always willing to learn whenever Kalsom taught her how to do certain chores to her standard, Kalsom terminated the employment after only a couple of months. She caught Pari in a compromising situation with a construction worker, so Pari was returned to her agency.

When Kalsom fell pregnant, she had to find another domestic helper. Wahyuni, from East Java, came to work for her. During the time Wahyuni worked for her family, Kalsom gave birth to her first and second child. When her second child was two years old, Kalsom decided to be a full-time mother, so she did not continue employing Wahyuni.

After one whole year of being a full-time mother, Kalsom realised that she did need some help, so in 1996 she employed Titi from Semarang, Central Java.

Titi was the most educated of the three domestic helpers she had employed so far, and the most religious. They got on well immediately. Kalsom liked Titi because she was good with the children, as well as a good cook. She taught the children how to count in Indonesian, and some Indonesian songs.

During the time Titi worked for her family, Kalsom gave birth to her third child.

Now seven years on, Kalsom felt that Titi had been working for her too long. She was beginning to take Kalsom for granted, and became too familiar with her and the family.

'She comes and goes as she pleases. During school holidays, she'll get up at 8:30, and helps herself to breakfast,' she recounted.

Kalsom felt that Titi was increasingly becoming like a dependent relative. 'Instead of preparing my youngest child's bath for instance, she'll call out to him to have a bath while vacuuming the floor. She'll yell at the other children to do this and that. I thought, I don't need her yelling at the children. I can do that myself. That doesn't help. I need her to get the children organized,' Kalsom said.

When they went for holidays overseas, they always took Titi with them. And they would not always leave Titi to look after the children. They would give her some time to go shopping while they looked after the children, but Titi never thanked them. She obviously felt she was entitled to whatever she was given, and continued taking them for granted.

One day Kalsom mentioned to Titi that not every domestic helper had the opportunity to travel overseas with their employers, to which Titi replied petulantly that she wasn't on holidays on those trips, because she had to look after the children. Kalsom was really annoyed. 'Did she forget about the shopping excursions? Did she forget she had a separate room? What did she expect? Her going on holidays and I looking after the children?' Kalsom asked hotly.

Overall, Kalsom admitted, during the seven years of employing Titi, there had not been major problems.

Kalsom planned not to continue employing Titi when the current contract expired in 2005. She would once again become a full-time mother, she said.

THE SOCIAL VALUES SHARED BY SINGAPORE AND INDONESIA

Domestic work is for those who cannot do anything else

Some social concepts are inherent, and rarely discussed, but often come up in private conversations, one of these being that those who work as domestic helpers are not skilled in anything else, and are most often than not, uneducated.

In Indonesia, where the origins of domestic help go back to feudalism and colonialism, despite the fact that increasing numbers of domestic helpers are secondary school graduates, or at least secondary school drop-outs, the inherent values are still very strong. Domestic helpers are the lowest paid full-time workers in the country, with a social status so low that women who have had any formal education at all would do almost any other type of work, rather than domestic work. In fact, when socializing somewhere else, many of the women who have been forced by circumstances to take up domestic work will hide the fact.

For a large number of people who cannot find work in any other field, the lure of working overseas as domestic helpers has not come merely from the promise of high salaries, but the lure is also weighted with promises of better status (being somewhat associated with better pay) and last but not least, the romance of anonymity. It is a fact that the promised land depicted by sponsors of employment and recruiting agencies in Indonesia is a lot better than what the women eventually face in reality.

Then, in relation to Singapore, the values which the women are hoping to evade in their own country, are waiting for them in their destination.

Seen as a low status job not worth having, Singapore women shun it. Furthermore, they themselves look to employ someone else to do this job for them, and since Singaporeans are not prepared to do it, they have to import those workers who are.

Understandably, there is an inherent prejudice that those who are prepared to do the job must come from a poorer country and have fewer skills than any Singaporeans. There is even a convenient cultural distance – they are not part of us -, which may suppress any feeling of guilt when they are abusing these workers.

'Domestic helpers are not real workers'
The concept which has rarely been articulated but is implicit in many employers' understanding of the nature of domestic help is that it is not real work. It has no formal job description or the certainty of working hours.

Even a contract cleaner who comes to clean the house has a job description and clear-cut working hours.

In Singapore as well as in Indonesia, domestic helpers are expected to work, or at least be 'on call' from dawn till midnight. Whether they get breaks during the day depends very much on the discretion of their employers. Many indeed do have long breaks between chores, but this arrangement is not a fixture of the employment situation. A domestic helper who has become used to being able to have breaks may find that with the next employer she has to work non-stop.

Many Singaporeans in informal interviews revealed that if they did not see their domestic helpers working hard, they would feel they were wasting all the money they committed to hire them. Since they themselves are hard workers, they did not take kindly to people receiving money from them just to sit around.

In Indonesia, meanwhile, the argument put forward by families who employ domestic helpers is that they are part of the family, therefore there is no need for a definite job description; it is understood. On the one hand, there is the grating fact that they are the part of the family who has to do all the unpleasant work, and eat separately in the kitchen instead of at the family dining table. On the other hand, there is an unspoken latitude in many of the employment situations which the helpers enjoy and in their own way, take for granted. Many employers extend assistance to the helpers' family members, such as the costs of medical treatment, accommodation during the treatment, the costs, or some of the costs, of a family member's wedding, and various other benefits. It can also be argued that the helpers may be thus bound indefinitely to the employers by a debt of honor.

The situation described above may not apply when they work outside their home country, in this case Singapore. The kind of latitude many helpers enjoy disappears in the geographical and cultural void. Devoid of this latitude, it is a narrow groove the helpers find themselves falling into. They are not real workers, they are not legally entitled to any rest days - their rest times depending on the discretion of their employers, they are certainly not part of the family and they are not even compatriots. Despite all this, they may still be expected to be available and 'on call' from dawn till midnight as if they were part of the family.

The employers are also aware that the domestic helpers they are employ-ing are paid a lot more than they would have been in their own country, so there is an expectation that they should feel grateful. Not all employers verbally remind them of this, but many do. And some of these employers go one step further by feeling they have the moral right to abuse them if they do not show gratitude by working like quasi-slaves.

In Hong Kong, the foreign domestic helpers are referred to as 'helpers' but are regarded by the law as formal workers and receive legal protection under the Labour Law. In Singapore they are referred to as 'workers' but regarded as informal workers, and do not receive the legal protection of the country's Labour Law.

The Singapore Ministry of Manpower provides an orientation video which both employers and helpers can access via the internet on its website. Strictly speaking, however, the video is more useful for employers. Described in the video are points of which employers may not be initially aware, such as the fact that the helpers, arriving from a different country, may not necessarily speak fluent English, know Singapore's legal and cultural environment, be familiar with Singapore's standard of personal hygiene and proper ways of carrying out daily tasks, or even be acquainted with modern electrical and electronic appliances. The employers are encouraged to train the helpers to the extent that they feel necessary for the purpose of their employment. The employers are even encouraged to train them in good behavior, good man-ners and good morality, such as being courteous, honest, reliable, diligent, show initiative and be responsible.

While the video encourages employers to have open communication, absent are explicit warnings against abuse of the helpers.

Since foreign domestic helpers are regarded as informal workers, they do not have official entitlements such as minimum allowable wage, obligatory rest days and leave, and job descriptions. They are virtually only protected in these areas by the employers' implicit moral code, or a contract if the employers agree to have one.

Protection, therefore, has to begin from the institution which recruits and places them in the homes of their employers. It is important to see what kind of regulation binds these agencies, what kind of people are operating them, and to whom they are accountable.

Just as important is the role of the Indonesian Embassy that is responsible for the well-being of its citizens living, visiting or working in Singapore.

THE ROLE OF THE EMPLOYMENT AGENCIES

Given that most of the foreign domestic helpers, including those from Indonesia, find their employment through local employment agencies, it seems appropriate for Singapore to have instituted control in the form of accreditation of its employment and placement agencies. The surprizing aspect is that it took the government until 2002 to have the issue first mooted in Parliament.

Once brought up however, the major players in the market moved quickly. By July that year, the Association of Employment Agencies in Singapore (AEAS) was founded. The AEAS is the first single association in the business, prior to that there being several, making it rather difficult to monitor the industry practice.

Initiated by the Ministry of Manpower (MOM), the founding of the association was the result of sustained hard work by a program committee which was tasked with upgrading the industry, based on the criteria set up by the Ministry.

In an interview on Saturday, 13 November 2004, with the office bearers of the association, I was informed that as of May 2004, the Ministry of Manpower would only renew licences of accredited agencies.

Before AEAS was founded, the only body able to handle accreditation for these agencies was the Consumer Association of Singapore, known as CaseTrust. According to the AEAS office bearers, however, the costs charged by CaseTrust had discouraged many agencies, who did not see accreditation as necessary. When the MOM announced that accreditation would be a condition for licence renewal, many agencies petitioned the Ministry to defer the requirement regulation. They asked for some time for a further feasibility study.

On the resumption of Parliament however, the Minister of Manpower rejected the petition, but offered an alternative: if there was an organization which could come up with definite suggestions on how to handle accreditation in conformity with the Ministry's guidelines, the Ministry would consider giving it approval.

A group of agency operators submitted a petition, taking up the challenge of the offered alternative. 'We believed we could do it ourselves. And by doing it ourselves, we'd help bring down the costs. On that basis, we championed it, we got the mandate, and we were elected into office,' Helen Tan, the president of the association, explained.

They spent the first six months of their office-bearership lobbying for the authority to handle the accreditation, and won the official approval in July 2003. AEAS has a definite edge on CaseTrust because the agencies did not see CaseTrust as a body involved in the employment industry, while on the other hand, AEAS was regarded as comprising industry peers.

AEAS also covers agencies that handle the placement of foreign domestic workers/helpers as well as the employment and placement of local workers and has forced the costs of accreditation requirements down by hard work. They drew up an affordable scheme, where members were coached at no charge, showing a major benefit of being a member of the association.

At the same time, AEAS imposed stringent requirements containing fifty-two criteria, which is aimed at rendering the industry a lot more professional, thus adding more prestige to it. It succeeded in bringing in 540 members.

Helen Tan emphasized that the purpose of the accreditation was, indeed, to upgrade the employment agency to be more professional, with a written code of ethics and policy statement. An audit is done every four years, by independent auditors.

The policy regarding complaints received from clients, be they the employers or employees, is to first assess their severity and nature. Those that can be solved by mediation will be passed on to the mediation chairman on the association committee. The more severe ones may bring sanctions to the offending member agencies, or even be taken to higher authorities, such as the Commerce Trust, or also the court.

The employment and placement agencies have no obligation to settle employer-domestic helper disputes, though the AEAS offers a mediation service. The agencies are in many cases, the first point of contact for foreign domestic helpers from Indonesia, so the way they handle complaints from the helpers is very crucial in making the helpers feel they have not been abandoned. Indeed many agencies prove to be competent in settling disputes and counselling, but there are also those who tend to show reluctance in becoming involved in disputes. Theoretically the clients, the employers as well as the domestic helpers, can complain to the AEAS if they are not happy with their agencies, however, in practice, it is the employers who are more inclined to do so. The helpers, in times of difficulty and despair, have another avenue for recourse, the Indonesian Embassy.

Many employment agencies are keen to improve the negative image associated with their industry, for instance the image of greed, of only caring about profits, of being abusive to the domestic helpers and prone to being dishonest in their dealings with clients.

One employment agency owner, Chew Kim Whatt, gathered his knowledge and experience of thirty-six years as a human resource manager and eight more years operating his own employment agency, and wrote a very hands-on and useful book, *Foreign Maid: The complete handbook for employers and maid agencies.*

In this book he highlights the need for employer-candidates to think why they need a domestic helper now, and if domestic help is really what they need, then they also need to plan carefully how to set up a workable arrangement for all parties. Chew does not pull punches, he does not paint anyone as without faults, neither does he paint anyone as totally evil. Based on realistic expectations of human nature, on the part of the employer, the domestic helper and the agent, he reveals where caution and consideration are called for.

THE ROLE OF THE INDONESIAN EMBASSY

Indonesian migrant/guest workers, including domestic helpers, form part of the brief of First Secretary Fachry Sulaiman, who heads the Protocol and Consular Affairs section at the Embassy.

There are over 70,000 Indonesian domestic helpers working in Singapore. Even if it were true that only two per cent – an oft-mentioned arbitrary figure in informal conversations with government officials – experienced problems in the course of their employment, in human terms, that would translate to almost 2,000 people needing help and assistance in various degrees, in

Singapore alone. In fact, figures provided by police and the Ministry of Manpower showed that at least 117 of these helpers have died since 1999 falling from high-rise apartments while cleaning windows or hanging laundry, and there are debates of whether a number of these actually committed suicide. The suspicion of suicide was brought on by the number of abuse cases which came to the surface and reached the court, with their employers ending up in prison or receiving large fines.

Despite the volume of work related to domestic helpers, there are no dedicated consular officials to handle the issue. My observations indicated that Fachry Sulaiman and his staff at the Protocol and Consular Affairs section worked beyond the normal embassy office hours.

The protection provided by the Embassy comes in two forms: vetting, as far as it is able, the agencies handling the placement and employment of Indonesian domestic helpers in Singapore homes, by enforcing its own accreditation requirements on them; sheltering the helpers who fled their employers' homes where they had been abused or had themselves committed crimes against their employers; and continuing to assist them by cooperating with the police and the court. Another form of protection the Embassy provides is of a social welfare kind: by providing the venue for meeting once a month, where various workshops are conducted to enhance the helpers' skills and self-esteem.

Vetting the employment agencies

In addition to the mandatory accreditation imposed by the Ministry of Manpower, the Embassy requires agencies which handle placement and employment of domestic helpers from Indonesia to be accredited by the Embassy. The power to enforce this comes from the requirement for job orders to be endorsed by the Embassy before they can be sent to the PJTKI in Indonesia. In other words, the Embassy only gives its endorsement to those agencies which have received its approval, in the form of accreditation.

In the arrangements for employment agencies obtaining accreditation, the Embassy in effect has taken a proactive step in the protection of the domestic helpers working in Singapore, rallying the resources and official power it possesses, to make the agencies reach out beyond the minimum requirements officially imposed by the Singapore Government.

In this step the Embassy is also aware that it can only drive the agencies to come to the party if it also offers a service in return.

The agencies are, in the arrangements, responsible for the welfare and well-being of the domestic helpers, such as providing assistance to the helpers they placed when disputes with employers occur. In more serious disputes, the agencies are to cooperate with the Embassy in the day-to-day activities of mediation, including accompanying injured or abused helpers to see medical professionals for the purpose of examination or treatment, and accompanying helpers to the police, the Ministry of Manpower, or the Immigration Office. Even in cases where certain helpers are being housed in the temporary shelter belonging to the Embassy, the agencies are required to continue to monitor their cases. In cases where certain helpers have to be repatriated, it is the agencies' responsibility to make sure that repatriation is carried out appropriately.

The agencies in return, receive regular updates on new requirements and regulations passed by authorities in Indonesia which affect their business and ability to perform their business activities. Conversely they also can expect the Embassy's assistance and endorsement in dealing with their domestic helper clients, and on issues relating to the clients' involvement with the police or the Ministry of Manpower. In the long run, the agencies benefit from their clients' participation in the free weekend skill and self-esteem enhancing courses at the Embassy.

Providing shelter and paralegal counselling to domestic helpers in trouble

Domestic helpers who leave their employers' homes for various reasons, need to go somewhere safe, often even before they can go to the police or other authorities. The Embassy has a temporary shelter for this purpose. It is in the Embassy grounds, and can house up to fifty people.

Once their cases have been taken up by the police or the Ministry of Manpower, they can stay at the shelter while waiting for the settlement of the dispute.

The shelter also houses relatives or family members of domestic helpers who are in police detention or whose cases are being heard or are waiting to be heard in court.

Since there almost always are domestic helpers who are in police detention or in prison charged with various crimes, First Secretary Fachry Sulaiman goes to visit them twice a month to offer paralegal counselling. Sulaiman, being himself a legal counsel, understands how unsettling and disturbing it is for the domestic helpers to find themselves in foreign police detention or prison. He visits them and explains their situation to them, in order for them to know what to expect.

Limitations

The Embassy can only be proactive to the extent that circumstances allow. Sulaiman explained that it is constrained by the lack of data it can access quickly relating to domestic helpers who come to work in Singapore.

While the Embassy is able to trace the number of job orders going to the PJTKI in Indonesia, it cannot trace the identities and particulars of the domestic helpers who arrive in Singapore. It is not easy to request these from the Singapore Government. The process takes months to complete. The Embassy has to rely on the PJTKI or the domestic helpers themselves to report when they arrive, and many do not. According to Indonesian Immigration Law No. 20/93, an Indonesian citizen who is going to stay longer than six months in a foreign country, must report to the Indonesian diplomatic mission in that country. Presumably, many domestic helpers who come to Singapore are not aware of this law.

'We are supposed to protect our citizens here, whoever they are, whatever their jobs, but if we don't know they are here, and who they are, it becomes a very difficult task,' said Sulaiman.

Not having complete data about its citizens residing in Singapore also means that when one of them goes missing, the Embassy cannot easily have him or her traced. If one of them falls seriously ill and is unable to communicate, the Embassy, tasked with taking care of his or her welfare and repatriation, will need to find his or her next of kin in Indonesia quickly. The same problem occurs if one of them dies and the Embassy has to repatriate the remains but does not have the correct address to send them to.

Necessary measures yet to be taken

Employment agencies accreditation arrangements have been a step in the right direction to assisting the Embassy in controlling the situation it is tasked to handle. In an interview on 25 November 2004, Sulaiman laid out what was yet to be achieved.

- The full implementation of a one-gate or one-stop system, where all would-be workers/helpers are required to come via Batam, where they can be easily monitored beforehand by the authorities in order to ensure that all their documents are in order. This will also allow the Embassy to access the information quickly;

- The handling by the Embassy of the arrival in Singapore of each group of workers/helpers, to be given a half-day orientation program, where they are briefed about important things they need to know, such as the emergency telephone numbers of Embassy staff-in-charge as well as what to do and not to do while they are in Singapore to avoid getting into trouble with the law and with their employers. Only when this is done will the agencies' representatives or employers be able to collect them;

- The continuous implementation of skill-enhancement training, where the domestic helpers can attend classes of English and Mandarin, of work skills, and of additional skills to prepare for post-domestic work time, such as hairdressing, dressmaking and fine cuisine; and

- The establishment of radio programs, with editorials that include their views. These will run sessions such as consultation regarding work situations, social situations, or anything of interest to the community. The radio station can be set up in Batam and monitored by Radio Singapore.

With cooperation from the related government departments in Indonesia and the community itself, Sulaiman believes all these can be achieved.

RECENT MEASURES TAKEN BY THE MINISTRY OF MANPOWER

To minimize further problems related to the employment of foreign domestic helpers, the Singapore Government has taken measures aimed at raising the quality of the domestic helpers working in Singapore. The government wanted them to be better able to communicate with their employers and pose fewer management problems for employers.

Minimum educational level requirement of the foreign domestic helpers
Prospective employers who apply for new foreign domestic helpers after
1 January 2005 have to make sure that the domestic helpers they seek to
employ have completed at least eight years of formal education in their
countries of origin. A list of acceptable educational certificates is provided
for Indonesia, India, Bangladesh, Malaysia, Myanmar, The Philippines, Sri
Lanka and Thailand.

For Indonesia most official certificates of junior secondary school and
senior secondary school are listed:

- STTB SMP (*Surat Tanda Tamat Belajar Sekolah Menengah Umum Tingkat Pertama*),
- STTB SLTP (*Surat Tanda Tamat Belajar Sekolah Lanjutan Tingkat Pertama*),
- STTB MTs (*Surat Tanda Tamat Belajar Madrasah Tsanawiyah*),
- STTB SMA (*Surat Tanda Tamat Belajar Sekolah Menengah Umum Tingkat Atas*),
- STTB SMU (*Surat Tanda Tamat Belajar Sekolah Menengah Umum*),
- STTB SMK (*Surat Tanda Tamat Belajar Sekolah Menengah Kejuruan*),
- STTB MA (*Surat Tanda Tamat Belajar Madrasah Aliyah*)

Compulsory entry test for new foreign domestic workers
In addition to the minimum educational level requirement, an entry test is
made compulsory for first-time foreign domestic helpers seeking work in
Singapore from 1 April 2005.

When a domestic helper obtains an IPA (In-Principle Approval) following an application for a Work Permit, she can enter Singapore. Within three
working days of arrival, however, the domestic helper has to sit for an entry
test. If she passes the test, she will be able to proceed with the request for
the issuance of her Work Permit. If she fails however, she will have her IPA
withdrawn and the employment agency which arranged for her transfer to
Singapore will have to repatriate her at the agency's own expense.

Minimum age requirement of the foreign domestic helpers
The minimum age, previously eighteen years, has also been lifted to twenty-

three years. Older domestic helpers are expected to be more mature, and better able to manage difficult work situations and, consequently, cause fewer employment-related problems.

There is no doubt that both the Singapore and Indonesian Governments are taking steps to improve the situation of the domestic helpers working in the city-state. It is, however, also obvious that the steps taken by the Singapore Government have employers as the uppermost of its considerations.

The welfare and well-being of the Indonesian domestic helpers working in Singapore, it appears, are the responsibility of the Indonesian authorities, via their diplomatic representatives. Considering the apparent constraints of human resource limitations on the Embassy, the implementation of First Secretary Fachry Sulaiman's plans for the improvement and better coordinated action of the many implementation stages before the actual arrival of the domestic helpers in Singapore are crucial.

THE ROLE OF NON-GOVERNMENTAL ORGANISATIONS

TWC2

The death of Muwanatul Chasanah shocked many, many people in Singapore, yet eventually most of them had to move on. A number of highly socially conscious and civic-minded individuals however, decided to do something concrete. These individuals consist of activists from AWARE (an advocacy group dedicated to promoting gender equality and understanding), Singapore employment agents, social workers from various church organizations, and other individuals. They formed a group and named it TWC2, an acronym for *Transient Workers Count Too* after the original TWC, or The Working Committee of Civil Society, set out in 1999 to identify present and future roles for civil society activities in Singapore.

The group's objectives focus on the dignity of labor and the right of workers to respect and fair treatment regardless of the nature of work, race, color, gender, language, religion or class of the worker.

TWC2 began lobbying the government for better legislative protection for foreign domestic helpers, as well as offering concrete programs such as classes and workshops for employers in order for them to be able to communicate more effectively with their helpers. To enhance public awareness, the group also has a website complete with a lively discussion board where people can write in their opinions and recount their own experience, or encounters, with foreign domestic helpers.

Several foreign domestic workers advocacy groups started out of TWC2, some running shelters, counselling, and help centers for foreign domestic workers in trouble.

Since the founding of TWC2, the government indeed has made some legislative changes such as increasing the penalty for employers who abuse their helpers, and introducing accreditation requirements for employment agencies applying for renewal of licences.

Darul Arqam

Darul Arqam Singapore is also known as The Muslim Converts' Association of Singapore. It is a friendly and welcoming center where, apart from a conversion procedure that accompanies its orientation sessions, it runs courses on Islam and marriage guidance.

Since domestic helpers from Indonesia are not allowed to marry Singapore citizens or permanent residents, they will only be in a position to take advantage of the marriage guidance classes in the small likelihood of their meeting, with a view to marrying, non-citizens or non-residents when they have completed their contracts. The center has also established Multinational Clubs and Sister Pool, which are informal, and which have been popular among foreign domestic helpers. They generally come to recreational activities organized by the Sister Pool, and attend prayers and celebrations for Eid-ul-Fitr and Eid-ul-Adha.

For those who like to explore further, there is also a bookshop with up-to-date books on aspects of life relating to being a Muslim.

Darul Arqam however, is more than a place where the domestic helpers from Indonesia come to take part in courses. It is also a meeting point, where they find a friendly network and comfort zone, where they meet people from other countries as well. Darul Arqam is a also a place where they see themselves in a wider context, outside their employers' homes.

ACMI (Archdiocesan Commission for the Pastoral Care of Migrants and Itinerant People)

The Archdiocesan Commission for the Pastoral Care of Migrants and

Itinerant People was founded on 15 June 1998 by a Filipino priest as a support group for the communities of migrant workers from various countries. Over the years, the organization has provided advocacy and counselling services to migrant workers who have encountered problems with their employers.

In 2004, the organization decided to refocus its role, and retreated from direct advocacy to concentrate more on conciliation and counselling, and maintain its role on pastoral care. To make it easier to remember, it adopted a shorter acronym, ACMI.

Chairperson Elizabeth Tan, who joined the organization in 2000, believes that over the years there have been increasing numbers of Singaporeans becoming aware of the problems faced by migrant workers.

Everyday ACMI handles an average of three cases, and approximately five calls for telephone consultations, some needing further consultations, others stopping at the telephone contacts. Here are some sample scenarios:

Scenario One

ACMI receives a call (increasingly now from a third party) reporting a problem relating to a domestic helper who has not received her salary for six months, and whose passport and other documents are held by her employer.

The ACMI officer who takes the call will ask the domestic helper, or if it is a third party, will ask the person to obtain the answers from the domestic helper involved, how long she has been working with the employer. ACMI officers are aware of the arrangements where Indonesian domestic helpers repay their recruitment agencies at home by hefty deductions of their salaries for the first few months, ranging from three to seven months. In many cases, the Singapore agencies make arrangements with their employers to pass on the repayments direct to the agencies, who then pass them on to the recruitment agencies in Indonesia. Unfortunately, it appears that in many cases the domestic helpers themselves are the last persons to be informed of these arrangements.

In the case where the domestic helper involved is aware of the arrangement regarding her repayments, and that the period of repayments is over but she still has not received any salary, the ACMI officer will counsel the domestic helper on how to approach her employer and broach the subject in a manner not deemed abrasive by the employer. There might also be another arrangement of which the domestic helper is not aware, such as an agreement between the employer and the agency to hold the salary for safekeeping until the end of the contract. Such arrangements are not uncommon in Singapore. Usually, however, the domestic helper concerned has been consulted, and has then agreed to the arrangement.

If, after bringing up the subject with the employer, the domestic helper still faces stonewalling – some employers become abusive and deliver threats -, the ACMI officer usually suggests that the helper write to ACMI detailing her problems. ACMI will then take it on her behalf to the Ministry of Manpower. The Ministry will then deal with the employer. This usually results in the employer paying the money owed to the helper, but also in the helper being repatriated following the employer refusing to continue employing her. Being responsible for her repatriation, the employer can do this. Understandably, the ACMI officer will first explain to the helper of the likelihood of this eventuality and, consequently, the domestic helper involved often decides not to continue with the case.

Scenario Two
ACMI receives a call from an abused domestic helper or a third party. The ACMI officer taking the call will ask the abused helper, or if it is a third party call, will ask the caller if he or she can accompany the abused helper to the nearest police station, and an ACMI officer will come and meet them there.

When the helper has made a formal report to the police, ACMI will take her to a shelter belonging to one of the two church organizations which link up with ACMI. The helper will need somewhere to live while waiting for her case to be heard in court, and in many cases, the helper will need counselling.

The police will usually inform the Indonesian Embassy of the incident. ACMI provides counselling for those who come to them for help, such as this hypothetical domestic helper. Like Darul Arqam, ACMI also provides short courses of which many migrant workers take advantage. In fact, during the class breaks the different ethnic groups socialize, to the extent that they take turns in bringing their ethnic lunch or afternoon tea to share together.

Elizabeth Tan believes that over the years the advocacy of ACMI and other groups with similar objectives have yielded results. 'Now in cases where the employer and employee are in dispute over whether the helper's salary has been paid, the employer has to prove the payment. If he or she is unable to do so, he or she will be compelled to pay within seven days of the due date determined by the Ministry of Manpower,' Tan said, citing an example.

THE SITUATION THROUGH THE EYES OF A SEASONED LAWYER

Mohamed Muzammil Mohamed has defended many migrant workers from Indonesia, the most high-profile being Sundarti Supriyanto who, charged initially with double murders, evaded a death sentence by hanging, and was eventually convicted of culpable homicide and sentenced to life imprisonment.

During an interview on 22 June 2005, at his law firm offices at Suite 11, Thirtieth Floor, International Plaza, Tanjong Pagar, Singapore, he shared some of his views on the situation.

His first case of an Indonesian national was in 1998. Muzammil was assigned by the Supreme Court to defend three Indonesians who were charged with murdering another Indonesian while working illegally at a construction site in Singapore's River Valley area. They were stranded in Singapore with no money to return home, so they decided to rob another compatriot who was working at the same construction site.

'We fought the matter in court for forty-five days. If found guilty they would have been sentenced to death. In the process, I had to get witnesses who had since gone back to Indonesia. I had to get help from the Indonesian Embassy. That was how I got in contact with the Embassy. And since then I've been asked to work on cases involving Indonesian nationals, especially domestic helpers, who are either charged with criminal offences or were victims of criminal offences in Singapore,' he explained.

Muzammil is a firm believer in the even-handedness and fairness of the country's law. 'In Singapore the law applies to everyone. If you are found guilty of murder, you face the death sentence. If you are acquitted, you are free. This is irrespective of where you come from, geographically, socially or politically,' he said.

He then gave an example where a member of the royal family of one of the states in Malaysia was charged with murdering a lady with whom he had had some business dealings. He had to go through the whole process. He had a trial. He was defended by counsel. At the end of the day, he was convicted of murder and was sentenced to death. He appealed, the appeal was dismissed and he was eventually executed.

Revisiting the trial of Sundarti Supriyanto, Muzammil summarized, 'She faced two charges of murder. The prosecution proceeded on one and dropped the other. If Sundarti had been found guilty of the murder charge, the court would have sentenced her to death. Fortunately we managed to raise reasonable doubts by raising the defence of a sudden fight. So she was found guilty on the lesser charge of culpable homicide instead of murder, and was sentenced to life imprisonment.'

Muzammil is proud of the fact that the court in Singapore is uncontaminated by any corruption.

'In Singapore,' he said, 'political figures are not allowed to gain political mileage by visiting their constituents in prison, during an election campaign or at any other time. And when you are in prison, no matter who you were or are in public life, you go through the same prison rigors as any other prisoner.'

In regard to the domestic helpers who come in contact with the law, he said, 'If they are victims of abuse by their employer and it is proven, they can claim compensation for the injuries they suffer and their employer will be prosecuted. If they are the perpetrators of abuse against the employers or their family members, they are charged with criminal offences.'

When he is assigned to defend them, Muzammil gives all he has. 'I spend a lot of time in court, and a lot of time with them. I think it is a duty as an officer of the court to assist those who need help,' he said.

Muzammil does not wax lyrical about the foreign domestic helpers who come to work in Singapore, but he believes that nobody would want to leave their home and the comfort network of their family, especially if they themselves have children, to travel across the sea to a foreign land to work and earn money, unless they really need the money. 'They are forced by circumstances,' he observed, then continued, 'Then when they come here, they face a culture shock. Since most of them come from rural areas, the lifestyle in their own kampongs would be a lot more slow-paced and tranquil compared to that in Singapore. There everyone knows everyone else, while here we have an urban lifestyle, where everyone is in a hurry, and everything needs to be done fast.'

He did not learn about this in books or films. Muzammil has seen for himself the domestic helpers' home towns or home villages. He makes a habit of visiting the place of origin of the person he is defending in court. For the defence of Sundarti Supriyanto for instance, Muzammil visited her family's home in Magetan.

'I wanted to have a profile of the family. With the assistance of the Indonesian Embassy, I met the family members: her mother, her sister, and some others, in Surabaya. They were accompanied by some of the village elders. On the next trip I went to visit her house in Magetan. About two or three hours from Solo. Apart from her mother, I met her grandparents, and her uncle.'

Being a Singaporean whose own family has employed Indonesian domestic helpers, he knows the exasperation of Singapore employers having to tell their domestic helpers what to do and what not to do, again and again. On the other hand, he also understands that it takes a long time for a domestic worker who comes from a completely different lifestyle and living pace, to adapt to everything that prevails in Singapore and to appreciate that the employer's demands are serious and immediate.

'This often sparks off anger on the part of the employers, some blowing their tops and using violence on the helpers. We have seen one-off incidents like that. More serious is where the maids are subjected to continuous abuse for a period of time. There have been burning and scalding using hot water and hot iron, hitting with cane or wood. Some abuse is unimaginable,' he recounted.

Muzammil also believes that it is important for women who want to come to Singapore to work as domestic helpers to be more mature, so the Singapore Government's policy of increasing the minimum age is a step in the right direction. A more mature person is more able to handle the culture shock and overcome the emotional stress encountered in the job.

He related some of the cases he defended where the helper's glibness and immaturity were dangerous to those around her and eventually to herself.

'In one case this domestic helper was recently employed to look after a baby. She was very angry with another helper who was already working for the same employer. She suspected that the helper had been bad-mouthing her to the employer. She was also angry with the child's grandmother for scolding her. So she poured hydrochloric acid into the baby's milk and fed it to the baby. The six-month-old baby suffered burns on his lips, inside his mouth, and inside his intestines. It caused long-lasting injuries. The child's intestines had to be cut open, and the badly burnt parts had to be removed. She admitted to the offence. The court was very unsympathetic to her. She got eight years.

'In another, a helper used a hot iron on the child. Then there was another case where a helper used a knife to cut a two year old's penis. Lucky for everyone around that it was not deep enough to cut off the penis, only the skin. She denied that she had used the knife to cut off the boy's penis, she said it was an accident. But the evidence was overwhelming. The doctor testified that the cut was found almost on the whole circumference of the penis. So there were no mitigating circumstances. She got twenty-four or thirty-six months. And very recently a domestic helper put insecticide in her employer's soya milk, because her employer had scolded her about her boyfriend. She maybe just wanted to hurt him, without appreciating the seriousness of her action.'

Sundarti Supriyanto's case, Muzammil admitted, was the most trying for him, because being such a high-profile case it was covered by the media in the region, and a great deal of sensationalizing went on.

'I had to go to Jakarta to explain to the media and some non-governmental organizations about what was actually being done,' he said. 'Some of the non-governmental organizations activists were saying that the laws in Singapore were draconian and unfair. I said, the laws are always there. You know what they are. It's up to you not to break them. I don't think it is up to me to say, for instance, that the laws in Indonesia are not fair. Do you?'

Since his first case handling an Indonesian national, there have been a lot of improvements brought about by the authorities. He said, 'The law has been passed to increase the penalty for those who abuse their domestic helpers. The police are very prompt and relentless. Once they receive a report about an abuse of a domestic helper, they will fully investigate. The government is fully aware. No one can say that the Singapore Government has not done anything to protect the domestic helpers.'

Muzammil agrees with the observations that the community in Singapore are a lot more aware of the situation with the foreign domestic helpers. 'A month ago I had a case where an employer and her daughter were abusing their helper. It was a neighbor of theirs who reported it to the police. Another recent case was a celebrity, a television compere, who abused her helper, and again it was a neighbor who reported it to the police. Yes, things are changing,' he said.

He also pointed out that the Indonesian Embassy is very sensitive to the needs and the situation of the Indonesian domestic helpers. 'I know for a fact that when they receive any complaints they inform the police, and they make sure that the helpers are not subjected to further abuse by their employers,' he said.

Now it is up to those in Indonesia to train the women who want to be domestic helpers in Singapore to be more prepared for what they are going to face. At present, Muzammil observes that many of these domestic helpers cannot cope with the demands of the work, and do not know the seriousness of the consequences of their actions. He said, 'I have had talks with officers in the Indonesian embassy, and suggested that the maids be briefed on the do's and don'ts of working in Singapore. In their current training, I presume they are taught how to do household chores and some English language. But I think what is missing is the social, cultural and legal parts. They have to be taught emphatically that committing offences with serious consequences will land them in prison. On the other hand, if they are subjected to abuse themselves, they should know their rights, and what they are entitled to do.'

CHAPTER THREE
MALAYSIA

SETTING THE SCENE

At a glance, Malaysia and Indonesia share many aspects of the Malay-based culture, and their languages enjoy a fair degree of overlap. If you look closer, however, you will find that Malaysia and Indonesia are like two siblings who are reluctant to concede to each other's seniority. Indonesia as a nation was born twelve years before the birth of Malaysia. So as nations go, Indonesia is, metaphorically speaking, the older sibling.

Economically, however, Malaysia has moved ahead of Indonesia, thus playing a more prominent role in the international political economy.

What is more, Indonesia, not fully recovered from the economic crash of 1997-98, and yet to properly regroup following the political reform of the post-Suharto era, has an economy that is lackluster in terms of performance and growth, resulting in high unemployment. According to official data from *Badan Pusat Statistik* or the Central Bureau of Statistics, in February 2005 the unemployment rate reached 10.3 per cent, while underemployment reached 31.2 per cent. This, coupled with Malaysia's rapid economic growth, has triggered a boost in the flow of migrant workers from Indonesia, some entering the country illegally. While work migration from Indonesia has been encouraged in different stages since the colonial era, and has served Malaysia well, the recent flow has caused some problems.

In the 1960s, actively encouraged migrants from Indonesia included a fair proportion of professional people, such as teachers and doctors, and most of these migrants have to a large extent blended into the Malay community. The recent Indonesian migrant workers however, consist mostly of construction workers and domestic helpers, whose presence in the country, legal or otherwise, does not blend readily into the local community. This is not necessarily caused by the migrants' reluctance to blend in. The fact is that the men are in construction work, a type of employment generally shunned by the locals, not in the natural environment to mingle with the locals, and therefore tend to mix among themselves. They thus become very visible and audible in concentrations and clusters, causing some resentment. When some of these workers commit crimes, they stand out even more, because in the media reporting, the fact that the perpetrators are Indonesians is usually mentioned, often in the headlines. The women, in the meantime, are mostly in domestic work, which in Malaysia is generally regarded as of very low status, thus neither the men nor the women are the type of people with whom the locals seek to socialize.

Aware that it is at least a richer sibling, with a 2004 per capita income of US$4,650 according to the World Bank's data, Malaysia is therefore not keen on admitting that it is the younger sibling.

MALAYSIA AS USER OF INDONESIAN DOMESTIC HELPERS' SERVICE

There are approximately 220,000 Indonesian domestic helpers in Malaysia, the number fluctuating marginally from time to time.

The way Malaysia developed into a user-country of the Indonesian domestic helpers' service cannot be separated from the social and cultural aspects that have tied the two countries together. Of the three country-users covered in this book, the standard salaries here for domestic helpers from Indonesia are the lowest, yet there has never been a shortage of Indonesian women who want to work in the country.

This may have a lot to do with the fact that these women feel that going to Malaysia is more like extending their comfort zone, rather than moving out of it. This, however, is where the mis-match begins. The employers in Malaysia do not necessarily regard them as part of their world. Many of these people employ the Indonesian women to work as domestic helpers because they are cheaper and generally more compliant than their Filipino counterparts who are known to be more confident about their skills, hence more self-assertive.

Today's Malaysia and today's Indonesia may well underestimate how much they have moved apart. Without the common language and some common cultural values they may, in fact, be as diverse from one another as Malaysia and the Philippines, or as Indonesia and Thailand.

In Indonesia, Malay was indeed used as the language of the national independence struggle. In the beginning of the twentieth century, the independence activists, aware that they needed a unifying force to rally the people of the far-flung regions each with its own language, adopted a *lingua franca* which had been naturally used throughout the archipelago. Malay was used at first by traders, then spread from the coasts to further inland. In 1928, the independence activists declared the language as Bahasa Indonesia, the Indonesian language, for the nation they aspired to have, Indonesia.

Bahasa Indonesia then developed into a language with characteristics different from those of the original Malay, or from those of the current Bahasa Kebangsaan Malaysia, Malaysia's national language, though both derive from the same roots.

There are further differences, such as different systems of government and, not least of all, the collective temperaments of the populations of the two countries. This may have a great deal to do with the fact that while ethnicity-wise Indonesia is overwhelmingly Malay, the ethnic Malays in Indonesia have been very much tempered with other cultures not present in Malaysia.

Interestingly, the presence of a Malaysian in Indonesia is not noticeable. The cultural diversity resulting from the many different ethnic groups throughout the country, allows people to have markedly different accents and different sets of body language while still speaking Indonesian. A Malaysian-speaking Malay in Jakarta for instance, may very easily be taken for someone visiting from West Sumatra or the Riau Islands.

Conversely, an Indonesian in any Malaysian city stands out, especially if he or she tries to speak Malay. The accent and the body language of the Indonesian are indicative enough of his or her Indonesianness, because nowhere in Malaysia is there a region or province to which the Indonesian's accent and body language can, even remotely, be attributed.

For two neighboring countries with a shared culture and history, Malaysia and Indonesia do not have major business ventures with each other. In fact, they both compete for roughly the same sources of foreign capital to invest in their respective countries. Most of the business ties between the two countries themselves are too small for a large contingent of Malaysian business people to be in an Indonesian city at one particular time, and vice-versa.

When contact occurs, it is usually fraught with tension. There have been the on-going mutual-blaming bouts over illegal migrant workers from Indonesia who have been forcefully deported, some having been previously detained and penalized, and the near-skirmishes between the two countries' navies in April 2005 over the sea border, the bone of contention, ostensibly at least, being the Ambalat blocks, an area off the eastern coast of Kalimantan rich in oil and gas.

Despite all this, at government level, Malaysia and Indonesia claim to be fairly amicable. At grass-roots level, the relationships are a lot more complex.

While the Malay roots are still, and will always be, present, Indonesian culture consists of a lot more than the Malay world. Its literature has developed independently of its Malay origins. And in their content, Indonesian literature, and now its media as well, have very few Malay components and hardly any Malay consciousness to speak of. In everyday life, the word 'Malay' generally invokes something of the deep past among Indonesians.

It has been a long time since Indonesian migrants have blended into the Malay community. The recent Indonesian migrant workers are now conspicuous, in a manner far from salubrious, to be resented and despised.

The going rates for Indonesian domestic helpers in Malaysia are between MR250 (US$66) and MR450 (US$120), with a handful receiving over MR500 (US$133). These rates are basically market-driven, based on the perceived levels of the helpers' skills, and the amounts employers are prepared to pay.

Foreign domestic helpers are not covered by the country's employment law, therefore there is no clear job description and the accompanying entitlements for them. Those who are recruited and placed by responsible accredited employment agencies have some recourse when they encounter problems with their employers, because most of these responsible agencies offer conciliation counseling. As many domestic helpers however, are recommended by friends, or friends of friends, and have entered the country using the service of illegal employment agencies, they do not have such a recourse. Most likely they themselves have no legal documents.

There are also those who initially entered the country legally, but after encountering problems with their employers, inadvertently become illegal. They run away from the homes of their employers who hold their documents and report them to the Immigration Department to cancel their work visa. If they have been placed by responsible employment agencies, they may receive assistance from them, but if they have been placed by irresponsible agencies that only concern themselves with profit and turn them away in times of need, they may be in real trouble. Unless the helpers are aware enough to seek the help of non-governmental organizations such as Women's Aid Organisation (WAO), they would be regarded as illegal, and as such, liable to be detained, penalized, and eventually deported.

It is not known how many of the domestic helpers from Indonesia are illegally working in the country, because these people are not registered at the embassy, nor are they willing to come forward to speak to strangers. They are, in reality, the most vulnerable of all foreign domestic helpers, because they are effectively in constant fear of being reported and eventually deported. Their existence is confirmed by those who are working legally but are not willing to divulge their illegal friends' whereabouts.

If the employment situation works well for a domestic helper from Indonesia – and many indeed do – she will be able to save some money and help her family's finances at home. The precariousness of the situation of these domestic helpers is, however, amply illustrated by the cases where the employment situation has gone wrong. Many of these cases have from time to time been made public in the media, while many others have gone unnoticed except for those closely involved.

A sample of cases where the employment situation went wrong
Case One
On 25 June 2004, local media reported on a Malaysian court that had charged a sixteen year old boy with assault for abusing his family's Indonesian maid.

The boy's identity has been withheld because of his age. The Bernama news agency reported that the court was told that he beat the maid, Misriani Muntono, thirty-six, with a sofa leg and burned her with a cigarette lighter at his home in northern Malaysia's Penang state.

Magistrate Priscilla Rajan fixed bail at MR2,000 (US$525), and instructed the trial to be held on 29 July.

If found guilty, the boy could be sentenced to three years imprisonment or fined or whipped, or any two of the punishments, according to the report.

Case Two

On 24 June 2005 a Malaysian businessman was sentenced to twenty years' imprisonment for beating his Indonesian domestic helper to death.

Judge Akhtar Tahir, at the Kuala Lumpur Sessions Court, found Gan Chun Loong, forty, guilty of the manslaughter of Sonirih Casnawi, twenty-eight. 'This is the most brutal and inhumane case of physical abuse that I have seen,' the judge was quoted as saying. 'The injuries on the body tells of the severe abuse and serious injuries inflicted on the maid before she died. Her internal organs were ruptured. There was bruising on the abdomen suggesting heavy blows causing the pancreas to be pressed hard on the backbone before it was ripped apart.'

The court heard that the attack on Sonirih Casnawi left her with forty-five injuries. Gan's wife told the court that she found the domestic helper lying motionless on the bathroom floor. She also testified that she had heard her husband arguing with their domestic helper about household chores shortly before that.

A SOURCE OF EMBARRASSMENT ALL ROUND

It is an irony that while the issue of domestic helpers itself took a long time to receive the kind of attention which is followed by appropriate action from the governments of Malaysia and Indonesia, each time a bad case hit the media, it became a source of embarrassment all round. After a week or so, however, life would then return to normal, and people would begin to bury their heads in the sand again, pretending that the situation was actually not as bad as the media made it out to be.

In the meantime, the temporary shelter in the Indonesian Embassy in

Kuala Lumpur continued to house domestic helpers from Indonesia who had been abused, mentally and physically. And employment agencies continued to place more Indonesian domestic helpers in Malaysian homes throughout the country.

Then in mid-May 2004, in the middle of an election campaign in Indonesia, a case exploded in the face of the incumbent president, Megawati Sukarnoputri.

THE LANDMARK CASE OF NIRMALA BONAT

A nineteen year old domestic helper from West Nusa Tenggara was reported to have been repeatedly abused for a period of four months. Nirmala Bonat, the helper, had been subjected to abuse by beating, burning and scalding by her female employer, thirty-six year old Yim Pek Ha, in their home in Villa Putera, Jalan Tun Ismail, Kuala Lumpur. Pictures of the young woman covered with injuries reportedly dismayed Malaysians. Even Prime Minister Abdullah Badawi was quoted as being shocked and appalled, and his government promptly offered a formal apology to the Bonat family.

On Friday, 21 May 2004, Yim Pek Ha was charged in the Sessions Court with four counts of voluntarily causing grievous hurt. The prosecution demanded that Yim be sentenced to twenty years imprisonment for each of those charges.

She wanted to augment her family's income

Nirmala, born on 27 August 1984, is the only daughter of Daniel Bonat and Martha Toni, of the village of Tuapukas, Kualin Regency, North Central Timor. Keen to help augment her parents' meager income from subsistence farming, Nirmala agreed to be recruited as a domestic helper by a Kupang branch of a PJTKI in Surabaya, *PT Kurnia Bina Rizki*. According to the local government's official record, she was sent to Malaysia via Surabaya on 25 June 2003, together with twenty-six other domestic helpers.

Nirmala herself however, stated that she came to Malaysia in September 2003. No explanation as yet has been offered for the discrepancy. Is it likely that she made a mistake about the date? Having completed nine years of schooling, it is reasonable to believe that she would know such a major fact.

How the abuse started

According to Nirmala, her employer, Yim, began abusing her when she accidentally broke a mug in January 2004. 'She then threw boiling water on me,' Nirmala told the media.

After that, things went downhill for the young woman. Yim seemed to lash out each time Nirmala did something which displeased her. She would beat the domestic helper with whatever she could lay her hands on, such as a clothes hanger and an iron mug. The most serious physical attacks Nirmala was subjected to, however, were scalding with boiling water and burning with a hot iron.

The hot iron was used because it was the first thing that Yim could grab. One day Yim was not happy with the way Nirmala had pressed her clothes, so she slapped her, and grabbed the hot iron and pushed it on to Nirmala's breasts.

Attempts at running away from the employers' home

People often ask why a domestic helper would stay in the home where she was being abused. The first and most likely reason is that the helper has been bullied to such an extent that she is convinced if she runs away she will be caught and be further, and even more severely, punished. The second reason is that she feels she has nowhere to go.

To consultant psychiatrist Dr Salina Abdul Aziz, Nirmala confessed that she had, in fact, tried to run away twice. Each time she had left the apartment, however the prospect of facing strange surroundings made her turn around and come back. When the abuse went well beyond her endurance, she walked out again, and not sure where to go, she sat on a box, crying in desperation. Lucky for her, a security guard saw her, and asked why she was crying. When she told him about how her employer had abused her and showed him her injuries, the guard eventually took her to the nearest police station in Dang Wangi.

This event then led to the arrest of Yim Pek Ha, Nirmala's employer. And Nirmala was later taken to the main hospital in the capital, *Rumah Sakit Pusat Kuala Lumpur* for further examination, which involved, among others, the hospital's forensics team.

In July, however, Malaysia's High Court in Kuala Lumpur, after accepting that she was suffering from high blood pressure and asthma, and that she had a child under one year old in her care, allowed Yim to be held under town arrest with a bail of MR85,000, and on condition that she hand in her passport and undertake not to employ any foreign domestic helper.

The Trial

On the first day of the hearing, 26 July 2004, the defendant Yim Pek Ha was absent from the Kuala Lumpur High Court, allegedly because she was receiving treatment for asthma in Damansara Specialist Hospital. Judge Akhtar Tahir then adjourned the hearing until the following day.

The hearing on 27 July was also adjourned for a further two months and resumed on 27 September 2004.

The trial, as it turned out, was not an open and shut case. The defendant, Yim, had hired a very astute and sharp defence team, who went straight onto the offensive, by claiming that the charges against Yim were defective, because the first three of these did not specify dates and times. 'Without specifying the date and time, the defence is handicapped, and assuming we want to rely on a defence of alibi, we cannot do as we cannot place the time,' said defence counsel Jagjit Singh.

Jagjit Singh continued and contended that the three charges under section 320 of the Penal Code for 'grievous hurt' should best come under section 319 of the Penal Code for 'hurt', as under section 320, hot water not being an instrument or weapon, such as an instrument used in offences like shooting, stabbing or cutting.

The defence team pointed also to weaknesses pertaining to the accuracy of details in the reports of the night Nirmala was found by the security guard, followed by her questioning by the police and examination by the hospital staff.

One of the most disconcerting suggestions he made was that Nirmala could have inflicted the injuries herself. During his cross-examination of Dr Afnizar Akbar of the Kuala Lumpur Hospital emergency unit, Jagjit Singh suggested that Dr Afnizar had not directed her mind that Nirmala could have self-inflicted the injuries, to which Dr Afnizar agreed that she had not. And to the next question, 'You found scratch marks, which were caused by fingernails, on the left and right side of Nirmala's neck during your examination. Do you agree they could have been self-inflicted?', Dr Afnizar had to reply, 'Possible'.

Yim's defence team tried to establish that Nirmala 'was suffering from mental illness' because of her background and her 'station in life'.

This suggestion was weakened, however, by the testimony of an expert witness, consultant psychiatrist Dr Salina Abdul Aziz, who with other senior consultants, medical officer Dr Phang Chee Kar, and the Head of the Psychiatric and Mental Health Department, Datuk Dr Aziz Abdullah, had examined Nirmala on 26 May 2004. Dr Salina Abdul Aziz testified that they had not found any symptoms of psychosis in Nirmala. 'We diagnosed her as having major depression and started her on treatment. We gave her anti-depression drugs to lift her mood,' she said.

The defence team also succeeded in cutting short Nirmala's testimony by obtaining the court decision to stand down the trial after thirty minutes.

One thing the team was not able to stem was the out-pouring of sympathy for Nirmala from around the region, which has made the waiting at the Indonesian Embassy's shelter in Kuala Lumpur easier for Nirmala.

At the time of writing, no verdict as yet had been reached.

INDONESIAN DOMESTIC HELPERS AS SEEN BY EMPLOYERS

Malaysian employers of foreign domestic helpers are not a monolith. They consist of people of lower to upper middle classes, as well as the transient expatriates. Of the local employers, there are those from different ethnic communities: Malay, Chinese and Indians.

Unfortunately for the domestic helpers from Indonesia, while they are employed by people of different socio-cultural backgrounds and social strata with varied attitudes, not many of the employers interviewed, even in informal chats, have many good stories to tell about them. Given that employment agencies claim that there have been many happy stories involving happy employers and happy domestic helpers, it is a pity that these happy stories are overshadowed by the unhappy ones.

To begin with, many of the expatriates who pay better salaries prefer employing domestic workers from the Philippines, because they speak English, and are generally more appropriately skilled and better presented. An Indonesian helper who is employed by an expatriate family usually regards herself as lucky and outstanding, because she is, more often than not, better educated than the average Indonesian domestic helper working in Malaysia, and this fact is reflected in the higher salaries they receive.

There is also a perception on the part of the ethnic Malay employers that Indonesian domestic helpers, most of them being Muslims, are better off being employed by Malay Muslim families, rather than by Chinese or Indian families. 'They are less likely to be abused for praying five times a day, or for refusing to cook food containing pork,' some said.

This perception may be true to a degree, but many of the current and former domestic helpers interviewed told of happy employment situations in the homes of Chinese and Indian families, where they managed to come to a working arrangement agreeable to both parties.

Too young

Even the more enlightened of local employers invariably and independently observe that too many of the domestic helpers from Indonesia are too young. A retired senior diplomat recounted the experiences of some friends of his, who requested domestic helpers about twenty-four or twenty-five years old, but ended up with ones very obviously barely sixteen years. 'So they (the domestic helpers) come here, having falsified their ages on their passports. But their behavior soon betrays them. How much can you expect from a sixteen year old girl, who hardly knows how to do any household chores?' he asked.

A Western-educated business woman recounted how she hated having to watch over her Indonesian domestic helper like a hawk. 'It is against my human rights principles. But what can I do? I have to think about my young children's well-being. She invited her boyfriend when she was supposed to look after the children!' Asked how she found out, she said, 'It was by accident. I caught my four year old son and three year old daughter playing what I thought was a rather weird game, called 'loving'. I asked them what they were doing, my daughter told me that was what the helper did with her male friend. I realized with dismay that something had been happening for some time under my roof, in the full view of with my children, apparently.' Her first reaction was to sack the helper, so was her husband's. However when she calmed down, she realized that her helper was a typical sixteen year old who had just busted out of an environment where she was watched closely by the whole community, and thought that she had just entered a different reality. 'So I just reprimanded her severely, and threatened her with dismissal if it ever happened again. I said she could see her boyfriend once a week, outside the apartment building, where we could see them. But the boyfriend didn't hang around. She didn't seem to mind too much either. Now from the office I call home several times a day, and also pay surprise visits home, just to show her that I mean business. Looking back now, we should have known better,' she concluded.

Dubious moral principles and incompetence

A young journalist friend related her experience when her parents employed Indonesian domestic helpers. During the employment of one, she would find some of her better clothes missing, and would blame her sister for taking them without asking for her permission. Then by accident, she found out it was the domestic helper who had been 'borrowing' them and wearing them before sneaking out of the apartment at night to party with the construction workers several blocks away. Another helper disturbed and irritated the family so much by her strange behavior that they decided not to employ any more Indonesian helpers.

A lawyer told of her experience with one of her Indonesian domestic helpers. After five years of what she had regarded as a good working relationship, her helper told her that her husband wanted to come over to work in Malaysia, so she had to go home to look after their own children. She was very apologetic that she would have to leave her charges, the lawyer's children. The lawyer encouraged her to go, thinking that it was the right thing for the helper to do, and that she could always find someone else. Not long after that the helper brought a man home for a visit, whom the lawyer understood as the husband. Then she told the lawyer that she needed to go away with him for a couple of days before she left for Indonesia. The lawyer thought it was only natural that they would want some privacy together before parting again. After that, the helper left, supposedly for her hometown. Several days later, the lawyer received a telephone call from the helper's children in their hometown, wanting to speak to their mother. The lawyer said, 'I told them their mother had left and should have reached home by then, but the children told her that they had not been aware of that, and that their mother was not home. Then my other domestic helper told me the whole story. The man she had brought for a visit was not her husband, but her Malaysian boyfriend. She had gone with him.' Like the business woman, after the initial anger of being cheated, the lawyer took it philosophically. 'Well, she had been earning the family's income for five years, with very little recognition. It is understandable that she finally wanted to reclaim some of her life. Good luck to her!' she said.

A female employer from a respected family told of how her Indonesian helpers flagrantly used their telephone to call friends and family at home in Indonesia, swelling their telephone bills. She also related an incident which she only found out about in retrospect. One of the Indonesian domestic helpers she employed would take her infant grandson to meet the construction workers down the street where another condominium was being built. She was so appalled that she did not know what she would have done if she had discovered the misdeed then.

Stories which cause the most concern are those of the domestic helpers who do not like children, yet are charged with looking after the employers' children. Former employers told of how they had to sack their young domestic helpers when they found bruises on their children's arms and legs. The helpers invariably, when confronted, would at first deny pinching the children, but when pressed, confess that they had been exasperated by the children's constant attention-seeking behavior. One employer even showed a video taken secretly in the home during the day when the helper, who had since been dismissed, was alone with the children, revealing how the helper pushed the toddler's head harshly, then pinched his arm. The stories about mistreatment of Malaysian children by Indonesian domestic helpers are widespread enough to be described, and thus immortalized, in some short stories.

Underskilled

Most current and former employers interviewed, complained that the Indonesian domestic workers they employed were seriously underskilled. The only work they do rather well, according to them, is simple cleaning. 'They and their agencies always claim that they have been trained, but the reality is that it takes months to train them to do other chores, especially complicated ones, like looking after children and old folk. They have no idea,' was usually what the employers said.

PREJUDICES ABOUT INDONESIAN DOMESTIC HELPERS INHERENT IN THE COMMUNITY

The Women's Aid Organisation (WAO) has documented the negative perceptions of foreign workers that contribute to the frequency and severity of abuse cases. These women, according to the WAO's findings, are regarded as culturally inferior and wanton women who have the full intention of seducing local women's husbands.

In a presentation prepared by Ivy N. Josiah and Meera Samanther for the 'Women at the Intersection of Racism and Other Oppressions: A Human Rights Hearing' at the NGO World Conference Against Racism, organized by the Center for Women Global Leadership, in Durban, South Africa, 2001, the conference heard:

'... they are not deemed deserving of our respect and consideration. Many Malaysians view foreign domestic workers as having a corrupting influence on Malaysian society. Thus the institutions also reflect this underlying prejudice.

'Racist comments from officers ranging from 'you cannot trust these women. They must have secrets. They are not educated. They have negative influence on our children. They are stupid,' are said with utter conviction.

All this is certainly not helped by the widespread knowledge in Malaysia that the domestic helpers they are employing do not have the respect of government officials in their own country. Informal conversations with Malaysians revealed that they were aware of how, after completing employment contracts overseas, the domestic helpers had to go through a special terminal on arrival at the Cengkareng airport in Jakarta where they were subjected to extortion by officials, from immigration, customs and foreign exchange services to the transport operators. This terminal is known to them as the 'collect toll'.

The inadvertent message sent through to employers in Malaysia is that these women are easy targets for bullying. The fact that many are not bullied or abused is a credit to the humanity of the employers.

THE WORKING WORLD FROM THE DOMESTIC HELPERS' POINTS OF VIEW

I have selected a sample of stories that were related first-hand, some happy ones, some not-so-happy ones, and some very bad ones.

Story One: Zaenab

In the mid 1990s, in her hometown of Makassar, South Sulawesi, Zaenab, now thirty-two years old, found that despite having completed secondary school, jobs eluded her. Her extended family happened to be spread out as far as Sabah, so she went to visit one of her aunts, and ended up staying there after meeting a Malay restaurateur who offered her a job in his restaurant.

At first Zaenab was happy being paid just under MR200 a month. The work demand of long hours, however, finally took its toll on her overall health. After seven months, she called it a day and moved on to Kota Kinabalu. After a brief stay in Kota Kinabalu, Zaenab continued to Kuala Lumpur, where by chance she was introduced to a family that was looking for a domestic helper.

They employed her immediately, with a starting salary of MR300. Zaenab was charged with cleaning the house and cooking the family meals. She found the work pleasantly spaced out so that she was able to rest several times during the day. Her employers were happy with her work and gradually increased Zaenab's salary to the present MR800.

Zaenab has worked with the family for eight years and have seen the couple's two children (looked after by a separate nanny) grow up. She has no complaints about her employment situation. 'I don't have any definite rest days, but I can take any days off whenever necessary. I have gone on holidays with them to Australia, Brunei, Singapore and Japan. I make friends with people in the neighborhood. I can call my family in Indonesia anytime I want. In addition to that, I have my own cellular phone.'

Zaenab has never signed an employment contract, and does not feel she needs one. 'My employers pay me my salary every month without fail. After sending money home twice a year, I still have plenty left for myself and my savings,' she said.

Asked if she ever thought or worried about her future, she said, 'From time to time I think about what I'd do if I no longer wanted to continue working here, or if my employers no longer wanted to have me. Maybe with my savings I could start a small business, such as a shop or a café. But so far I know they still want me, and I see very little incentive to leave.'

Zaenab also believes that she is lucky working for a Malay family, because she is sure that working for a Chinese or an Indian family she would have to face the problems of not being able to pray, or having to cook food containing pork.

Story Two: Sirat

Unlike Zaenab, Sirat does not have misgivings about working for a Chinese or an Indian family, because she has worked for both, and concluded that ethnicity has little to do with the quality of the employment situation.

Working in Malaysia is not her first experience overseas. Twelve years ago when she was barely seventeen, a sponsor known to her family in Purwokerto, Central Java, took her to a PJTKI in Jakarta, who recruited her and sent her to Singapore to work as a domestic helper. Five years later, and wiser, Sirat returned home. She soon found that she had to go back to work. She tried working in Hong Kong, but did not find any employment situation agreeable to her. Three months after her arrival, she returned home. The PJTKI who had recruited her, employed her to teach English to new recruits. She met her now husband, and got married.

Having been used to being able to save some money, Sirat and her husband decided that Sirat should find further employment overseas. They had heard that in Taiwan domestic helpers could get good salaries, so Sirat asked the PJTKI to find her a job in Taiwan.

The PJTKI, however, told her that for Taiwan, they needed an up-front fee of Rp1.5 million, which she did not have. She was going to save up the amount, but her husband urged her to find a job elsewhere, where the fee was affordable.

'That was how I came to Malaysia,' said Sirat.

Her first job was with a family who treated her with no respect, so after five months, she ran away from their home. She went and stayed with friends, and was worried about her situation. She had heard about police raids on illegal migrant workers. While she had come to Malaysia legally, she knew by running away from her place of employment she might become illegal. And she had had a taste of being apprehended by the police during the five months she was working.

She was on her way to the shops to buy groceries for the family, forgetting to carry her passport with her. A police officer stopped her and asked for her passport or travel document. When she said she did not have any on her, the officer was going to arrest her and take her to the detention centre for illegal migrants. Some negotiations took place, and she got out of the sticky situation by paying him off. When she took out her purse, he demanded that she give him all the money in it.

'It is a common occurrence here,' said Sirat.

While she was looking for another job her visa ran out, but she did not dare apply for a new one, because she did not have a job. Fortunately for her, she found the present employers, who then renewed her visa for her.

The present employment situation is much better. She is charged with cleaning the house, then helping her employers at their shop. 'I work from nine o'clock in the morning till 8.30 at night, but with a lot of rest periods in between. My employers are good and they respect me and my work. I am happy,' said Sirat.

Nonetheless, she does not want to live too long in Malaysia. 'I've worked here for three years now. I think if I work another two or three years, I will have saved enough money to return home to start a small business,' she said matter-of-factly.

Story Three: Rita

Rita came to Kuala Lumpur in the middle of 2004 from North Sumatra where her family lives. She got the job on the strength of the recommendation of her elder sister, who has been working for the same employer at several of her shops.

It has not been a happy employment situation for Rita, however, because she seems to receive the stroppy end of her employer's moods every day.

Her work necessitates her getting up at five in the morning, because she has to prepare breakfast for the family, which means her employer, her employer's husband, and their five children. After that she has to clean the house, pick up the dirty clothes and wash them, and make sure the youngest child gets to school in time. In the afternoon she has to do the ironing, and then begin preparing dinner.

She works non-stop, yet her employer is never happy with her or her work. Worse than that, her employer is always angry with her, always finding faults in everything she does. 'And she calls me several times a day, asking me what I am doing. And I have to tell her exactly what I'm doing, otherwise she yells at me,' Rita recounted.

Whenever she asks her sister, she is told that their employer is very nice to her customers. 'Yet, at home she is always in a bad mood. She fights often with her husband, who works shifts, so he sleeps three nights at home, and three nights out. I don't think she is a good Muslim either, because she seems to pray only when her husband is home,' observed Rita.

Rita feels generally humiliated because, after all, she herself is the mother of grown-up children, so she knows how to keep house properly. 'But I'm at my wit's end trying to find out why she always finds something wrong with me and with what I do. I have tried to talk to her, but she always cuts me short. So no communication,' said Rita.

One good thing about her employer, according to Rita, is that she never withholds her salary. And when Rita once asked for a loan for family matters, she did not refuse it. Rita feels trapped, however, because her employer keeps her passport, so she cannot leave.

Rita believes that the police are always on the lookout for Indonesian migrant workers who are out and about without passports. And she has friends who have been thrown into police lockouts until their employers came to bail them out.

Asked why she wanted to leave or run away, she replied, 'I heard about her previous helpers who all ran away. She abused them. I heard one of them ran away after she bashed that one's head against the cupboard. I don't want that to happen to me.'

Rita said, 'I want to go back to my hometown. I still have my family there.'

Story Four: Erwina
Erwina confessed she was only seventeen years old, but sitting in the interview room in a shelter of a women's organization, she looked even younger.

Almost two years previously in her village in a South Sumatran province, at the age of fifteen and just finishing year nine at school, a sponsor who knew the family came to visit and asked if Erwina wanted to work in Malaysia, promising her an easy job and a good salary. Her parents were persuaded, and allowed the sponsor to take her to Jakarta to be recruited by a PJTKI.

For two weeks she was taught English and Malay, and shown how to do some household chores, then was sent to do her 'apprenticeship' in a household for three months. She was then given half her salary, the PJTKI keeping the other half.

She was then sent back to the PJTKI's training center and waited for a week, before being sent to Malaysia. The local agency who placed her arranged for a two years' employment contract for her to sign.

Erwina was not in the shelter because her employer or employers had abused her.

'No one abused me,' Erwina began, 'my employer did not abuse me. He abused someone else.'

Her employer operated a childcare center, where Erwina helped look after the children. Erwina had no complaints about his treatment of her, and her salary had always been paid. Something began to happen, however, which worried her to the extent of losing sleep.

Her employer took a particular dislike to one of the toddlers in the center. At first he only yelled at him, and then it gradually escalated to physical abuse. Erwina had no idea why he picked on that little boy. 'He didn't hide it from anyone around. He'd slap him, though not hard, but enough to hurt and frighten the two-year old boy. The more the boy cried, the crueler the man became. Once he locked the boy in a small cupboard and shook the cupboard. I was so shocked I didn't know what to do. I was shaking just watching it. When my employer was not looking I comforted the little boy and gave him a hug. But I was also scared that my employer would do something even worse to him. In fact, he'd tell me to slap the boy too, and watched. I pretended but I didn't hurt him. My employer realized the boy wasn't hurt so he took over. So I learned to hurt a little bit so that he'd cry, but later when my employer was not looking, I comforted the little boy,' Erwina related.

The abuse continued. Erwina was forced to bathe the boy in cold water, and when the boy cried, her employer told her to smack him. At lunch time, her employer would force her to put chilli in the boy's food. It became Erwina's preoccupation to devise ways to keep the boy away from her employer's attention.

A month later, Erwina, having reached the end of her forbearance, reported the abuse to a teacher of the school attached to the childcare center. The teacher explained to her that if they reported her employer to the police, Erwina would lose her job. Erwina said she was prepared to take that risk.

The police came to take Erwina's employer to the police station for questioning. In the meantime they also took Erwina's statement. Erwina told the police officers that she did not want to return to the employer's house, so she was taken to the shelter.

Erwina only knew that her employer denied the charges when questioned by the police. At the time of the interview she was waiting for the trial to give evidence.

'It is taking a long time,' said Erwina, 'but without my evidence he would go free. So I guess I have to wait.' She then added, 'When this is over I just want to go back home. Maybe I could find a job nearer to home.'

Story Five: Mira

When a sponsor approached Mira in her family home in a village in East Java, she told her about how pleasant and how profitable working as a domestic helper overseas would be. The sponsor, known to her parents, also told them that the money Mira would earn would help rebuild the dilapidated hut and even replace it with a brick house.

The farming couple, whose hut was not even on their own land, were understandably won over. After all, they had a cousin working in a Kuala Lumpur suburb. If Mira were to go to Malaysia surely she would be able to come and visit her aunt on her days off. They had visions of Mira working for a generous family who would allow her to have days off regularly.

They gave their consent. The sponsor took Mira to a PJTKI in Jakarta to be recruited and trained. After three months of training, where she was taught Mandarin and showed how to do normal household chores, Mira was sent to Malaysia.

Sitting in a room in a shelter for abused migrant workers, Mira, still showing scars and disfigurement (some permanent), described the training center as well-organized, and the teachers and instructors were good to the trainees. She felt as if she was just continuing her schooling. After all she was only eighteen years old then.

Mira arrived in Malaysia in mid-2003, where her employment arrange-ment was handled by a local Malaysian agency. Her first job was in Bukit Serdang. It was not as rosy as her sponsor had painted for her and her parents, but she was paid the salary promised to her. After a year, Mira wanted to move on, thinking she could find a better job with better pay and conditions. By then, however, Mira had lost her local agency's contact details, so she independently terminated the employment and went to stay with her aunt while looking for another job using a network of family and friends.

Two months later she found a new employer who agreed to pay her a sal-ary higher than that of her previous job, so Mira was happy. Barely a month after she started, however, her employer began to show abusive behavior. And the higher salary she had been promised, was never paid.

Her employer kept finding faults in whatever Mira was doing. At first she would hit Mira with her bare hands, then when she found that it hurt her own hands, she began to use a piece of wood or cane. Mira tolerated this for months, hoping that the situation would change. When it did not, Mira tried to talk to her employer, but she refused to respond.

After some time Mira tried talking to her employer's husband. She told him that she could no longer work in this hostile atmosphere, and that she would like to leave and go back to her aunt's place. Her employer's husband then had a brief discussion with his wife, followed by a brief period of respite for Mira. They said they wanted to continue employing her.

The period of respite did not last long. Mira's employer returned to her old ways, becoming worse each day. In addition to hitting her with wood and cane, she once even thrust a bottle into Mira's crotch.

Again, she spoke to her employer's husband, with no results. Finally, one morning she left the house. She was aware that she had no ID on her, since her employer kept her passport, so she went straight to a neighbor's house. The neighbor, upon being told of her predicament, called the police and located Mira's aunt.

The police came and arrested Mira's employer. And Mira, accompanied by her aunt, was also taken to the police station to make a statement: 'That was October last year,' said Mira, 'and I've been waiting here since. I'm waiting for my former employer's trial, and for her to pay all the money owed to me.'

And the interview was in February 2005.

Story Six: Lina

In her hometown in North Sumatra, Lina found it hard to find any work, so one day she borrowed some money from relatives and headed for Jakarta. In the capital city she had marginally better luck. She was able to find work in various garment factories. Four years later her homesickness brought her back home. After paying off her debts, she still had some savings left.

When a sponsor approached her and told her that there were jobs waiting in Malaysia, she was interested. 'She told me that working as a domestic helper there I would be able to earn Rp20 million from a two-year contract. Of course I was interested. Nobody in my family, or in my circle of relatives and friends could even imagine that amount of money! I thought at the time that I could help send my younger siblings to school. So I agreed to go. My parents were by then used to the idea of my going away to work, so they also agreed.'

The sponsor, according to Lina, had no links to any PJTKI, but had business ties with employment agencies in Malaysia. 'She didn't take me to any PJTKI, and I wasn't given any training in Jakarta or anywhere else. She handled everything herself, including my passport and other documents.' Lina used her remaining savings to pay her.

On her arrival in Malaysia, a local agent picked up Lina, and brought her to her own house. The following day she took Lina to a house where she was going to be employed.

Lina was totally unprepared. Told to do household chores immediately, she did not know where to start. The household itself did not have a friendly ambience. She had to learn by trial and error, and being reprimanded when she made too many errors. Then she noticed that the nanny employed to look after the employer's baby let the baby cry and cry for hours. When she asked the nanny why she would not pick the baby up and feed him, the nanny said that she was working according to a strict feeding time.

'Sometimes the baby would cry from one feeding time to another. I didn't understand what they were doing. I thought it was cruel. I couldn't bear hearing him cry non-stop like that. I would cry in sympathy. Whenever I confronted her, the nanny became angry and accused me of interfering in her duties.'

One day her employer came home and caught her crying. 'Why are you crying? Don't you like working here?' she asked.

Lina replied she was not happy, and would like the employer to return her to the agent. She believed the agent would be able to find her another job elsewhere.

Lina's employer called the agent at the office, saying that she was going to bring Lina back, at her own request. Curiously, the agent asked the employer not to bring her to the office, but to her home. 'Your agent said she would send you back home to Indonesia,' her employer told her after the telephone conversation.

The agent did not, however, send her back to Indonesia. Instead she found her another employer, where Lina worked for four months. It is interesting to note that before sending her to this employer, the agent had made modifications in her passport. Her name had been changed. 'She said she needed to do that because I changed employers after a short time. I worked for four months, but the agent took all my pay, and only handed me one month salary, saying that I had to pay her back for the costs of renewing my passport and my visa. She then found me yet another employer, and I worked there for two months. And she took all the pay, without explanation.'

By this time, Lina did not want to continue working in Malaysia, so she asked the agent to send her back home to Indonesia. 'But she said if I wanted to go back to Indonesia, I would have to repay my debt to her, worth Rp10 million,' Lina recounted.

When Lina insisted, the agent told her husband to beat her up. 'I had no choice. I stayed,' Lina said.

The agent then found her another employer. Despite having taken most of her pay from the previous jobs, the agent still took the first three months of Lina's salary in this job. Interestingly, just when she was supposed to start actually receiving her salary, her employer told her that she was keeping the money and would give it to her at the end of the employment before Lina returned to Indonesia. Nonetheless, Lina was still forced to sign a receipt every month.

At the same time also, her employer began to abuse her. She also forcefully cut Lina's hair very short. 'Everyday when her husband came home, she'd tell him to beat me for all the things she said I had done wrong. Sometimes she'd even call her husband in the middle of the day to come home and beat me up until he drew blood,' recounted Lina, revealing scars on the side of her head, her mid-riff, her thighs, and her arms. 'He used a metal pipe,' she added. Later on to the police, her employer would say that Lina was accident-prone and often hurt herself.

At first she was too scared to leave the house, because she did not know where to go, her agent not being any better. So she stayed, until she could bear it no longer. It got to the point where she became reckless and fled to the nearest police station.

After seeing the fresh and old scars, the police brought her to a shelter belonging to a non-government organization.

The Women's Aid Organisation took up her case, and Lina's employer was brought to court. 'But my employer denied that she withheld my pay. She said in court that she had always handed over my pay, which I had kept in my own cupboard. She was able to show all the receipts I had signed,' Lina continued her story. 'I don't know what happened, but the organization was able to help me get MR2,400, out of my real entitlement of MR5,950.'

'The police then came to arrest me, and detained me overnight in the lockup. They said it was because I changed my name on the passport. I explained that the agent had told me they had done that when I changed employers. The police did not believe me. Luckily the social worker came to bail me out. I don't know what she told the police.'

When interviewed, Lina was still in the shelter, waiting for the completion of the trial, and for the WAO to try to get her full wage entitlement.

[note: the social worker from WAO who handled Lina's case explained that her file had been returned to the Labour Office. They encountered a problem with the modifications made on the passport, which did not match the name she identified herself with. Her agent modified the name and even changed her photograph for her own reasons, but Lina thought the agent had done that because it was necessary when she had changed employers. The social worker and the lawyer had explained the problem to her, but Lina failed to appreciate the seriousness of the problem.]

ASSISTANCE GIVEN BY NON-GOVERNMENT ORGANIZATIONS

Two main organizations that extend assistance to migrant workers are WAO and Tenaganita. WAO is increasingly active in helping foreign domestic helpers who run into problems in their employment situations. WAO has lawyers working *pro-bono* as well as paid social workers and volunteers, so it has the capacity to handle cases of, as well as run shelters for, domestic helpers in trouble, who are unable to deal with the authorities in the course of seeking justice and, in many cases, compensation.

WAO was originally an organization advocating for the elimination of domestic violence, and sought to enlighten the public on instances of domestic violence, such as how to recognize it, how to help prevent it, and how not to perpetrate it. In the last ten years, it has taken up the cause of abused foreign domestic helpers as well, because it regards their treatment as a kind of domestic violence.

Interviews with Jessie Ang, a WAO social worker, and Meera Samanther, a lawyer and President of WAO, revealed a great deal about the situation of the foreign domestic helpers in Malaysia.

Jessie Ang, Social Worker

As a social worker for WAO Jessie Ang is acquainted with the kinds of problems foreign domestic helpers come across while working in this country, even if not all of them escalate into conflicts they are unable to solve themselves.

'I have worked with WAO for ten years now. I find the domestic helpers who got into trouble and who came or were brought to us are very unaware of the situation generally in Malaysia. They accept everything the agents, and to a great extent also, the employers, tell them. There is a need for them to learn about what they are going to face and experience in Malaysia before they leave their original countries and there is a need for them to know what kind of things some agents or some employers unscrupulously do which can seriously disadvantage them later on,' she began.

Ang gave an example, 'Take Lina (referring to the domestic helper whose story was described above). When her photograph and her name in the passport were changed, she did not question the agent the reason for this.

She got into trouble, got thrown into detention, yet she still didn't know the real reason she was locked up. She only knew it was because she changed employers.'

Ang learned about the inherent submissiveness of the Indonesian domestic helpers and their almost blind trust in those who hold power over them, such as the agents and the employers. They tend to believe that these people will do the right thing by them, so they are comfortable to remain ignorant of the social and legal aspects of their employment situation.

'Over the years of my working with WAO, I've seen how this lack of awareness can get them deeper and deeper into trouble. When they go to court for instance, the judge asks them their names and ages, and in all innocence they'll give the judge their real names and ages, while in the passports they have different names and ages. All this goes against them, because they are seen as lying. If it is their agents or their employers who have been lying, then they need to prove the fact. And most of the time, they cannot.'

When Lina's employer refused to hand over her salary, WAO in handling her case, had to go to the Labour Court to force the employer to pay up. The WAO officers came up against strong resistance however. As a result, they were not able to get the full amount. 'What went against her was that when her employer made her sign a receipt every month, she did it without questioning. So the employer had the proof that she had paid Lina her salary every month. Yet in reality she never received a cent. So the court finally awarded MYR2,400 to her, payable by the employer,' Ang explained, before continuing, 'But then the employer got the police to arrest her for using a false name in the passport. Lina was consequently arrested and remanded for one night for investigation. Then she was released because we argued that there was no case.'

As for the criminal case where the employers abused her, the WAO lawyer representing her managed to get them convicted. Since they immediately pleaded guilty, the process was relatively fast.

Ang recalled, 'During the first year I worked here we already had migrant workers coming to seek our assistance. At the beginning there were very few, but the numbers increased each year. The police around here now know about the shelters, and they send the women here. Most of the residents in our shelters are referred by the police.'

'We have not had migrant workers from the Philippines coming here,' Ang observed. 'I understand not many of them have been abused. And when they are abused, they usually know what to do. They are more educated, and have fair resources, such as friends and networks. Their embassy is also well prepared to help their workers in Malaysia. Filipinas who are referred here have not been domestic helpers, they have been women who are victims of domestic violence or have been involved in trafficking cases.'

As for Indonesian workers, Ang said, 'The Indonesian embassy is increasingly prepared and very helpful. During my first two years here, the embassy seemed unaware of the abuse of Indonesian domestic helpers. Over the years, however, there has been a rapid increase in awareness of the problems, and I have met several embassy officials who are really helpful. They also have a temporary shelter at the embassy. Sometimes they are put up here because of the large numbers needing shelter at a particular point of time.'

'The migrant workers who stay here in our shelters however, stay longer. They wait for the trial, and for the Labour Office to process their cases,' said Ang.

Cases where the employers refuse to hand over the workers' salaries take longer for the Labour Office to process. And when a worker's case involves criminal charges, it takes longer again.

Ang also explained that WAO had been looking at the cases of Indonesian domestic helpers in Malaysia. She said, 'We found that the workers begin to accrue debt the moment they are recruited by their sponsors. Since there are so many layers of authorities they need to go through, by the time they arrive in Malaysia they are already heavily in debt. That is why for the first three, four or five months they are effectively paying back their debt, and not a single cent passes through their hands.'

If the employment situation goes well, they can start receiving their salary and start saving or spending, but if the employment situation goes wrong, it can go very wrong. She continued, 'While we can assist them, house them and arrange for their temporary visas, during their stay in the shelters they cannot work, which means they are not earning any money, and they don't get any allowance. They are given free board and food. We help them by giving them some casual work here and there, for their pocket money. That is about all they get. It is far from the ideal situation for them.'

Meera Samanther, President of WAO

Meera Samanther is an advocate and activist on equal rights for women and a safe working and living environment for those who hold very little power over their own situation. She is also the Co-Chair for the Law and Policy Sub-committee of the Malaysian Government's Steering Committee on Violence Against Women.

'Perception', said Samanther, 'is very important.' She is opposed to the domestic helpers being called 'maids', because in her view, they are workers, 'So I call them domestic workers. The word maid connotes a very master-servant relationship. When we have that kind of connotation in the back of our mind, we inevitably tend to treat a person in a manner prescribed by the concept. When we emphasize the term domestic worker until it is ingrained, we'll realize that she is a worker in her own right. She is an employee in my house,' she said, then continued, 'Because she is not protected as a formal worker, people do not recognize her as a worker. We have to change this.'

She does not like the fact that the media tend to use *maid* instead of *domestic* worker.

Samanther told how WAO became involved in doing a lot of advocacy work in the cases of migrant workers. At first the cases came and were handled on an ad-hoc basis. 'We did not have enough migrant workers to have studied and done analyses from the few cases we had,' she said, 'Then later on, in the early 2000s we started getting many more.'

They became really involved at the World Conference Against Racism where Samanther presented a paper, 'Is the domestic worker safe at home?', where racism and xenophobia were discussed. 'We realized that racism and xenophobia colored our migrant workers' situation in Malaysia. In addition to that, class consciousness and feudalism,' said Samanther.

'We began consciously to check ourselves within our organization for prejudices. We must recognize that we all have our own prejudices. To deal with the issue we need to be constantly challenging ourselves,' Samanther continued.

She confessed to being guilty of prejudice herself. 'I have to constantly challenge myself. So do my children,' she said emphatically.

As a lawyer, Samanther is familiar with the court system. She has done a lot of employer-employee negotiations. She has also done watching briefs. Here she painted a scenario:

'Domestic worker abuse is a criminal case. So prosecution takes over. I come in as a watching brief lawyer to make sure that the process is fair. Once a criminal suit is in process we also advise our clients that they have a right to file a civil suit, where they can claim compensation. In a criminal case you can claim compensation too, but it is hardly ever awarded. So you have a civil remedy for your unpaid salary, claims and damages.'

'We find that when we have a criminal suit in process simultaneously with a civil suit, we attract a lot of media attention. So we call a press conference. All this helps to bring the employer to the negotiating table. It is unfortunate that it has to be done this way, because the cases we bring to the criminal court are otherwise not priority cases. Our clients are forced to stay in this country for up to two years and during that time they are not allowed to work, so they are not earning any money. On top of that, they have to pay for a special pass, MR100 per month.'

'Often what happens is, seeing what she is facing, the domestic worker will say, look, I've got the money or some of the money owing to me. I don't want to go through the grueling process. So please drop the case.'

In cases where the domestic worker has been raped or assaulted in other ways, we usually advise her to pursue the matter. However I can understand if she refuses. How do you think she feels, waiting around for one to two years, unable to do anything productive?'

In the meantime, the publicity causes a great deal of embarrassment as well as negative implications in the relationship with Indonesia.

'So if we don't pursue the case, we are criticized. Our argument is, it is the right of the client to do what she thinks is in her interest. WAO is not going to decide for her. We have to make her aware of the choices available, and we can only advise. For an organization promoting individual rights, we have to practise it.'

Samanther is known to Indonesian Government officials as well as Malaysia's Ministry of Manpower, because each time there is a problem with an Indonesian domestic worker, these people became involved in her advocacy.

WAO has also advocated for a standard contract of employment to the Ministry of Manpower, but it has not been officially accepted.

The organization's advocacy has borne some fruit, because now at least the police will bring abused Indonesian domestic workers to WAO. The Indonesian Embassy is also aware of WAO shelters, and trusts the organization with housing and handling the cases of their workers.

Asked what she saw as the strongest reason why people abuse their domestic workers, Samanther named class consciousness and xenophobia as prominent causes.

'The authorities, when it comes to treating migrant workers' cases, appear to have no respect for them. I don't know what the real reason is. Is it the low educational level of the Indonesian migrant workers in general? As for the domestic workers, the fact is, they are so easy to bully. And as it is usually the case with bullied people, they're too scared to speak up, either to stand up for themselves or to tell people what happens to them. Then there is the element of impunity. Because they are confined to the house, nobody knows they are bullied,' she said.

Samanther believes that this kind of attitude is found among the lower middle class to the upper middle class.

Asked if she agreed with the popular belief, that 'families who have been employing domestic workers for generations treat their domestic workers better', she stopped and pondered, then said, 'I see what you mean. I remember my Chinese friend whose family used to have an *amah*. The amah was respected as part of the family, always well presented, and paid well too.'

Then she began to recall, 'When I was growing up, we had this girl who used to take care of me and my three brothers. She was from the estate. Only seventeen at the time. As she grew up, my father found her a match. They got married and had a child. Now whenever we have a family function she and her husband always come over. I remember those instances. And I remember my uncles and aunties having similar situations. And their domestic workers are still in touch with them, too.'

Dislocation, Samanther believes, plays an important part in the problems encountered by domestic workers from Indonesia. 'The domestic workers we had in those days were local Malaysians. They had the option to go back.

Even if they run away or however they do it, they have their home nearby. Whereas the Indonesian domestic workers are trapped. Many employers or agents keep their passports. It is a violation of the Passport Act. I found that many Immigration officials don't know of this Act,' she said.

'The domestic workers from Indonesia are thus at the mercy of the employers. When you have a bit of power, it is human nature to abuse it. It is very similar to domestic violence,' Samanther continued.

If xenophobia is an aspect, how come the domestic workers from the Philippines fare much better?

'Probably because they are better off to begin with. They speak English. They are able to negotiate to have every Sunday off. They go to church, where they meet up and get informed of their rights and exchange stories about conflict-solving strategies. I believe that before they leave their country, they have an orientation program. The kind of orientation program the Indonesian migrant workers get is very poor,' replied Samanther.

She then related some of her experiences with the Indonesian domestic workers she had employed. 'They are scared. They always ask if they can do this, and do that, which in reality is their right. A domestic worker I once employed was amazed when I said she could keep her passport and her pay. 'Oh, can I do that?' she asked. 'Of course you can,' I said, 'it's your right. It took her some time to realize I wasn't joking or testing her. So I asked her, 'Weren't you told you were allowed to keep your passport and your pay?' She said no. She said the most emphasized phrases were, yes sir, no sir, yes ma'am, no ma'am!'

'In the meantime, the recruitment and employment agent told me, 'Don't give them all the money. They'll spend it and when they go back, they'll have nothing.' Well, maybe they're well-meaning, but I couldn't help asking them, 'Do you tell that to the staff working in your office? Don't spend all your money?' They said, well no. 'Then why do you have to tell these people that?' I asked. And they said, 'because these are simple people.' I guess it is good to advise, but to take such a patronizing attitude? That's the way the Indonesian domestic workers are treated by everybody.'

Samanther is well aware of some recruitment and employment agents who keep unhealthily tight control over their recruits, who are also greedy and unscrupulous.

'Some of the migrant workers I know, not only work in one household. They are told to work in several households. And when there is friction, and they feel their employers don't like them or treat them badly, they have no one to complain to. Their agents keep telling them to work harder. They can't go out. If their passports and documents are kept by their employers, they'll be too scared to even step out of the house. They know that when they go out, they must make sure they take their ID card, the card they are given when they are employed in Malaysia. And they must also carry a photocopy of their passport.'

As one of the leading advocates for migrant workers, Samanther revealed the extent of legal protection that the workers can rely on. She painted the situation in a number of scenarios:

Scenario One
'Say she is assaulted, or raped. She gets the same legal protection as any other person in Malaysia has. Penal Code, assault, Section 323, or Section 324, assault with a weapon.'
    'She lodges a police report. Then the government prosecution takes over, and prosecutes the case against the defendant, the employer. Now that is in terms of the criminal.'

Scenario Two
'Sometimes a domestic worker reports some unpaid salary. So we go to the Labour Office to report that she hasn't been paid, say 300, 400 dollars, or several months' salary. The Labour Office will fix a date, and send a letter to the employer to come to the Office. So we, meaning my social worker, my client and myself also go to the Labour Office. Sometimes the employer doesn't turn up. Sometimes he or she does.'

'Say in this case, the employer turns up. She tells her side of the story, and the domestic worker tells her side of the story. The employer may say, 'I paid the salary. Here are the receipts she signed', or she may say, 'I didn't pay such and such months salary because she owes me this amount of money, money she borrowed for her brother's wedding at home', or 'She took my jewellery, so I would have deducted the amount.' Then the domestic worker may deny all the employer's claims. It's very much 'your word against mine', and may become protracted. Sometimes it's all resolved amicably, and the employer pays.'

Scenario Three
'Say the employer in *Scenario Two* refuses to pay and a dispute arises. The Labour Office will decide that the case will go to the Labour Court, because the Labour Office is strictly a stepping stone before the Labour Court. Here, we have the employer's lawyer and the employee's lawyer representing their clients.

'The Labour Court then gives an order: employer X has to pay employee Y 2,000 dollars. You win. But you cannot execute on the order. That order has to be registered in the High Court. So you take that order to the High Court. Once you have registered it, the order becomes a proper High Court judgment, then it can be executed.

'What do you do to execute an order? Say you have a judgment registered for the amount of 2,000 dollars. What are the avenues you can go about executing this judgment? Avenue one: since the employer is not paying the money she owes, you want to bankrupt her. The law in Malaysia specifies that, the claim must be more than 5,000 dollars in order to bankrupt someone. You are stumped.

'Even if for argument's sake we manage to increase the claim to 12,000 dollars. But to file a bankruptcy petition you must have money. Where on earth do you get that money? So bankruptcy is out of the question.

'Avenue two: using writ of seizure and sale. That means you seek the service of a bailiff. The bailiff will seize whatever assets belonging to the employer, and auction them off, then take the proceeds. But you also need money to do that.

'So you see, execution of a judgment, even if it is registered, is only available to those who have money. That is how employers who withhold payment of their domestic workers' salaries, can get away with what they do.

'And in WAO, we have lawyers doing pro-bono work, but there is no money necessary to cover the costs of bankruptcy petition and issuance of writ of seizure and sale. That's why if the worse comes to the worst, we try

to negotiate, because even if you win, whatever judgment you have won, is
a paper judgment.'

Samanther also further depicted the hopelessness of someone without money
successfully bankrupting anyone and obtaining money from the bankrupt.
'Even if you do bankrupt the person, you are an unsecured creditor. Secured
creditors such as banks and other financial institutions will have the first bites
of the cherry. Say they get 15,000 dollars out of the person, after the court
awards the money to the secured creditors, there may be nothing left for you.
So it doesn't make sense going to court for the domestic workers,' she said.

Samanther then related a case she was handling. 'It's a criminal matter.
A lady abused her domestic worker. At first she pleaded not guilty. Then she
changed her mind, she pleaded guilty. Then she changed her mind again,
and pleaded not guilty. Then at the next hearing she didn't turn up. Her
lawyers didn't know where she was. A warrant arrest was issued. But they
still can't find her. In meantime, I have this domestic worker waiting to be
compensated. What can I do?'

An illegal migrant worker, according to Samanther, may well have started
out as a legal worker. His or her passport may have expired and not been
renewed. 'He or she may be given a work permit of one or two years. The
employer is supposed to renew the work permit. If this is not done, intentionally or unintentionally, the worker becomes undocumented, thus illegal,'
she explained.

'It is also possible that he came on a temporary social pass, with the hope
of getting a permanent visa. Right from the start the recruitment and employment agency should have told him that that kind of visa transfer is not
possible. An actual work permit must be applied in the country of origin,
not when the applicant is in Malaysia. Some unscrupulous agencies would
tell a client that his documents were in order, but in reality nothing has been
done. In the meantime the migrant worker has paid the agency all the fees
charged, came in and became an illegal worker.'

The picture painted is thus not very bright for the migrant worker, in the
case of this book - the domestic worker/helper from Indonesia who seeks
legal protection. Legal protection is readily available for the employer, the

Malaysian citizen, but not the migrant worker, who does not even count as a formal worker.

THE BUSINESS OF EMPLOYMENT AGENCIES

There are over 300 employment agencies in Malaysia which have been licensed to recruit and place Indonesian domestic helpers in this country. To operate legally as an employment agency in Malaysia, a company has to obtain a licence from the Ministry of Human Resources, and to be able to handle recruitment and placement of foreign domestic helpers it has to obtain another licence from the Immigration Department.

'Then specifically for bringing in Indonesian domestic helpers, we have to seek registration with the Indonesian Embassy, and similarly with other embassies if we want to recruit their nationals,' explained Jeffrey Foo, Vice President of the Malaysian Association of Foreign Maid Agencies (*Persatuan Agensi Pembantu Rumah Tangga Asing Malaysia* – PAPA).

According to Foo, there were then (February 2005) over 200,000 registered foreign domestic helpers, eighty to ninety per cent of whom were Indonesians.

When Foo started his employment agency fifteen years ago, there were fewer than a hundred agencies. The number began to increase in 1997-98, and within a couple of years the number jumped from approximately 200 to over 300 agencies.

Can you describe the normal and accepted modus operandi of employment agencies that recruit and place Indonesian domestic helpers?

We build business ties with PJTKI which are listed with the government. There is no limit to the number of PJTKI we can do business with. To obtain the number of domestic helpers needed at one time, we may need to link up with two or three PJTKI simultaneously. After several business dealings, we drop those we find unreliable and unethical, and conversely, they may drop us if they find us unreliable or that we don't play the field fairly.

Do Malaysian employment agencies screened prospective employers, seeing that they were dealing with vulnerable human beings?

We do not actually screen the employers. First, legally we cannot do that. We don't have any legal power to screen them. And without the legal power, it comes across as intrusive. We come up against the pride of these people, who no doubt regard themselves as enlightened and principled middle-class people. And we have to assume that they have the knowledge, decency and capability to employ domestic helpers and treat them appropriately. Proposing to screen them is not only intrusive, but can be taken as questioning their integrity and credibility.

What we do in lieu of screening, is look at their income levels. We can do this, because we are required to give assurance to the Immigration Department that these people can afford to employ domestic helpers, pay their wages and lodgings and all the necessary things, without going into debt. Then we ask questions like, why do you need to have a domestic helper? Do you have young children or old relatives to take care of?

From our experience, while it is not well-mannered to tell people off, we can always make up excuses for not supplying a domestic helper to a particular employer. Via internal communication among employment agencies or information from friends, we do get to know employers who abuse their domestic helpers or who don't pay their wages. We don't like them any more than the abused helpers like them, because they are bad for the business' image. We care about our image, because we are not fly-by-nighters, and we take pride in satisfied clients, be they employers or domestic helpers. We can say to them, sorry, we don't have the right person for you.

We also receive feedback from the domestic helpers we recruited and placed. We assess their feedback continuously. If a number of helpers have reported the same complaints about some particular employers, then we know they are telling the truth, and we do our best not to supply them with any more domestic helpers. That is our own screening process.

Do the agencies keep monitoring the situation of the domestic helpers they have placed?

Most of us certainly do, if nothing else, because it is good business practice. And to have an on-going business, good business practice is a must. The helpers that my agency recruit and place for instance, when they finish their contracts, they come back to us to arrange another contract, or to go home. When they want to return to Malaysia to work in future, they contact us. That way we maintain our good clientele. Clients who have good records and good relationships with us will always come back. But we ourselves must have a good reputation; otherwise nobody will use our service. Now part of good business is concern about the domestic helpers we recruit and place.

Why do some agencies had very cavalier attitudes in relation to their domestic helper clients?

I am aware of some bad agencies, that manipulate the domestic helpers, tell them to work for several employers in rapid succession so that they can collect fees from each of them. However, there is another side to this story. The purpose of allowing employers to try out another domestic helper is cost-saving. We used to have a rule which prohibit employers from changing their helpers. You employ a helper, you keep her until the end of the contract. Or, you either keep her or you send her back. It is a costly practice. Don't forget it costs a lot to bring in the helper in the first place. You pay a recruiting fee to the PJTKI (now MR2,500 to MR2,700, it used to be MR600 to MR700).

Can you describe the recruitment process?

Employment agencies in Malaysia have no access to the women in their villages at home in Indonesia who may be interested to work as domestic helpers in Malaysia. We are dependent on the service of local sponsors, who know them and their families. The sponsors approach them and make them offers. If they agree, the sponsors will take them to the closest town or city where he or she knows a PJTKI. The moment a sponsor takes a woman away from her home, she has to start paying the woman pocket money. It may also happen that the sponsor passes on the woman to another sponsor, then this sponsor passes her on to yet another sponsor, until the woman is finally taken to a PJTKI. Each time a sponsor takes over from an earlier sponsor, he or she has to reimburse the earlier sponsor's expenses and pay her a fee.

Why does it have to be so protracted?

It may begin with a particular sponsor who received a request from a PJTKI for thirty candidates for domestic helpers. He or she cannot get such a big number from one sponsor, so has to send messages to several sponsors. Each sponsor may also send messages to her own contacts. Then the PJTKI pays the final sponsor, let's say MR300 000. The final sponsor then pays his or her contacts, who may have to pay their own contacts. That is how it goes'.

The PJTKI then takes the women to be trained and taught in the appropriate languages and skills. They house and feed them, send them to have medical check-ups, and prepare their necessary documents. When the women arrive, we, the agencies of the destination country, go and meet them, and interview them to select those we think are the most suitable for our particular clients. We stream them: who are suitable for general household work, who for baby-sitting work, old folk carers, and so on.

We handle their documents in Malaysia. Then we prepare orientation programs for them. When they are ready we take them to their employers. Up to this point, the women have not spent one single rupiah. That's why if after all that, some are not suitable for their nominated employers, who have paid a lot of money to their agencies, both the employers and agencies are out of pocket.

Whatever fee the employer pays her agency, does not quite cover the cost of bringing and training and preparing the woman for employment. So we usually have an agreement with the PJTKI to allow us to recover the difference by deducting the woman's salary once she is employed.

What happens when employers return the helpers to the agencies?

A: If an employer returns a helper to us for some reasons other than abuse, we will try to find her another employer. Under the previous regulations, we would have to send her home. In that case we would have to pay for the cost of her repatriation ourselves. We couldn't ask the sponsors and the PJTKI to reimburse us. It was very costly.

Can you explain the process of how an employer finds a domestic helper he or she wanted?

Say employer A approaches Agency B, expressing intention to employ a domestic helper with specifications C, D, and E. Agency B then sends a job order to PJTKI F. PJTKI F then sends a candidate with the required specifications. Agency B pays PJTKI F the amount of somewhere between MR1,500 and MR1,700. Employer A pays Agency B MR2,300 to MR2,500. The difference between what Agency B receives from Employer A and what it pays PJTKI F is not enough to cover the costs of processing the candidate's documents, medical check-up, orientation program, insurance, and after-sale service such as counseling for two years, so Agency B needs to recoup the costs from a deduction of two months salary from the domestic helper. On top of that it also collects on behalf of the PJTKI through further salary deduction.

The MOU between the Government of Malaysia and those of the sending countries specifies that expenses in the countries of origin are borne by the candidate domestic helpers themselves. In the case of Indonesian domestic helpers, however, they have no money to begin with, so the PJTKI effectively loans them the money, to be paid later when they begin to earn.

Some of the costs of training and processing the documents are charged by the PJTKI to the employers. And like their counterpart employment agencies in Malaysia, the PJTKI recoup the differences from the domestic helpers themselves.

Why do Malaysians increasingly need to employ foreign domestic workers?

The higher standard of living accompanied by the economic boom in Malaysia drove women who previously stayed home to look after the family to try to follow their own career aspirations. So they need someone to take care of the household, look after the children and the old folk. And nobody wants to be domestic helpers anymore in Malaysia. So they've had to turn elsewhere. Indonesian domestic helpers are favored because they are affordable and reliable.

I am aware of the dissatisfaction of some employers who end up abusing their helpers. They are not representative of the majority of employers I come across. There are a lot of happy stories. But they are not told.

Initially the Indonesian domestic helpers were paid MR250 per month. Now they are generally paid MR400. In Malaysia the average worker's salary is MR3,000 or MR4,000 per month. If both husband and wife earn, they'll have MR6,000 or MR8,000 between them. They can afford to employ a domestic helper to look after the children or their old folk.

Despite the fact that the government allows Filipino, Cambodian and Thai, as well as Indonesian women to come and work as domestic helpers, most agencies concentrate on recruiting and placing Indonesian women as domestic helpers, because the demand for them is the highest.

Foo's own agency does not handle recruitment and placement of Filipino domestic helpers. 'The numbers are too small to be a viable business proposition,' he explained. He commented nonetheless, that people who employ Filipino domestic helpers are much wealthier than the average Malaysian, because the going rate for a Filipino domestic helper's salary is between MR750 and MR850 per month.

What assistance do the agencies provide in cases where their domestic helper clients are abused?

Our clients usually tell us and seek help when they are abused. Like most responsible agencies, we try to find and assess what the root causes are. We provide conciliation service. If the causes are rooted in irreconcilable conflict, then we'll ask the employer to return the domestic helper, and we'll try to find a more suitable employer for her.

My company handles 200 or 300 domestic helpers a year. Not big by any measure. But I have encountered many cases. Problems are caused by employers as well as domestic helpers. I think it is important to give them the opportunity to express their anger, but not at each other. So the agencies should lend themselves to that. They shouldn't just collect the money then forget about their clients.

They should be able to find out why a particular employer suddenly wanted to return her domestic helper, or why a domestic helper ran away from her employer, then try to solve the problems. If possible, they should try to find a way satisfactory to both parties, and save the situation from getting to the stage where the helper will have to be sent back to Indonesia, because then everyone loses.

What would happen if the employer prevented the domestic helper from contacting the agency?

Most employers know that if they prevent the helper from contacting her agency, they run the risk of the helper doing something drastic, which would land them in legal trouble, even physical danger. We have seen in Singapore, how some domestic helpers reached such a stage where they harm their employers or members of the employers' family.

How would the agency know that a domestic helper who claimed she had been abused was telling the truth?

This is why agencies should carefully interview the candidates, so they have a fair idea of their character. In my agency, I interview them and select them personally. Before then I have even met them in Indonesia. They know me, and they trust me. When counseling them I know if they are telling the truth or not.

Inexperienced agencies tend to rush the process. Their clients come to Malaysia not knowing who will be receiving them when they arrive. They feel apprehensive and uncertain. That is not a good start. If, during the individual interviews and the orientation programs, they tell the women about the situation and any likely problems, the women tend to come back to you if later on they encounter any of the problems.

Many agencies have good business links with their PJTKI partners in Indonesia, so they can go and meet the candidates even before they are sent to Malaysia. Employment agencies are basically human resources businesses, so those that are comfortable dealing with people are the more successful ones.

Unfortunately, there is no monitoring mechanism in place for the government to make sure all employment agencies maintain their service quality. Industry self-regulation does not work either, because even PAPA or the Malaysian Association of Foreign Maid Agencies is not empowered to regulate the industry, and not all agencies are happy to be members of the association.

Foo said, 'If all employment agencies are our association members, we may be able to lay down the rules of do's and don'ts. We have good reasons to want all foreign domestic helpers to come through appropriate and legal channels. In that way they also can have protection. However, we have to face the fact that some people simply don't like being told what to do and what not to do by anyone other than those with authority to do so.'

THE ROLE OF THE INDONESIAN EMBASSY

Interviews and informal conversations with parties who are concerned with the welfare of Indonesian domestic helpers in Malaysia indicate that the Indonesian Embassy is playing an increasingly bigger role in the situation. Conversations with the domestic helpers themselves, however, have not fully supported this notion. Those who have had contact with the Embassy have not shown a feeling of warmth or trust in it, saying that they only went there if necessary, or if their employers allowed them to attend the Idul Fitri celebrations.

This may be because, while the Embassy is a lot more aware of the situation of the domestic helpers, it is yet to take a more overt role in reaching out to them, or in making them believe that they have the Embassy's respect. The following interview with the Indonesian Ambassador to Malaysia, Rusdihardjo, on 24 February 2005, may shed light on the position of the Embassy vis-à-vis its role as assigned by Jakarta.

How many transient workers from Indonesia are there in total in Malaysia?

There are approximately one and a half million transient workers registered at the moment, 200,000 to 225,000 of them are in the domestic work. As for the illegal workers, it is not easy to ascertain their number.

Are many in the domestic work, illegal?

Yes, we understand there are many domestic helpers here who are illegal.

Is it true that many of the illegal workers started off legal, but became illegal because they neglected to renew their passports or visas?

Yes, it is true that some people come here legally, on a tourist or social visit visa, then go on to work. I don't believe that they don't know that their passports have expired. They can read the date of expiry which is clearly shown on the passport. Maybe some don't understand the situation of the visa.

Some people have recounted experiences in Cengkareng airport in Jakarta, of being approached by domestic helper returnees from Malaysia who asked for help. These domestic helpers needed help to fill out their disembarkation cards. Maybe they don't understand the complexities of the documents. Some even had passports that had expired. How could that happen?

I would say that these people may have taken illegal paths through dubious means in the first place. In Indonesian we call that *jalan tikus* (mice burrows). You realize of course, that there are small vessels sailing backward and forward between Malaysia and Indonesia operated by illegal syndicates. They can depart anytime. We also know that there are many informal entry points in Malaysia they can access. The vessels don't even have to come too close to the coast, because as soon as they get within sight of land, many of their passengers are just told to jump and swim the remaining distance. Some don't make it. Those who don't make it usually become the Embassy's responsibility. It is the Embassy's business to investigate. Now, back to your domestic helpers who arrived back in Cengkareng with expired passports, it is very possible they have been victims of those syndicates.

Considering the number of problems in Malaysia regarding transient workers from Indonesia, is the Embassy well prepared in terms of manpower?

In the countries of destination of Indonesian workers, there are now consular staff in charge of Indonesian manpower. However, only two diplomatic missions throughout the world now have a Manpower Attaché, that is in Malaysia and in Singapore. Six more will be posted in various countries, where the needs have arisen.

So far, which destination country, do you think, is the most conducive for Indonesian workers to work in?

Certainly in Hong Kong. There Indonesian workers have even outdone those from the Philippines.

You mean, people prefer employing domestic workers from Indonesia to those from the Philippines? Why, do you think, is that so?

In short, because Indonesian workers are more compliant and flexible. If they are asked to do something beyond what is defined as their tasks, they oblige.

What limitations or problems does the Embassy encounter in handling the Indonesian workers cases?

We only have records of legally documented workers. This is because the legal ones usually come using the service of PJTKI. When they come via PJTKI we will certainly have their records, because all job orders for PJTKI have to be endorsed by the Embassy.

Initially domestic helpers from Indonesia came here informally, such as in situations where they accompanied those who were going to employ them. Gradually when the needs for domestic helpers increased sharply in this country, domestic work became a field of work in its own right. This followed Malaysia's economic boom, where employment opportunities opened up for women who previously would have stayed at home looking after children, old folk and general household.

This sudden increase posed an array of problems for the Embassy. We have been able to be more pro-active in handling the cases of the legal workers. We organize open house dinners, karaoke competition and things like that for them, so we can meet them. But we can't reach the ones who are working illegally. We don't know who they are, and where they are. We only find out about them when they encounter social problems, commit crimes, or die.

Of those who work legally or illegally, what problems do they encounter which you end up having to handle?

The most common are conflict with employers, abused by employers, sometimes they themselves are the perpetrators of abuse. Many of the illegal ones fall victims to their syndicate's or middlemen's dirty tricks. They were brought here on false pretences, having been promised jobs in restaurants and bars, but finding themselves trapped in brothels. Some of these even jumped from windows of high-rise buildings to escape.

How does the Embassy respond to all these?

We come to the place, and quickly contact the police. We take the victims to the hospital. If they don't have any money, we raise the funds. For those who died, we try to find their contacts in Indonesia. Here we usually encounter protracted problems. They are not documented, so contacting their family is not a straightforward matter. They use false names and false addresses in their false documents. The authorities here don't have their real identities, neither do we. Say the name is Nani, from West Java. The hospital cannot wait forever, so they bury her. When the burial is done, news comes from Indonesia, saying that she was actually Nurhalimah from Banten, her family in such and such address.

You see how difficult it is for us to provide assistance, let alone protection, if they are not legally documented.

Is it not possible to obtain the necessary information from Malaysia's Immigration?

They don't have information on illegal workers.

Do you have a good relationship with Immigration here?

Yes, indeed we do. Every morning by 9 o'clock they have informed us on the number of Indonesians who leave the country. That way we also can monitor. And if we ask them, they'll also give us the names of those leaving. It is also a boon that they have implemented the biometric system here, where they take the prints of all fingers and thumbs of the Indonesian workers leaving Malaysia.

Why do they have to take such care recording the details of those who leave?

They do that so they can give priority to these people when they return to seek further work here. Starting 1 March this year the government here is going to post Immigration officials complete with their computers at twelve entry points.

What does the Embassy do to assist Indonesian domestic helpers who encounter problems?

Say a domestic helper complains to us that her salary is withheld, and the employer denies the claim. We have a civil case. We assist in data collecting. Does she have any witnesses? Who are these witnesses? What documents does she have? We go to the police with all the facts. The police will call the employer. Many instances stop here, because most of the time, the employer will pay up. If the employer still refuses to pay, then it will go to the Labour Office, and it is then a Malaysian Government matter.

If the domestic helper is physically abused, it is a criminal case. We also assist in data collecting, finding witnesses and evidence, and finding a lawyer. We then accompany her until the trial is over. It is our duty to assist and protect Indonesian citizens in this country, but we have to do this according to the law of the land.

In Nirmala Bonat's case for instance, we sought out all the doctors and psychiatrists who examined her. We obtained statements from all of them. In Adi bin Asnawi's[1] case we did the same. We discovered that he had been treated in a psychiatric hospital in Malang. We sought out the doctor who had treated him and obtained a statement from him. We tried to find mitigating circumstances in the case to help him.

What we cannot do is smuggle someone who has been charged with committing crimes out of the country. People who have violated Malaysian law, have to go through the legal process here.

---

[1] Adi bin Asnawi is a plantation worker from Lombok who in early 2005 was arrested and charged with murdering Acin, the owner of the plantation in Selangor where he had been working.

What do you perceive as the role of the employment agencies in Malaysia who recruit and place Indonesian workers?

They have their job, which is recruiting, distributing and placing the manpower where it is needed. And they are licensed to do that.

How do you respond to comments that most employers who abuse their Indonesian domestic helpers are ethnic Chinese?

It is a fact that many employers who abuse their domestic helpers are ethnic Chinese. I think because in a Malay household, the domestic helper, who is most likely a Muslim, will be in a Muslim household, so the likelihood of conflict such as prayer time, is minimal. In a Chinese household for instance, the helper might want to pray just at the time when the family is preparing their meal. Then the employer objects, and the helper protests. Apart from that, Chinese, and Indian families also, are known as hardworking people. They are more disciplined. While Malay people are more laid back. These things can contribute to friction.

How come in Hong Kong, instances of conflict caused by religious differences are not so numerous?

We must remember that those who go to Hong Kong are mostly from East Java. In Malaysia we have workers from Nusa Tenggara and other regions. It is a fact that Javanese are more compliant and tolerant. If they have to wash dishes that have been used for food containing pork, it's OK, provided they don't have to eat the food. If they have to look after the family pet dog, fine, provided they can wash their hands afterwards and don't have to sleep in the same room with the dog. Muslims from other areas are not so easy-going. They object, they protest. The employer gets annoyed and irritated. Tension starts. And so it goes.

Yesterday I happened to meet some plantation operators. I asked them, if you have a ranking system for workers from Indonesia, who is the most popular, and who is the least popular? Almost all of them named Javanese as the most popular. Next in line is those from Flores, after that Sundanese, and last of all Sumatrans. These are Malaysians who have been employing Indonesian workers for decades!

Javanese work quietly asking very few questions. North Sumatrans often ask many questions why they have to do certain things a certain way. We are talking about manual workers. When people employ manual workers, they want them to work, not to argue. So they prefer Javanese.

As for West Sumatran women working as domestic helpers, it is against their natural psyche. In West Sumatra they are the bosses, so working as domestic helpers where they are bossed around by their employer makes them resentful. Tension arises.

If you look ahead now, what prospects do you see in terms of Indonesian workers coming to work in Malaysia?

I think the prospects for Indonesians to work in Malaysia are better than those for Saudi Arabia, or Taiwan. Some political glitches need to be straightened out. In addition to that, the workers have to be mentally prepared to work outside their own cultural environment. They have to be ready to work hard, and work for all kinds of people, not only for Muslims. And most importantly, they have to come in legally. That way we in the Embassy can protect and serve them. I have written to the President giving him my inputs regarding the situation of the Indonesian workers here. I have tried to have the workers SPLP (*Surat Perjalanan Laksana Paspor*) or travel document in lieu of passport made gratis starting 1 January 2005. Then without warning, the charge for the workers SPLP rose again in February. I complained to the President. I said that, as his representative in this country, I object to the fact that the decision I have made here was reversed without any consultation. In Medan, the workers were forced to pay Rp3 million for their SPLP!

Some workers claimed that they were driven to become illegal, because to be legal, they have to use the service of PJTKI *which charge them high fees.*

In reality, if they do their sums properly, they'll find that whichever way they take, it will still cost them roughly the same amount. If they use the service of PJTKI, they are paying for medical check-ups, training, induction courses, document processing, and so forth. If they come in illegally, they skip all that, and their passports are processed by some syndicate people who can disappear overnight. Most likely they are given recycled passports bearing names and details which do not belong to them. Then once here they find that their employers who obviously know they are illegal, exploit them and do not pay them for months. And when they pay, the salary is much lower. The women are often raped, forced to work as prostitutes, and they are powerless to seek help. So where is the advantage of being illegal?

CHAPTER FOUR

FROM INDONESIA
WITH A DREAM?

WHEN AN INDONESIAN WOMAN SEEKS WORK AS A DOMESTIC HELPER OVERSEAS

We have learned about a number of reasons – by no means exhaustive – why Indonesian women want to seek work as domestic helpers overseas, the most prominent of these, it appears, is the scarcity of work, let alone decent paying employment situations, in their own home towns, or in other cities in Indonesia.

We have also learned how the idea occurs, or more precisely, is suggested to them, and what kind of picture is painted for them about the employment situation in the countries of destination.

From the moment they hear about the employment opportunity, and then agreeing to 'seize' that opportunity, to having their documents made by a third party, they generally believe that it is only a matter of time before they achieve the ambition. In many cases, they are indeed right.

For many others, however, achieving the ambition in itself is like embarking on a big problem, because what awaits them beyond that, is the daunting part. The pictures painted by their sponsors are very different from the world they step into. At this point, they are thrown metaphorically into the deep end. They either sink or swim. Miraculously, many can swim, and survive.

Those who cannot swim, however, sink.

What happens? There are a number of possibilities:

1. They do not possess the skills expected by their employers, who have paid

a large sum of money to send for them,

2. They do not possess the skills expected by their employers, but they themselves fail to see the nature of the situation,

3. They do not possess the skills expected by their employers, but all they know is that something is not right, and they are scared, confused, and cowering, so infuriating the employer further,

4. They possess some of the skills, and they land an employer who wants someone perfect for what they pay,

5. They possess a lot of the skills expected, but they are emotionally unprepared for the culture shock of an entirely new environment and the continuous demand of work, and they do not have the strength to recover quickly enough to negotiate the workload with their employer,

6. They possess a lot of the skills expected, are well presented, but they land an employer who is totally self-centered and inconsiderate of other people's feelings and needs,

7. They do not possess the skills expected, are poorly presented and emotionally unprepared for the culture shock of the totally new environment. It can be argued that these people should not have been sent in the first place.

What happens between the time a woman decides to go overseas to work as a domestic helper, and her arrival in her employer's residence – her place of work?

If she is completely taken by surprize by the situation, she may have been recruited by a dubious sponsor, who may have sent her to an equally dubious employment agency, or as we have learned in the earlier chapters, she may have been sent directly to an employer overseas without going through the proper channels.

Supposing she goes through the proper legal channels, who are the parties who play determining roles in taking her to her destination? Are these parties in any way accountable to the public?

INDONESIAN RECRUITMENT AGENCIES
Perusahaan Jasa Tenaga Kerja Indonesia (PJTKI)
The new Law No 39 of 2004, or *UNDANG-UNDANG NOMOR 39 TAHUN*

2004, passed by the Indonesian Parliament on 18 October 2004, concerning Placement and Protection of Indonesian Workers Overseas, refers to the Indonesian Recruitment Agencies as the Administering Agencies of Indonesian Workers' Placement Overseas (*Pelaksana Penempatan TKI di Luar Negeri* – PPTKILN).

I shall however, except when discussing the new law, continue to refer to the agencies in this book as PJTKI, as they have been known since they became proper business entities.

There are currently four known associations of PJTKI which send workers, including domestic helpers, overseas: *Asosiasi Perusahaan Jasa Tenaga Kerja Indonesia* (APJATI), Indonesian Employment Agency Association (IDEA), *Asosiasi Penempatan Jasa TKI Asia Pasifik* (Ajaspac), and *Himpunan Pengusaha Jasa TKI* (Himsataki).

On 28 September 2004, shortly before the new law was passed and the bill was still being deliberated in Parliament, I conducted an interview with Hussein Alaydrus, President of the Indonesian Manpower Services Association, or APJATI, in the association's office in Jalan Buncit Raya, Jakarta. Present also were a number of the association's executive office bearers. By then the content of the bill was widely known among people involved in the migrant workers business.

There were then 400 PJTKI registered as members of APJATI, 196 of which were servicing the Asia Pacific region. The rest focussed on the Middle East.

During the interview, the president and the executive office bearers, each of whom operates a PJTKI of their own, painted a picture of the situation from their points of view.

PJTKI began recruiting and sending workers overseas in 1979. 'We had begun sending Indonesian migrant workers to the Middle East before the government had any mechanism in place for regulating or monitoring the flow of migrant workers out of the country. A monitoring unit was only set up in 1982,' said Alaydrus.

That a government is rather slow in reacting to the needs in the community is not unique to Indonesia, but it is interesting to note that it took Indonesia twenty-five years and twelve successive ministers of manpower to finally come up with a proper law designed to regulate and supervise the sending of workers overseas. This oversight or neglect especially stands out considering that the migrant workers have been brought in revenue of over US$3 billion to the state.

PJTKI operators believe they receive unfair treatment from the government. To begin with, they never receive any government support. Instead they are continuously forced to fork out bigger and bigger expenses and capital outlay.

'Just think,' said my interviewees, 'The tourism industry receives generous support from the government, yet they bring in less revenue than we do. Our migrant workers' remittance alone is worth US$32 million per annum. Can you imagine what it would be like if we did receive government support? Now banks are falling over one another trying to seize the business of remittance.

'We have always been used by the government as a kind of bumper to absorb any attack and blame from the community, especially through the media,' said Alaydrus, 'We operate on our own, without government support or protection. Do you know, even banks are reluctant to lend us money, because they know that the government could change its rules and regulation on the industry any time. Without warning, let alone consultations, the government can ban sending of workers to a particular country. In the meantime, what happens to the investment we have made in that country? How are we supposed to recoup our losses?'

The new law (Law No 39 of 2004 passed on 28 October 2004) indeed is ushering in several changes to the ways the PJTKI must conduct business.

For a long time on the ground, PJTKI, according to my interviewees, were hamstrung by the fact that they had to rely on 'sponsors' to bring in recruit candidates, yet neither they, nor the government authorities, had any authority to monitor these sponsors and their practice.

'Only the sponsors were able to reach the recruit candidates in their often remote rural regions, because we were only allowed to set up branches in provincial capitals,' they explained.

'This all added to the costs. The sponsors were not legally bound to anyone. They make their own rules and *modus operandi*. Generally, as soon as the recruit candidate agreed to go with a sponsor to a PJTKI, the sponsor would extract a sum of money from the candidate. When the sponsor brought the candidate to the PJTKI, he or she would also charge the PJTKI a certain fee for providing it with the candidate.'

While PJTKI were legally bound to send a candidate to a particular country only if there was a job order for a candidate possessing the required skills nominated in the job order, the sponsors were not limited by such requirements. They brought any number of people they had themselves recruited from the candidates' home towns, and the PJTKI would then give them training for various vocations, according to their aptitudes.

Alaydrus gave an example of the usual process: 'Say our company receives a job order from Japan for a hospital worker and we don't have anyone in training for that job requirement, we will contact a sponsor, because we ourselves are not allowed to go to places outside the provincial capital. The sponsor will then bring us the appropriate person and charge us a fee. We'll give the candidate an aptitute test. If the test results are good, the person will go through a medical check-up before training.'

Not all PJTKI have their own training centers or *Balai Latihan Kerja* (BLK), but each has working arrangements with a particular accredited BLK.

At the completion of the training, the candidate will have to pass the competency test prescribed by the government, then the PJTKI will arrange the candidate's passport and other documents, including the air ticket to the country of destination. Before the candidate's departure, the PJTKI will have to arrange for a pre-departure orientation program or *Pembekalan Akhir Pemberangkatan* (PAP).

The going rate for a sponsor's fee for a candidate for Malaysia was, at the time of interview, Rp1.5 million, higher for Singapore, Hong Kong, Taiwan and Saudi Arabia.

The length of time between the handover of the candidate by the sponsor to the PJTKI and her departure for the country of destination, depends on the amount of training needed, combined with the length of time the prospective employer or their agency, which is a local business partner of the PJTKI, comes up with the candidate's visa.

Employers in some countries, such as Hong Kong and Taiwan, often request a video or a CD of several candidates. They will then choose the one they deem the most appropriate, and will approve the visa of the nominated person.

The new law requires everybody who aspires to work overseas to register with the local region's Office of Manpower, and the PJTKI will then have to draw on the register instead of relying on sponsors. How this is going to be implemented is not yet known.

What has happened so far, in terms of the workers themselves, in this case the domestic helpers seeking work in particular countries, is that it is in their interest to work toward the success of the whole process, because in most cases they are already indebted to the sponsors. The PJTKI recruiting a particular domestic helper does not necessarily know the amount of money the helper owes a sponsor unless it has to forward the money to the sponsor, which the domestic helper will repay when she begins receiving her salary.

It is unlikely the domestic helper will default on the debt because the sponsor knows her family. It is, in fact, the sponsor who knows the most about the recruit's family. In most cases, the PJTKI receives the recruit's documents, such as photo ID or *Kartu Tanda Penduduk* (KTP), written permission from the recruit's parents or spouse, from the sponsor.

Problems can arise when candidates are not processed by an accredited PJTKI. There are individuals or illegal syndicates who go around 'recruiting' women who are gullible enough to take their words at face value. They use false or recycled passports for the women. According to Hussein Alaydrus, Malaysia is the most vulnerable to the work of these dubious middlemen, because it has seventy-three entry points from Indonesia. 'Singapore only has two, by sea via Batam and by air via Changi. Hong Kong has only one,' he said.

It is not known whether the existence of these individuals or syndicates is known, or partially known, to the authorities in Indonesia.

Regarding the inadequate training perceived by employers in the countries of destination, Hussein admitted, 'Yes, we are aware of that. But we send our recruits to the *BLK*s recognised by the government. And at the end of the training the recruits have to pass a competency test conducted by a body accredited by the government. It is incumbent on the government to make sure that the training and the competency test are up to industry standard. We have no control over them, though as you know, we usually get the blame.'

All kinds of blame, according to Hussein, are piled on PJTKI, despite the fact that it was PJTKI which opened the market in the first place and that has since developed into an enormous one over the last twenty-five years. 'There is no indication as yet that the government recognizes, and is taking concrete steps in solving, the problems which exist and are still growing in the industry. Some government bodies allegedly provide protection to the migrant workers, but in reality they add to the workers' burden. For twenty-five years we have been working on finding work for those who did not complete their primary schooling, who found it very hard to get employment in this country. At least, from where they are now, they can send money back to their home-towns, money which generates more work in the community. For what we do, we have not received any assistance from the government.'

According to Hussein, the new law leaves much to be desired. In his opinion, it has the effect of making life difficult for PJTKI. Apart from significantly increasing the up-front costs for PJTKI, the law will necessitate PJTKI to compete to a degree with the government. 'Government and the private sector are now administering the placement programs. How could anyone be a player and a referee all at once? Shouldn't the government's function be a referee? Shouldn't the government play the role of regulator, law enforcer and facilitator? Why does it have to take over PJTKI's function as well?' demanded Hussein.

'We are placed under a Directorate of the Department of Manpower and Transmigration. We are required to make long-term planning. That is fair enough, if there is such a thing as long-term certainty. The problem is, the Director can be replaced any time followed by big changes in the regulations, leaving us scrambling for something safe to hang on to. So, for PJTKI, it is like a continuous gamble. There is no protection for our investment.'

Hussein and the other office bearers of APJATI present at the interview opined that there was an urgent need for more operational syncronization between the governments of Indonesia and those of the migrant workers receiving countries. They would also like to see Indonesia's diplomatic representatives in those countries being more proactive, or at least taking preventive measures. 'But until now they are still curative,' they said.

'Take Malaysia,' Hussein said, 'Malaysia is in great need of workers from Indonesia, but they don't take the employment arrangements seriously. The employers there, despite having to have their job orders endorsed by the Embassy, don't feel the need to come to the Embassy themselves. And the Embassy officials are reluctant to go out to the employers' places to meet them. Yet this personal relationship is very important. Admittedly this is beginning to happen in Johor.'

The APJATI office bearers present claimed that none of their members were happy with PJTKI which did not look after their recruits. Human resources being the core of their business, they said that good and responsible PJTKI would like to see their business go smoothly. 'We don't like to see our recruits being abused by their employers either. Who do you think brought up the case of Nirmala Bonat in the first place? We did, because we don't want the perpetrator of the abuse to get away with the crime,' said Hussein.

THE TRAINING CENTERS (BALAI LATIHAN KERJA)

According to APJATI's register of members, only eighty-one have their own training centers or *BLKs*, two of these have more than one BLK.

Those who do not have BLKs of their own, send their recruits to other *BLKs* which charge them training fees. It is worth noting that BLKs do not necessarily belong to member PJTKI of APJATI. Some are totally independent of any association.

And, while they differ in physical appearance, and in degrees of elaborateness of the curriculum among the BLKs, the core components of languages, cooking, laundry management, general cleaning and tidying up and familiarization with modern appliances are generally present.

Interestingly though understandably, the BLKs who welcomed me to have a look inside their premises were well organized and, to all intents and purposes, are abiding by the rules and regulations. From my interviews with domestic helpers or former domestic helpers as well as with employers or former employers in Hong Kong, Singapore and Malaysia, I am aware of other versions of BLKs which may have the tendency to cut corners.

The following are three BLKs I have chosen as case studies. They each have different enough story from each other to form a rather comprehensive overall picture.

PT SINAR MAKMUR JAYA
Pandaan Pasuruan, East Java

The Sinar Makmur Jaya Training Center belongs to a PJTKI with the same name. It is situated in the highlands of East Java, Pandaan Pasuruan, an hour and a half drive from Surabaya. From outside it looks like a grand house surrounded by high walls, without appearing forbidding. Once the guard opens the gate and you walk in, the ambience is somewhere between business-like formality and homely familiarity. There is a large long reception area with several settees for different groups to meet without intruding on each other. Throughout the day there are always two or three young women arriving, then being invited to wait. They are mostly fairly well-dressed and well presented. The staff do not show condescension or off-handedness when they are addressing clients, who are Sinar Makmur Jaya's own recruits and those of other PJTKI which do not have training centers of their own and use the Sinar Makmur Jaya BLK.

When you walk further in, you face a large oval with buildings alongside it and behind it. The oval is where the recruits do their exercise and play sports in the mornings and late afternoons.

It is a modern, well-kept and fairly new establishment, where recruits are mostly in various classes. In the class-rooms and language laboratories with modern equipment, the recruits are learning Cantonese and English. Sinar Makmur Jaya mostly handles workers for Hong Kong, where the two languages are spoken. The learning does not only occur in formal classes, however, because throughout the buildings, the public announcement systems are making announcements in Cantonese and English.

In another building, some rooms are arranged and furnished to simulate those generally found in houses in Hong Kong, where recruits receive instructions on how to take care of infants (some dolls and a real baby are used) and old folk (using role-play), make beds, do laundry, clean bathrooms and toilets and, in a simulated kitchen, they are taught how to use modern electrical appliances and cook Chinese dishes.

The curriculum is professionally designed by the company's staff qualified for it, where, apart from lessons, tests – both theoretical and practical – are regularly run. The dormitory is clean and airy, and the recruits have a locker each.

According to E A Tamara, Vice President of Sinar Makmur Jaya, the length of training ranges from six weeks to six months. Apart from the needs of the recruits, it also very much depends on how long it takes for a recruit's visa to be issued.

On arrival, a recruit is interviewed, physically checked, including her height, her eye sight and her hearing. At this stage, if she is discovered to have a disease, a curable one such as a skin disorder, she will be asked to go back home and get proper treatment for it before returning to the *BLK*. If she has a scar from a major operation she will not be admitted, because she may have difficulty lifting heavy items, which means she may have problems working. If she passes the physical tests she will be given more thorough medical tests. Then she will be IQ tested, before being evaluated for the purpose of placing her in a suitable level class, as well as determining whether to start preparing her bio-notes to send to the company's business partners, the local employment agencies in Hong Kong.

The management obliged when I asked if I would be able to speak to some of the recruits in English classes, in English.

The recruits I engaged in conversation were generally confident in their manner and communicate fairly effectively in English. In one class of approximately twenty recruits, I discovered from asking them in English, that they were all from Tulungagung, Bondowoso, aged between nineteen and thirty-five. Most of them were first-timers, with a few returnees from Singapore or Malaysia who now wanted to go to Hong Kong.

At least five of them were married with children. They wanted to work in Hong Kong because the salary is higher than those offered in Singapore and

Malaysia. They wanted to earn money to send their children to school.

One recruit, Dede Sukaesih, was a returnee from Taiwan, where she had worked for two years. She wanted to return to Taiwan, but was unable to do so because of the ban put on Taiwan by the previous Minister for Manpower (Yacob Nuwa Wea). She said she had had a very pleasant working experience there, and had had very good and considerate employers. 'I am very disappointed I cannot go back to Taiwan,' she said in English.

In the cookery classes, those who are Muslims are showed how to handle pork without compromising their own religious observance.

In one of the classes, I spoke with Aminah Ayu from Central Java, who had been training for three and a half months. When asked whether she was a recruit of Sinar Makmur Jaya, she said yes. When asked why she had to come to this PJTKI in East Java, instead of going to one nearer to home, this is what she said in English, 'I work in Hong Kong before, so I not new. I know other PTs (how the domestic helpers refer to PTJKIs) near my home, but all my friends sent by this PT very happy, so I come to this PT. No this time I not use sponsor. I come here myself.'

It occurred to me Aminah Ayu should have been given a large discount for this inadvertent promotion.

Apart from languages and practical skills, recruits are also given instruction on etiquette and how to negotiate with their employers in difficult situations. They are even given instructions on how to handle dogs. The *BLK* has at least one dog at the premises at any one time.

PT PERWITA NUSARAYA
Kriyan, Sidoarjo, East Java

For Hajjah Sri Murtiningsih and her husband, Haji Sunari Harijono, the Perwita Nusaraya Training Center is part of their life. Their place of residence, the PJTKI and the training center are all in the same vast, fairly new compound surrounded by high walls.

Behind the walls the ambience is more homely than business-like, though the long conversation with the owner-operator of the PJTKI and its training center will later reveal that it is a serious business she and her husband are running.

The reception area has comfortable seats and couches for people to wait. Apart from recruits, there are also sponsors who come to have regular meetings with Sri Murtiningsih.

No dedicated area has been set aside for physical exercise and sports, but the place is not short of open grounds for the odd informal game of sport.

Perwita Nusaraya does not focus on sending its recruits to any particular country, so the training rooms are set up in a neutral, generic but modern way. Apart from language classes, lessons are given in general household chores and infant care.

As for the curriculum, Sri Murtiningsih explained that they responded to needs appropriately, depending on the job orders they received.

The dormitory is airy, clean and well equipped with comfortable bunk-beds and generously-sized lockers.

Sri Murtiningsih admitted that Perwita Nusaraya was a new player in the field of domestic helpers. When she obtained her licence in 2000, her primary concern was formal workers, workers for factories. Maybe, being a retired secondary school headmistress, for Sri Murtiningsih, the business is an extension of her quest to provide education, in this case of a vocational kind. In fact, after her retirement from the school system, she set up a private teaching institution providing English, accountancy and computer courses.

Soon after she began her employment agency, she had a windfall. She received a job order for 200 workers for a garment manufacturing company in Brunei. The training, which had to be done immediately, and other accompanying costs would total Rp4.5 million. Fortunately the East Java Regional Government gave her a loan of Rp2 million, repayable in ten months.

She set up working arrangements with a vocational school in the area, and recruited their graduates, however it was not that simple. The graduates were young women who had never set foot in a working establishment, let alone left their home-towns. Because of the numbers, Sri Murtiningsih had to organize training for them at the premises of the Regional Office of Manpower for two weeks, followed by work training in a garment factory, which disconcerted many of the young women. Training became very slow. 'Even then, I had the problems of reconciling their skills with the skills expected of them in the factory in Brunei. The machines they had been using here were antiquated compared to the ones they were going to use in Brunei,' Sri Murtiningsih recounted.

They were behind schedule. When the time came for them to leave, they had not done their industry exams. So Sri Murtiningsih sent the teachers and examiners together with the recruits to Brunei, in order for them to organize the exams there.

The next job order came from Selangor, Malaysia. After that, job orders kept coming, and Sri Murtiningsih was operating a well-oiled machine. And being a natural paedagogist, she did not stop analyzing her operations and continuously built in improvements.

She then turned to recruiting informal workers, the domestic helpers. That was when she built the present *BLK*. She was determined to send only those who had mastered the language of the destination country and whose skills matched the expectations of their employers.

Most of the recruits currently undergoing training in the Perwita Nusaraya training center have expressed a desire to go and work in Hong Kong. Sri Murtiningsih observes that not all of them learn the Cantonese language easily. Those who are still struggling after four or five months, are usually persuaded to turn to Malaysia. If they persist, they will be asked to leave.

Such is her determination not to send underskilled workers.

PT BINAMANDIRI MULIARAHARJA
Malang, East Java
One of the oldest and most established PJTKI which have their own training centers, Binamandiri training center is also one of the best equipped, best run and most modern.

According to Arti, the company officer in charge of designing and monitoring the curriculum, the company's *BLK* strictly adheres to the curriculum prescribed by the Department of Manpower and Transmigration.

Arti and another staff member, Endah Nuraini, explained that each recruit had to undergo at least 600 hours of training.

Since Binamandiri, which has twenty partner agencies in Hong Kong, only trains its own recruits, and ninety-eight per cent of recruits are indeed sent to Hong Kong, the whole curriculum is geared toward working in Hong Kong. While English is also taught, Cantonese is the dominant language, filling the ambience of the place. Apart from a minimum of forty-two hours of formal lessons in Cantonese, the instructors mostly use Cantonese as their medium of instruction in practical lessons such as cooking and other household chores.

'We implement the learning by doing method,' said Arti. During the day, they are also required to speak Cantonese to each other.

The physical environment of Hong Kong is also simulated in the BLK, where the dormitory, situated upstairs, has windows closely facing each other, just like in high-rise apartment buildings in Hong Kong. In the rooms simulating different parts of the interior of an apartment, the electrical appliances, the furniture and soft furnishings and even the foodstuffs in the cupboards are of brands usually found in Hong Kong.

Apart from teaching recruits how to recognize different types of fabric, and how to care for them in the washing and ironing stages, the instructors also teach them how to hang them out to dry.

For those who specialize in taking care of infants, Binamandiri has an arrangement with the local hospitals to have them practise in the hospitals' mothercraft section.

Etiquette lessons also cover correct behavior as proper diners, in order for them to be presentable in case they are taken out to restaurants or to their employers' friends' homes.

To avoid cultural misunderstandings which can cause unnecessary tension, Muslim recruits are told not to wear white prayer capes, because white is a mourning colour in Chinese tradition. They were given floral capes instead.

One aspect which Binamandiri instructors emphasize and take time to allow recruits to learn properly is the use of western-style toilets. It is the only BLK I have seen so far which did not only have western-style toilets for recruits to learn how to clean and maintain, but also to use.

Tuti Sanarto, the Director, recounted how, in the past, a number of recruits had fallen ill from homesickness, and subsequent investigation had revealed that the root of the problem had been their inability to use the toilets. So they make sure all recruits have overcome that problem before they leave for Hong Kong. It seems a small thing, compared to passing the various compulsory competency tests and completing the final orientation program, but it certainly has the potential to undermine the success of the recruit's work.

Binamandiri does not wash its hands of its recruits once they have begun work. It has a follow-up program, monitored by its partner agencies in Hong Kong. I was able to see some letters of feedback from former recruits. The following is my own translation of one such letter, written in the domestic helper's handwriting:

> My employers are good, patient and not miserly. They, sir and madam, often take me to dine out in restaurants. They often buy me new clothes too. On Christmas Eve, they asked me to cook Indonesian food. They were so pleased with the Christmas dinner I prepared that they gave me a present. A box of chocolates. Their family and friends are also good to me. They all call me A Wah (a Chinese way of shortening my name Tri Wahyuni). Everyday I clean the house, prepare meals, wash the car, feed the two dogs, take the dogs to the park. I don't have to wash and iron every day. I don't have to go shopping to the market every day. My salary is HK$3,270 per month. They often take me to the beach, together with the dogs. They are very considerate of all my needs. I can pray five times a day, and I have my own food, no pork. I am very happy here. Thank you.

'If any dispute arises, we try to find solution through our local partner which placed the particular helper with the employer in question,' said Arti.

SPONSORS

There is no one single image we can use as a stereotype of sponsors. They range in age from approximately twenty-four to sixty-five. Most of them, however, live in the same regency as the women they seek to recruit. Some are even their own village heads, or the wives of the village heads.

Interestingly, a fair number of sponsors are domestic helper returnees. Having had the real experience of working as domestic helpers overseas, they feel they are in a better position than anyone to inform recruit candidates of what to expect.

One of these sponsors, also known in Indonesian as *Petugas Lapangan* (PL) or Field Officers, is Suprapti.

Suprapti (thirty-five years) lives in the Sub-District of Besuki, in Tulungagung. She worked in Hong Kong for six years. After that she felt she had saved up enough money for a house, and it was time for her to be near her husband and their child. Since then they have had another child.

Suprapti saw the potential in being a sponsor for domestic helper candidates, so she contacted her former PJTKI and suggested she recruit for them in her own sub-district. The PJTKI agreed.

'I bring people from the villages around the sub-district, to the PJTKI. I also brief them about the work situation in Hong Kong. I tell them it is not easy. They have to know the Chinese customs in Hong Kong if they want to have a good working relationship with their employers. So by the time they are recruited, they already know a lot from me,' said Suprapti.

Suprapti claims she never asks the candidates for money. 'I give them loans, and they repay me when they start earning in Hong Kong,' she said. 'I know that some sponsors ask the candidates for money. Then they don't look after them properly. They disappear. They give us a bad reputation.'

Suprapti explained that when she had several candidates agreeing to be recruited, she would take them to the PJTKI. 'It is a four-hour journey by bus from my village. So if I have rallied ten candidates, the company often sends a driver and a minibus to pick us up.'

Suprapti is happy with what she is doing, 'because I help other people while earning a good income,' she said.

THE GOVERNMENT

In the earlier chapters we have seen various manifestations of the fact that a great deal of improvement is needed in the legislation governing the recruitment, training and dispatch overseas of Indonesian workers, specifically those who seek work as domestic helpers. And just as important, proper control in the implementation of existing legislation has been sorely lacking.

After 18 October 2004, the Indonesian Government can finally claim it has a proper law governing the country's workers migrating to other countries.

It is called UNDANG-UNDANG NOMOR 39 TAHUN 2004 TENTANG PENEMPATAN DAN PERLINDUNGAN TENAGA KERJA INDONESIA DI LUAR NEGERI, or LAW NO. 39 OF 2004 ON THE PLACEMENT AND PROTECTION OF INDONESIAN WORKERS OVERSEAS.

On 13 June 2005, I conducted an interview with Andi Syahrul Pangerang, Head of the Legal Planning Section of the Department of Manpower and Transmigration's Legal Office, in their office in Jalan Jendral Gatot Subroto Kavling 51, South Jakarta. Also present were the Officer-in-Charge of Industrial Relations and the Officer-in-Charge of training transmigrant workers.

Before this law was passed by Parliament, workers' migration was governed by a ministerial decree, KepMenakertrans Nomor KEP-104A/MEN/2002 tentang Penempatan TKI ke Luar Negeri, or, for the purpose of this book, shortened to the Ministerial Decree 2002.

According to Andi Syahrul Pangerang, Law No 39 provides legal protection to migrant workers against abuse and deception before departure, during employment, and after completion, of their contracts overseas.

Under the Ministerial Decree 2002, Andi Syahrul explained, the government was only able to impose administrative sanctions on inviduals or PJTKI which abused their power or were negligent in their duty in handling the placement of the workers they recruited. Law No 39 puts these breaches under the criminal code.

'Anyone, be they individuals or legal companies, who breaks the law in the course of sending workers overseas can go to prison,' Andi Syahrul said.

Law No 39 comes down heavily on PJTKI, or the Administering Agencies of Indonesian Workers Placement Overseas as they are known in this law, and any individuals involved in sending workers overseas.

In terms of financial capacity, the minimum capital outlay for an agency has been increased from Rp750 million to Rp3 billion; and the agency is still required to have a monetary guarantee deposited in a bank nominated by the Minister of Manpower. The Minister has the authority to withdraw the funds or part thereof. The minimum amount of this monetary guarantee has, however, been reduced from Rp250 million to Rp15 million.

In addition to the above requirements, the new law stipulates that agencies must have prepared a business plan for three successive years.

The new law, according to Andi Syahrul, will have the power to protect migrant workers, including domestic helpers working overseas, through tighter control over the administering agencies which handle the recruitment and placement of these workers.

'In this law, the government has to arrange an MOU with the receiving countries, in the cases where these countries do not have laws providing protection to our workers,' he said, 'then in addition to that, every worker has to sign an employment contract where the rights and obligations of both employer and worker are specified. Another contract the worker has to sign is one with the administering agency where the rights and obligations of both parties are specified.'

The 'third eye' in the monitoring of the administering agency in the receiving country, if the new law works as intended, is its local business partner, which handles the placement of the worker. There is an equally legally-binding contract between the administering agency in Indonesia and its local business partner in the receiving country, or in the cases where the prospective employer (user) does not use the service of a local employment agency, the contract is between the administering agency in Indonesia and the user in the receiving country.

The drafts of all three contracts have to be checked and endorsed by the Department of Manpower and Transmigration, which will also send them to the diplomatic offices in the respective receiving countries before they are signed and ratified. If either of the above finds any weaknesses in a draft contract which are deemed to have the potential of causing problems, the said draft contract will be sent back to be rectified.

Andi Syahrul emphasized, 'Under this law, no workers are allowed to leave without proper contracts.'

The flow pattern may be described thus:

In terms of accountability, the Department of Manpower and Transmigration turns to the Administering Agencies of Indonesian Workers Placement Overseas, and the Agencies turn to their local business partners or their clients, the users.

The government may from time to time ban the sending of workers to a particular receiving country, if it deems the country to be negligent in carrying out its part of the obligations in the MOU, or that there are aspects which may endanger the lives of the workers.

To monitor the process of sending workers overseas, the government has approved the establishment of a special body, which will be in charge of monitoring the process, from the sending until the return, of workers. It is called the National Supervising Body for Placement and Protection of Indonesian Workers (*Badan Koordinasi Nasional Penempatan dan Perlindungan Tenaga Kerja Indonesia* – Bakornas PPTKI).

Bakornas PPTKI is a non-departmental government body, answerable to the President of the Republic of Indonesia. It will be tasked with providing service, coordinating and overseeing document processing, implementation of the Pre-departure Orientation Program, problem solving and finding funding sources. It will oversee workers' skill enhancement training programs and it will also be responsible for the smooth processing of the workers' return.

The membership of the Body will be drawn from the government departments and institutions which are related to workers' migration. In carrying out its tasks, the Body can co-opt professional people from various sectors.

'Eventually this body is expected to initiate the one-stop service program for the sending of workers overseas,' said Andi Syahrul. And when they can overcome the funding constraints, the service will make extensive use of online information dissemination and data collecting. 'We will then be able to know exactly how many people have been placed in particular countries, how many have completed their contracts, who their agencies are, and so forth,' he continued.

The new law will virtually make redundant the services of sponsors, because it requires domestic helpers aspirants like any other migrant worker aspirants, to be proactive and register themselves with the local Office of Manpower. And the PJTKI will then source this register. 'We are hoping that this way the migrant workers aspirants can no longer be manipulated or deceived by irresponsible people who act as their sponsors,' Andi Syahrul explained the rationale of this provision, adding, 'Anyone who recruits from outside the register, will be prosecuted. A PJTKI which recruits from outside the register, will at least lose its licence to operate.'

The Department of Manpower will have investigating officers in each regency who will assist the Police in supervising the process of recruitment and sending of workers overseas.

The new law also covers individuals who find their own employers without using the service of employment agencies. They will still have to complete documents issued by the Department of Manpower and Transmigration, informing the Department of the types of work they are going to do, and who their employers are, and other facts related to the prospective employment. Like those using the services of employment agencies, the individuals obtaining employment independently also have to obtain ID cards indicating they are migrant workers. These cards are issued by the Department of Manpower and Transmigration, and the diplomatic missions in the receiving countries will be appropriately informed in order for them to have their data, and will be able to monitor them, and provide protection if need be. And when the workers arrive at their countries of destination, they are required to report to the Indonesian diplomatic mission there.

'It is extremely important for the Indonesian diplomatic mission in the country where an Indonesian worker is working, to know of his or her whereabouts. The worker's confidence of being able to look after him/herself will become irrelevant once he or she is found missing for instance, because when this happens, his or her family will expect the diplomatic mission to find the missing person. Or if he or she encounters problems, again the diplomatic mission will be expected to provide assistance,' Andi Syahrul explained.

This possibility also motivated the government to require the workers to produce letters of consent from their parents or their spouses. Andi Syahrul cited an example in Taiwan, where a worker died. When the diplomatic office sent his remains to his parents, they received an expression of objection from his wife. To that point the diplomatic office did not know that he had a wife.

Andi Syahrul admitted the new law stipulated that apart from PJTKI, the government is also able to send workers overseas. He emphasized, however, that the primary roles of the government are those of regulator and monitor.

'In the rare cases where the government sends workers overseas, it is answerable to the Legislative Council,' he added.

PJTKI (or the Administering Agency for Placement and Protection of Indonesian Workers Overseas as they are referred to in the new law), have expressed objections to the more demanding requirements from the government in order for them to continue with their business.

Andi Syahrul justified this, saying, 'This is to prevent exploitation of the workers. These agencies have to realize that they are dealing with people. Their commodity is indeed human beings. So there needs to be tight monitoring. Considerations usually given for small and medium business in other fields, are not applicable here. It is true the government puts up a high entry barrier. They must have big capital outlays, very good and reliable management and long-term planning. This is no place for fly-by-nighters.'

The Department of Manpower and Transmigration is generally optimistic that once the one-stop service system is in place, the process will be a lot smoother. 'Now the process has to go through several government institutions, leaving it vulnerable to abuse and mistakes,' admitted Andi Syahrul, adding, 'The new law stipulates clearly what charges a recruit has to pay. Those who add illegitimate fees will be prosecuted.'

IN AN IMPERFECT WORLD

Seen cursorily, the world of the women seeking better opportunities working as domestic helpers overseas may not look very different from that of other people seeking work outside their own environment. They feel disoriented and an overwhelming sense of alienation. In terms of the working situation, they lose some bargaining power when they find themselves disconcerted by the unfamiliar environment in their new place of work. It is imperative to be as prepared as possible in terms of the appropriate skills required for the jobs, and to have a fairly extensive knowledge of the new environment. A combination of factors has, however, pushed the women who seek employment as domestic helpers overseas into a position that is more disadvantaged than those employed in most other jobs.

On 5 October 2004, I conducted an interview with Salma Safitri, an advocate and Program Coordinator of the National Executive Body of *Solidaritas Perempuan*, a non-government organization concerned with justice for women, in its office in Jakarta.

The feisty young advocate is convinced that domestic helpers are the least protected group of workers throughout the world. 'In almost every country in the world, including Indonesia, domestic helpers' work is not recognized as real work, to the extent that what they do is not covered by the country's Labour Law,' said Safitri. The exceptions are Hong Kong and Taiwan that both recognize domestic helpers' work as formal work, and thus provide a legal mechanism to protect them.

'In Hong Kong and Taiwan, if a domestic helper does not receive her salary, she can go to the Labour Court to seek redress. Then the Labour Court can order her employer to pay the salary owing to the helper. Failing to do that can land the employer in prison,' she elaborated further, 'This is yet to happen in countries such as Malaysia, Singapore, Korea, Japan or in the Middle East.'

Ironically, Saudi Arabia has a good Labour Law for its own citizens although, according to Safitri, foreign domestic helpers are not covered. Article 3 of the Law specifies that immigrant workers and those who work in a domestic situation are excluded from the provisions of the law.

As Safitri pointed out, 'In relation to Indonesia, even the new law to be passed (Law No 39 of 2004, which was still being deliberated in Parliament at the time of this interview) neglects to recognize migrant domestic helpers as the biggest component of the whole Indonesian labor force sent overseas, hence it does not take into account the specific needs of these workers'.

As for the provisions in the new law (Law No 39 of 2004) which requires the inclusion of hours of work, salary, days off and social support system in the compulsory employment contract, Safitri said, 'There is no indication that the law recognizes the work situation of domestic helpers. There is no mechanism regulating the work or the kind of social support system to which they are entitled. In addition to that, it imposes stricter conditions for domestic helpers. It requires them to be not younger than twenty-one, and to have at least completed junior secondary school (Year Nine). This is ignoring the fact that the majority of this country's population have not completed primary school. Does this mean they are denied the rights to seek work overseas?'

The idea of regarding those who have less than nine years of former education as gullible and vulnerable to exploitation is irritating to Safitri. 'If they are gullible, that is because they are not sufficiently informed. People who are not formally educated are not necessarily stupid. If they receive proper training and are suitably informed, they can be just as prepared as those who are formally educated,' she said. Then she continued, 'Having seen the debate between the government and the Legislative Council, it became obvious to me that the women who want to work as domestic helpers overseas were not much more than commodities to them. And this is very much reflected in the new law.'

'This is what the government sees: a group of people want to work, but there is no work available here, so they have to find it somewhere else. And if they find work elsewhere, the government has to draw profit from the process. So what does the government do? It makes a law which specifies how it can charge everybody, including the employment agencies, for every avenue the aspirant workers or recruit candidates have to take. It sets up a rigid and thickly layered process. Eleven government institutions are involved. Ten documents have to be completed, eight stages of recruitment have to be passed. In this country, everyone knows that each time you approach a government official's desk, you have to pay. You even pay for the cost of having your document typed, as well as the paper on which the document is written.'

'The recruit candidates are not regarded as citizens who have the right to find work, and therefore are entitled to have this right fulfilled. Instead of setting up a system easily accessible by recruit candidates, the government set up an expensive, complex, time-consuming and energy-taxing system. Yet there is no guarantee that the system will protect them from falling into irresponsible middlemen.'

Safitri also objects to the fact that there is no mechanism for the public to monitor the process. 'So far it has always been the community whose persistence has shed light on the cases that have gone wrong. There is no official access for anyone who wants to know,' she said.

While the new law stipulates that the government has the obligation to protect Indonesian workers overseas, no mechanism is offered as to how an aggrieved domestic helper can claim this protection. 'It is too abstract,' Safitri pointed out.

'There is no indication that the government is able to perceive the inherent subordination that a domestic helper is subjected to. Being a woman is enough to set the subordination going. On top of that, there is a perception that they are stupid because they come from low social classes,' she said. 'In a foreign country, a domestic helper is faced with three types of discrimination: based on her gender, her social class, and her place of origin, a rural village.

'So she does not have the employer's respect, because she is seen as someone carrying out inferior work. She may also be condescended to because she belongs to a minority race.'

To provide genuine protection to these women and subsequently empower them, according to Safitri, the government needs to recognize all these inherent disadvantages. 'But it does not even show any awareness of them,' she said.

Safitri also takes exception to the provisions of the new law requiring every migrant worker to report to the office of the local diplomatic mission. She offered a scenario:

Aminah has just arrived in Saudi Arabia. Having come by a cheap means of transportation, she has arrived not in Jeddah or Riyadh, where the offices of the Indonesian diplomatic mission are situated. She is in a strange place. She does not know anyone, she cannot read street names or traffic signs. At the place of her arrival, she is picked up by her prospective employer or the local agent. She does not have the courage to ask to be taken to the Indonesian Embassy or Consulate. In fact, she is immediately in the care, hence the power, of her employer or the agent. It is not up to her to decide where to go. So she does not report to the diplomatic mission as required by the law. That means she has broken the law. If her employment situation works well, then she is all right. But if she is subjected to abuse by the employer and she eventually finds her way to the Embassy or the Consulate, she will be told that, because she has not reported her arrival, her presence is not registered, and legally she is not there. Or worse, she has broken a law to begin with. Why can't the government make it easy for women like Aminah, by setting up reporting desks at all the usual entry points?

Another scenario Safitri offered:

> Masri does not use the service of an employment agency. The first possibility
> is that she found a job order on the web, applied, and was accepted. The
> second possibility, a friend of hers who works in Malaysia was asked by her
> employers if she knew someone reliable to work for them as well. Her friend
> recommended her, and the employers applied for her visa in order for her
> to come to Malaysia. The new law stipulates that people like Masri must
> register themselves as soon as they arrive in the country of destination. What
> if Masri's employers live in a remote place, far from the capital? Why make
> it so difficult and costly for these people? This is also where reporting desks
> at all entry points will be useful, not only for people like Masri, but also for
> the diplomatic missions, to save them headaches later on.

The situation, Safitri pointed out, does not apply to migrant workers
who work in other fields, such as in factories or plantation in Malaysia.
Interestingly, the new law appears to have them in mind, while in the
meantime, seventy per cent of the migrant workers, the domestic helpers,
are virtually ignored. 'Not only are they not properly protected, but they also
suffer discrimination,' said Safitri, then continued, 'These are people who pay
their way, benefitting various people in the private and government sectors,
and when they start receiving their salary, they benefit their families back
home, and even when they return, they become the victims of extortion of
greedy and unconscienable officials at the airport.'

There is still an overwhelming inclination to blame the domestic helpers
who encounter problems. Safitri opined that it was a kind of justification for
not doing anything to rectify the situation.

'You were beaten up? You were probably lazy or careless in your work! You
were raped? What were you wearing? Were you wearing revealing clothes?
Did you flirt with your male employer? If this kind of attitude is not changed,
the problems encountered by the domestic helpers will never be solved!'
Safitri said, and continued, 'Shouldn't we say, you were beaten up? What
happened which made your employer beat you up? You didn't understand
what he or she said? Maybe we should give you better language training. See
what I mean? If the domestic helpers are so used to being blamed when they

get into trouble, they will eventually give up reporting what happens. They can see the futility and the pain accompanying it. Any wonder that some were driven to such despair that they committed suicide?'

The tendency to blame the domestic helpers also reflects an inherent attitude in the community that those who work as domestic helpers are stupid, unskilled and worse still, so recalcitrant that they are untrainable. Safitri agreed with this suggestion, and suggested that unless there was an attitude shift, the problems would only be compounded.

'In my experience, they are just as intelligent as any other person. When they are treated like normal adults, they will behave accordingly. However, they are mostly given instructions like, don't shame your country, work hard, be good to your employers, you're going there to work, not to have fun, and so forth.'

'The fact that over decades problems have come up to the surface, instead of devising ways of preventing the problems from recurring, we blame them, and some people even say, stop the problem by stopping sending them. In the latest parliamentary session, the TNI POLRI fraction's statement reflects this, It is hoped that with this law we can stop sending domestic helpers or informal workers, and increase the number of formal workers instead. Does it solve the problem of unemployment here? Where do these women seek work, then?'

Another issue which Law No 39 of 2004 neglects to accommodate, according to Safitri, is the issue of illegal migrant workers. They still float in a legal limbo.

Given that it is the first law governing the placement and protection of Indonesian workers overseas, it is hoped that with the increasing awareness and community participation in monitoring the process, the law is going to be amended as frequently as necessary.

CHAPTER FIVE

CONCLUSION

THE STAKEHOLDERS AND
THE COMMUNITY

Researching this book has been a steep learning curve for me. I wanted to study the situation because I thought that I had a reasonable initial grasp on the topic, and that all I needed to do was flesh out the skeleton which had already formed in my mind. Halfway through the research I realized that it was the skeleton of a fat creature I was fleshing out.

When I started thinking about the issue seriously, I had not been leaning one way or another, realizing that in every situation where there was conflict, there would be more than one facet to the subject to look at, that it was very important for me to maintain balance.

By the time I decided to write a book about the situation of Indonesian domestic workers/helpers overseas, not only had I been exposed to news items and features about the events in various countries where the women were working, I had also spoken, albeit informally, with several overseas employers of Indonesian domestic helpers.

I realized there were many relatively happy situations where things either went well, or both employer and domestic helper were able to continuously negotiate any potentially tense situations before serious conflict flared up. Some relationships even developed and lasted well beyond the time of employment.

It was evident to me that not all domestic helper situations overseas were fraught with tension and conflict. In the cases where they were, however, I was able to see the main issues at play, the biggest one being the gap between expectations on the one hand, and discovery of the reality on the part of both the domestic helper and the employer, on the other. Unconsciously I began to look around for a third party who may have had a hand in creating this gap, or at least allowing it to remain in existence.

I was right, to a degree. And there was more than one third party in this picture. There was the employment agency, in Indonesia as well as in the receiving countries; there were the government institutions involved in the sending of the workers; and there was the sponsor. They each played a part. Furthermore, I came to see that all parties, including the employer, and the domestic helper herself, were stakeholders in this profitable business. And in deconstructing cases of conflict, it became clear that each of these stakeholders had not been impeccable in carrying out their part of the whole deal.

The reasons behind these flaws, however, vary according to where they stand on the ground, taking into account the fact that the ground is not level.

THE STAKEHOLDERS AS PROTAGONISTS IN HYPOTHETICAL SCENES OF CONFLICT:
THE EMPLOYER

In the following section I describe three stereotypical examples. There are naturally other types and many more variants of these types.

Employer Type One
It is human nature to seek the best bargain for what you want. The employer in this case forgets that it is a fellow human being he or she is bargaining for. In the effort of looking for the greatest gain at the cheapest price, the employer opts for a domestic helper from Indonesia. The agency he or she contacted, indicated that an Indonesian domestic helper would give the best value for their money. This is what the agency said to them: the Indonesian domestic helper is not only capable, she is also undemanding. She is not inclined to stand her ground, thus minimizing the potential for dispute. She is flexible. And her best feature of all: she comes cheap. She accepts a below-standard salary.

For some reason alarm bells did not go off: if she is so good, how come she comes cheap? Something did not add up, but the employer chose to ignore the anomaly, and believed instead that he or she had come across a miracle. So the employer now expects a real miracle. That is why when the domestic helper arrives, the employer, upon discovering that the expected miracle is a fraud, becomes disappointed, then frustrated, and eventually so angry that he or she begins to lash out, verbally and physically, at the helper.

Even if the employer stops at a one-off incident, it is still shameful. Unfortunately, in most cases, the employer feels good after beating up the helper. Instead of feeling guilty or contrite, the employer feels powerful. The abuse continues.

Employer Type Two
Life is a constant struggle for her. She has to help her husband in his small business employing four people, look after their two young children and keep house as well. When her husband travels for the business, she has to manage everything.

Her husband does not see her problems, but agrees reluctantly to their employing a domestic helper. Knowing that her husband thinks she is being self-indulgent, she feels guilty and resentful all at once. She goes to an employment agency and asks for the most economical solution: a domestic helper who agrees to be paid as little as possible, but who has the necessary skills to make life a lot easier for her.

She gets a domestic helper from Indonesia, who seems to her to be forever dreaming. The helper is slow at taking in her instructions, and even slower at carrying them out. When she rushes this helper, the wretched woman becomes so disoriented she drops anything in her hands. Within a short time she has broken some of the family's best crockery and glasses. Worse still, the helper will burst into tears often, slowing the process even further.

One morning she is at her wit's end. The helper keeps making mistakes. Her husband will be wondering what is keeping her; why she has not turned up at the shop, so she grabs the helper by the hair and shakes her head hard. The screams only make her more frantic. She pushes the helper's head against the wall, again and again, until she sees blood streaming from it.

Now she is overcome with fear. She lets go. The screaming stops. The helper falls in a heap on the floor. She checks. The woman still breathes, still conscious. She apologizes, and tells the helper to go and wash herself. In the meantime, she had better change her blood-spattered clothes and pacify her children before leaving.

At the shop her husband complains about her lateness. She becomes angry, not at her husband any more, because she now has a suitable recipient for her anger. The domestic helper.

The abuse repeats itself, until she is desensitized, and no longer feels contrite. The situation would have continued indefinitely, except one day the helper disappears, and two police officers appear.

Employer Type Three

The idea of employing a foreign domestic helper is actually his wife's, because as the main income earner she needs help with looking after the children and keeping house, which he cannot provide. After all he also works, though his job does not have to get him out of the house at certain times.

They go to an employment agency and select this 'little thing' from Indonesia. When the domestic helper arrives, he is not disappointed, though he does not show it, because his wife has very sharply-tuned antennae when it comes to things like that. The woman turns out to be a fairly good worker too.

It does not take him long to start sidling up to the cute woman when she is washing the breakfast dishes after his wife has left for work and the children are at school. But the little hussy is playing hard to get. She moves away. When she keeps moving away he becomes so infuriated he grabs her by the waist and is going to kiss her when she pushes him away.

What? What does she think she is, rejecting me? He grabs her again, and when she tries to push him away again, he hits her with a backhander, something he often almost did to his wife, except that the cow holds the purse strings. Now the hussy stops fighting, holding the side of her face with an open palm, her eyes brimming with tears. The sight of a finally subdued woman aroused him immeasurably. And he is not going to stop now.

When he has finished, he threatens to kill her if she tells his wife or anyone else about what happened.

That night, his wife sees the bruise on the helper's face, and asks her how she got it. The helper says she bumped into a door. To his horror, his wife turns to him, and he could see from the gleam of her eyes that she knows. He turns away. Luckily she does not say anything.

Encouraged by the impunity, he repeats the assault, again and again. Besides, the hussy must enjoy it, because she fights less and less as time passes. Except she is becoming very quiet. She is up to something! He repeats his threats every day, roughing her up while delivering them.

Then it happens. One afternoon when he comes out of the shower, feeling like another little adventure, the woman is no longer there.

He is agonizing, wondering what to do next, when there is a knock on the door. It is the little hussy but she is not alone. Two police officers are with her.

THE AGENCY

As is the case with the samples for employers, the following are stereotypical of agencies which, knowingly or unknowingly, contribute to the multiplication of problems in the employment situation. There are more types, and even more variants of the types.

Agency Type One

The owners started the agency because they were able to see a business opportunity and persuaded themselves that they were assisting the migrant worker aspirants who needed help. They discovered, however, that to start this business they needed a big capital outlay, so they pooled their money together and borrowed the difference. They obtain an entry into the network of local employment agencies in the receiving countries, and arrange partnerships with a number of them.

Getting recruit candidates is easy. Once they have plugged into the network of sponsors, the candidates keep coming. With the incoming flow of candidates is the outgoing flow of costs. The sponsors have to be paid; they charge a fee for each candidate. The agency owners cannot afford to be too choosy. Then the candidates have to be trained. The agency sends them to a government accredited training center, and fork out more money. Processing the documents is expensive; the stamps and approvals of each official institution cost money, not to mention time and energy. This adds to their determination to ensure that the candidates find appropriate employers. Only then will they begin getting their money back; by extracting instalments from the workers' salaries.

To save costs, the agency begins to cut corners. The 600 hours stipulated by the government regulation can be made up of formal training at the training center and 'informal' training' at associates' homes, from where the agency keeps half the trainees' salaries. It is fair. After all they also have to assist with the administrative costs.

Gradually there are more and more corners to cut. Though this means forking out more money to get the stamps and approvals, in the long run, it is more economical. The going rate for workers from Indonesia is always lower than those from the Philippines, who are better trained and speak better English, but that is also fair enough. The agency still gets its money back and in most cases, handsome profits too. Until of course, some workers misbehave, are sent back, and the agency has to shoulder the costs.

Agency Type Two

This agency is a local business partner, in one of the receiving countries, of several employment agencies in Indonesia. The company specializes in the placement of Indonesian domestic helpers in this country. In fact, the owners have lived in Indonesia, and can speak Indonesian.

Competition is fierce in the business of foreign domestic helpers, especially those from Indonesia. So agency fees have to be cut down at least fifty per cent, sometimes up to seventy per cent. Consequently, to make the business viable, the agency has to be creative and astute; it has to charge its business partners in Indonesia for its service, calling the charge something which does not contravene the local laws. If they have to follow the law to the letter, the business will not last for much longer, because the agency fees it can charge prospective employers are plainly inadequate. In addition to that, it has to restructure its human resources: cut down the time spent on 'after-sale' service and counselling, and increase the time spent on processing more workers, either the incoming ones or those requiring change-over of employers. Telephone calls for help from workers encountering problems with their employers have to be put in a queue, and gradually, the queue is becoming longer and longer.

THE SPONSOR

The sponsor has a kind of symbiotic relationship with the agency. Until the new law is able to be implemented, the agency cannot do without the sponsor. Even after the new law is implemented, it is doubtful that the sponsor can be completely dispensed of. He or she may emerge assuming a different identity playing the same role, possibly facilitating between the Regional Office of Manpower which holds a register of migrant worker aspirants, and the agency.

Sponsor Type One

He or she lives in the same locality as the recruit aspirants, and is known to the village or at least the neighborhood. The sponsor regards his or her role as someone who helps the villagers to improve themselves and their lives, and draws an income out of it. The sponsor is usually well-connected, on good terms with local authorities and able to get things done, such as having documents processed quickly.

He or she is often a mentor to the recruit aspirants, and has a way of gaining their trust. The relationship with the agency is usually good, though from time to time mutual suspicions may arise, causing some tension.

The sponsor tends to paint a rosy picture of the prospective job to the worker aspirants, probably because he or she believes it to a degree. And because of this belief, the sponsor does not see much harm in cutting corners, convinced that things will be alright once the recruit aspirant finds an employer. And interestingly, when things do turn sour, the sponsor is no longer responsible. It is the agency's responsibility.

Sponsor Type Two

He or she does not live in the same locality as the recruit aspirants, but has reason to visit the village or neighborhood, maybe selling items the people there need. He or she is outgoing, finds it easy to make friends, and always has interesting stories to tell about the countries where domestic helpers from other villages have been amassing wealth.

The sponsor does not necessarily feel attached to the women he or she eventually persuades to come to an agency in a big city to be recruited. In fact, after taking a fairly large number of young women away, the sponsor usually is no longer seen in the village, because he or she is heading for another locality.

THE GOVERNMENT INSTITUTIONS

It could not be said that the government was taken by surprize by the rapid increase in the flow of workers seeking employment overseas, and in this case, specifically women who seek work as domestic helpers in various countries which have the need for them. If the government were taken by surprize at some stage, then it dragged its feet in providing the necessary regulations in order to make sure that these workers' needs were well-served and they had legal protection in their places of work. The first comprehensive law to speak of was passed by parliament in October 2004.

The employment agencies, which later assumed the name of PJTKI, started sending workers overseas in the late 1970s. The phenomenon could not have eluded the government's attention because it became a type of industry which brought in significant revenue to the state, as well as benefiting the neighborhoods of the villages where the workers came from. The growth of this industry alone would have had the magnitude to stare the government in the face, let alone the increasing revenue to the government coffers and the added benefits to the business of banking and the communities of the workers' places of origins.

I would like to draw an example from the Philippines, a country that, since the beginning of 1970s, has been well-known as the source of workers migrating far and wide for the purpose of employment,. Its government responded to the phenomenon in 1982 by founding the Philippine Overseas Employment Administration (POEA), giving it a parliamentary mandate to optimize the benefits of the country's overseas employment program. It did not stop there. Five years later the POEA was reorganized to incorporate improvements as the needs developed. Seven years later, in 1995, the POEA was again strengthened by a parliamentary act, where issues such as the guarantee of migrant workers rights, stricter rules on illegal recruitment activities, repatriation of workers and a reintegration program, drew immediate legal attention.

The Philippine diplomatic missions in the countries of destination of their workers, are equipped with labor attachés, welfare officers, social workers and doctors, all trained to handle welfare and legal problems of their workers. Most of the labor attachés posted abroad are qualified lawyers.

In Hong Kong and Singapore, the Indonesian domestic helpers in employment-related trouble far outnumber their Filipino counterparts, yet there are Filipino – church-based or community-based – non-government organizations which provide assistance to the Filipino domestic helpers in trouble, as well as extending this assistance to their counterparts from Indonesia.

It appears that the Indonesian Government has been unjustifiably slow in coming to terms with the problematic situation of its migrant workers, and has only come up with a proper law some twenty-five years after the private sector had begun to take up the business challenge of handling the sending of worker aspirants overseas.

While the private sector was quick to seize its opportunity, the lack of strong legislation and monitoring mechanisms has made the business vulnerable to irresponsible and unscrupulous parties or individuals; and their most immediate victims, and those having the least bargaining power, are the workers.

The irresponsible and unscrupulous elements in the private sector have not been acting alone in making a mockery of the existing legislation for what it has been worth. The collusion with irresponsible and unscrupulous elements in the government institutions has been public knowledge, so public in fact, that it is known even in host countries of the Indonesian workers.

THE DOMESTIC HELPER

There are as many types and variants of domestic helpers who tend to get into trouble as there are employers, but I have selected the following two salient types.

Domestic Helper Type One

She goes with the sponsor to an agency in a big city, bursting with optimism, believing that the opportunity of earning a lot of money, helping with her family's finances and saving up for her own future, is in the palm of her hand. All she has to do is close her hand.

She has never worked as a domestic helper anywhere, ever. She is only seventeen, and has had to drop out of school because her family could not afford the expense of sending four children to school. She has no idea what is involved in being a domestic helper in a foreign country. But she knows that she will be earning an awful lot of money.

The sponsor tells her that he or she has had to 'increase' her age to twenty-one on the new photo ID the sponsor is arranging for her, but that it is all right. Many people do that, and they have never had any problems.

At the agency she does not know if the sponsor has told them that she is in reality only seventeen, but she is not going to upset the arrangement and scuttle her dream of making money, so she does not ask. She is sent to a training center in another city, where she has to learn so many new things all at once. The hardest part, she finds, is learning a language she has never come across before. She has only been learning for two weeks when the agency tells her that her documents are ready and her prospective employer's application for her visa has been approved – whatever that means.

Shortly before her departure, the agency tells her what her salary will be, which sounds like an exhorbitant amount when converted to rupiah. 'But this is less than the going rate, because you are still under-trained,' the agency manager tells her. She does not mind. She is also told that she will not start receiving the money until she has worked for four months, because she has to start repaying the agency for all the costs of training, medical check-up, processing her documents and air-fares. That sounds fair too.

Arriving in the employer's country, she is immediately whisked away by someone from the local agency, and taken to the employer's house.

She is totally disoriented. She is hardly prepared for the situation she finds herself in. To begin with, she and the employer and the employer's family have problems communicating. The amount of language she was taught at the training center is obviously far from adequate. Fortunately for her, the family seems resigned to the fact that they have to be extra-patient with her.

She learns as she goes, and for a while it looks like she is going to pull through but the whole situation is beginning to depress her. She feels in-credibly lonely. She cannot go anywhere on her days off, because she has no money. She begins to feel used, and resents everyone and everything around her. One afternoon as she is cleaning the house, she finds some money in her employer's bedroom. She looks at it, knowing it is not hers, but feeling that it could be hers. After all she has been working for two months, yet has not seen any tangible payment.

She quickly grabs the money and puts it in her pocket, not realizing that there is a closed-circuit television camera in that room.

Domestic Helper Type Two

She promises her widowed mother that she will send money home as soon as she has paid off her debt to the agency, which will take four months.

The local agency places her with a family of three, where both husband and wife work, and the child (six years old) goes to school.

She finds the work not too onerous. She has time to herself during the day. The problem is, during that time she is by herself because she has no friends to socialize with. She has no money to go anywhere. She feels cut off from other young people her age. She thinks she is going crazy.

Then she meets the young man. He is walking past as she is taking the rubbish bag out. The following day at the same time she looks out the window of the ground-floor apartment and sees him walking slowly, glancing around as if looking for someone. She comes out.

Her life changes after that. The family notices that she is no longer sullen, and that she smiles a lot. Then the male employer has to spoil her fun. He has seen her talking to the young man. 'He's one of the construction workers from the new development round the corner. I know his type. He changes girlfriends more than he changes his clothes. I bet he has a wife and children at home. I don't want you to continue seeing him. I don't want you to get into trouble. Remember we're responsible for your well-being.'

She is so angry she nearly throws the dirty plate she is holding at him. He sees her face, glares and says, 'If I see you talking to him again, I'll send you back home. I have no choice!'

She can't sleep that night. The following morning she has made up her mind. She wants to teach him a lesson.

At the breakfast table, he is going to drink his soya milk. But as he puts the glass to his lips he grimaces. It has a strange smell. He looks up and catches her stare. He gets up and grabs the telephone and calls the police.

In court later that week, she is charged with attempted murder. To the defence counsel she says, 'I only wanted to hurt him, teach him a lesson for saying bad things about my boyfriend.' She swears she did not know that the amount of rat poison she put in his glass of soya milk could have killed him.

THE COMMUNITY AS RETARDANT TO PROGRESSIVE CHANGE

Over the years since independence, Indonesian society has continuously evolved. On the surface, with the spread of formal education – albeit unevenly – throughout the country, people have been growing more aware of their rights and obligations, thus presumably eroding the collective feudalistic mores steeped in the society ever since the pre-colonial era.

Feudalism, however, proves to be a great deal more difficult to uproot from the collective psyche than what most people with high ideals are hoping it is. In every sector, the hierarchical structure is still as strong as ever. In the formal employment situation everybody automatically positions himself or herself in this structure almost without questioning. Anyone who puts a step out is uncompromisingly pushed back to position or cut out altogether.

This structure is mirrored, in a more truncated manner, in a domestic situation, where the husband is accepted as the head of the household, and below him comes the wife, then the children, and last of all, the household staff. This may consist of the children's nanny, the driver, the gardener cum guard, the cook and the general household helper - popularly known as the maid -, all in that pecking order. The staff may be friendly toward each other, but are nonetheless aware where everyone stands in the hierarchy.

The office cleaner and the maid, the lowest positions respectively in the pecking order of the hierarchy, are at the bottom of the heap because their work is regarded as not requiring any real skills.

The actual role of the maid is disproportionately bigger than the credit given to her. She is responsible for the smooth operation of the household without having access to budget planning; she is the de facto telephonist of the family; she has to make sure that everybody - meaning the husband, the wife, and the children -, have the specific clothes they need, ready on the right day and the right time of day; and above all, she has to be polite and well-presented, but not better presented than her female employer. And she has to be near-invisible.

When the family has a dinner party, the cook, while also invisible, at least has a 'presence' in the preparation of the food the diners are enjoying, but the maid? She serves quietly, then disappears until summoned from time to time to carry out specific tasks. Then when everyone has finished, she comes to clean up. She does not leave any lingering impression on anyone. She is indispensable yet nobody recognizes her indispensibility.

There are gradients of the maid's 'invisibility' in the households which employ domestic helpers, especially considering that among the less affluent families, it is also common to have the domestic helper charged with the responsibility of being a cook as well as a general household helper. The core premise of her irrelevance in terms of status in the family is, however, immutable.

This subconscious notion is so prevalent in the society that it is reflected in the government, and specifically in this case, in the Department of Manpower and Transmigration which in principle should have the responsibility of having a workable system in place, in order for the women who work as domestic workers/helpers overseas to have proper legal protection.

This protection has been so far lacking, because as Salma Safitri of *Solidaritas Perempuan* pointed out, even the new law protects workers other than migrant domestic helpers, despite the fact that they are the largest segment (seventy per cent) of all Indonesian manpower sent overseas. It seems that the notion of the maid's irrelevance is so strong that it has even permeated the government structure as well. After all, in everybody's perception, these domestic helpers are 'just maids', and as such, do not deserve serious attention.

The problems of Indonesian domestic helpers overseas are chronic and basically rooted in a system which can be described as makeshift, propped up by ad-hoc regulations here and there, to treat symptoms which have come up and which cannot be ignored. What is needed is an overhaul, a remedial surgery instead of symptomatic treatments.

Time will tell, if the new law and the mechanisms which are yet to be set up to enforce it, will be able to effect this remedial surgery. One thing is for sure, it needs the support of the community to implement the changes, because most of them are in the collective psyche.

APPENDICES

APPENDIX 1

*The following is the **Hong Kong Standard Employment Contract** and **Schedule of Accommodation and Domestic Duties** (compulsory and recognized by the Labour Law), known as ID 407*

D.H. Contract No._____

EMPLOYMENT CONTRACT

(For a Domestic Helper recruited from outside Hong Kong)

This contract is made between ....(the "Employer", holder of Hong Kong Identity Card/Passport No*...............) and .... (the "Helper") on .... and has the following terms:

1. The Helper's place of origin for the purpose of this contract is ....

2. (a)† The Helper shall be employed by the Employer as a domestic helper for a period of two years commencing on the date on which the Helper arrives in Hong Kong.
   (b)† The Helper shall be employed by the Employer as a domestic helper for a period of two years commencing on ...., which is the date following the expiry of D.H. Contract No .... for employment with the same employer.

(c)† The Helper shall be employed by the Employer as a domestic helper for a period of two years commencing on the date on which the Director of Immigration grants the Helper permission to remain in Hong Kong to begin employment under this contract.

3. The Helper shall work and reside in the Employer's residence at ....
....

4. (a) The Helper shall only perform domestic duties as per the attached Schedule of Accommodation and Domestic Duties for the Employer.

   (b) The Helper shall not take up, and shall not be required by the Employer to take up, any other employment with any other person.

   (c) The Employer and the Helper hereby acknowledge that Clause 4 (a) and (b) will form part of the conditions of stay to be imposed on the Helper by the Immigration Department upon the Helper's admission to work in Hong Kong under this contract. A breach of one or both of the said conditions of stay will render the Helper and/or any aider and abetter liable to criminal prosecution.

5. (a) The Employer shall pay the Helper wages of HK$.......... per month.

   (b) The Employer shall provide the Helper with suitable and furnished accommodation as per the attached Schedule of Accommodation and Domestic Duties and food free of charge. If no food is provided, a food allowance of HK$.............. per month shall be paid to the Helper.

   (c) The Employer shall provide a receipt for payment of wages and food allowance and the Helper shall acknowledge receipt of the amount under his/her* signature.

6. The Helper shall be entitled to all rest days, statutory holidays, and paid annual leave as specified in the Employment Ordinance, Chapter 57.

7. (a) The Employer shall provide the Helper with free passage from his/her* place of origin to Hong Kong and on termination or expiry of this contract, free passage to his/her* place of origin.

(b) A daily food and travellling allowance of HK$100 per day shall be paid to the Helper from the date of his/her* departure from his/her* place of origin until the date of his/her* arrival at Hong Kong if travelling is by the most direct route. The same payment shall be made when the Helper returns to his/her* place of origin upon expiry or termination of this contract.

8. The Employer shall be responsible for the following fees and expenses (if any) for the departure of the Helper from his/her place of origin and entry into Hong Kong:

(i)   medical examination fees;

(ii) authentication fees by the relevant Consulates;

(iii) visa fee;

(iv) insurance fee;

(v) administration fee or fee such as the Philippines Overseas Employment Administration fee, or other fees of similar nature imposed by the relevant government authorities; and

(vi) others ....

In the event that the Helper has paid the above costs of fees, the Employer shall fully reimburse the Helper forthwith the amount so paid by the Helper upon demand and production of the correspondent receipts of documentary evidence of payment.

9. (a) When the Helper is ill, or suffers personal injury, whether or not it is attributable to his/her* employment, the Employer shall provide free medical treatment to the Helper. Free medical treatment includes maintenance in hospital and emergency dental treatment. The Helper shall accept medical treatment provided by any registered medical practitioner.

(b) If the Helper suffers injury by accident or occupational disease arising out of and in the course of employment, the Employer shall make payment of compensation in accordance with the Employees' Compensation Ordinance, Chapter 282.

(c) In the event of a medical practitioner certifying that the Helper is unfit for further service, the Employer may, subject to the statutory provisions of the relevant Ordinances, terminate the employment and shall immediately take steps to repatriate the Helper to his/her* place of origin in accordance with Clause 7.

10. Either party may terminate this contract by giving one month's notice in writing or one month's wages in lieu of notice.

11. Notwithstanding Clause 10, either party may in writing terminate this contract without notice or payment in lieu in the circumstances permitted by the Employment Ordinance, Chapter 57.

12. In the event of termination of this contract, both the Employer and the Helper shall give the Director of Immigration notice in writing within seven days of the date of termination. A copy of the other party's written acknowledgement of the termination shall also be forwarded to the Director of Immigration.

13. Should both parties agree to enter into new contract upon expiry of the existing contract, the Helper shall, before any such further period commences and at the expense of the Employer, return to his/her* place of origin for a paid/unpaid* vacation of not less than seven days, unless prior approval for extension of stay in Hong Kong is given by the Director of Immigration.

14. In the event of the death of the Helper, the Employer shall pay the cost of transporting the Helper's remains and personal property from Hong Kong to his/her* place of origin.

15. Save for the following variations, any variation of addition to the terms of this contract (including the annexed Schedule of Accommodation and Domestic Duties) during its duration shall be void unless made with the prior consent of the Commissioner for Labour in Hong Kong:
    (a) a variation of the period of employment stated in Clause 2 through an extension of the said period of not more than three months by mutual agreement and with prior approval obtained from the Director of Immigration;

(b) a variation of the Employer's residential address stated in Clause 3 upon notification in writing being given to the Director of Immigration;

(c) a variation in the Schedule of Accommodation and Domestic Duties made in such manner as prescribed under item 6 of the Schedule of Accommodation and Domestic Duties.

16. The above terms do not preclude the Helper from other entitlements under the Employment Ordinance, Chapter 57, the Employees' Compensation Ordinance, Chapter 282 and any other relevant Ordinances.

The Parties hereby declare that the Helper has been medically examined as to his/her* fitness for employment as a domestic helper and his/her* medical certificate has been produced for inspection by the Employer.

Signed by the Employer_____

(Signature of Employer)

in the presence of _____   _____

(Name of Witness)   (Signature of Witness)

Signed by the Helper_____

(Signature of the Helper)

in the presence of _____   _____

(Name of Witness)   (Signature of Witness)

* Delete where inappropriate

† Use either Clause 2A, 2B or 2C whichever is appropriate.

SCHEDULE OF ACCOMMODATION AND DOMESTIC DUTIES

1. Both the Employer and the Helper should sign to acknowledge that they have read and agreed to the contents of this Schedule, and to confirm their consent for the Immigration Department and other relevant government authorities to collect and use the information contained in this Schedule in accordance with the provisions of the Personal Data (Privacy) Ordinance.

2. Employer's residence and number of persons to be served
   a.   Approximate size of flat/house.................... square feet/square metres*
   b.   State below the number of persons in the household to be served on a regular basis:
   ... adults ... minors (aged between 5 to 18)
   ...minors (aged below 5) ... expecting babies,
   ... persons in the household requiring constant care of attention (excluding infants).
   (Note: Number of Helpers currently employed by the Employer to serve the household...)

3. Accommodation and facilities to be provided to the Helper
   a.   Accommodation to the Helper
   While the average flat size in Hong Kong is relatively small and the availability of separate servant room is not common, the Employer should provide accommodation with reasonable privacy. Examples of unsuitable accommodation are: The Helper having to sleep on made-do beds in the corridor with little privacy and sharing a room with an adult of opposite sex.
   [ ]   Yes. Estimated size of the servant room .... square feet/square metres*

[ ]   No. Sleeping arrangement for the Helper:
    [ ] Share a room with......child/children aged......
    [ ] Separate partitioned area of.... square feet/square metres*
    [ ] Others. Please describe...
    ....

b.   Facilities to be provided to the Helper:

(Note: Application for entry visa will normally not be approved if the essential facilities from item (a) to (f) are not provided free)

(a) Light and water supply	[ ] Yes	[ ] No
(b) Toilet and bathing facilities	[ ] Yes	[ ] No
(c) Bed	[ ] Yes	[ ] No
(d) Blankets or quilt	[ ] Yes	[ ] No
(e) Pillows	[ ] Yes	[ ] No
(f) Wardrobe	[ ] Yes	[ ] No
(g) Refrigerator	[ ] Yes	[ ] No
(h) Desk	[ ] Yes	[ ] No
(i) Other facilities (Please specify)	_____	

4. The Helper should only perform domestic duties at the Employer's residence. Domestic duties to be performed by the Helper under this contract exclude driving of a motor vehicle of any description for whatever purposes, whether or not the vehicle belongs to the Employer.

5. Domestic duties include the duties listed below
    Major portion of domestic duties:
    1.   Household chores
    2.   Cooking
    3.   Looking after aged persons in the household (constant care or attention is required/not required*)
    4.   Baby-sitting
    5.   Child-minding
    6.   Others (please specify)...
          ....

6. The Employer shall inform the Helper and the Director of Immigration of any substantial changes in item 2,3 and 5 by serving a copy of the Revised Schedule of Accommodation and Domestic Duties (ID 407G) signed by both the Employer and the Helper to the Director of Immigration for record.

_____   _____

Employer's name and signature   Date

_____   _____

Helper's name and signature   Date

* Delete where inappropriate
[ ] tick as appropriate

APPENDIX 2
EMPLOYMENT ORDINANCE, CHAPTER 57

The Employment Ordinance is the main piece of legislation governing conditions of employment in Hong Kong. Since its enactment in 1968, the benefits provided for under the Ordinance have been substantially improved. It now covers a comprehensive range of employment protection and benefits for employees including:

- Wage Protection
- Rest Days
- Holidays with Pay
- Paid Annual Leave
- Sickness Allowance
- Maternity Protection
- Severance Payment
- Long Service Payment
- Employment Protection
- Termination of Employment Contract
- Protection Against Anti-Union Discrimination

EMPLOYMENT AGENCY REGULATIONS

The Employment Agency Regulations made under the Employment Ordinance regulate the operation of employment agencies in Hong Kong.

The major provisions of the Regulations are:

- Every employment agency is required to apply for a licence from the Labour Department before undertaking any job placement business.
- An application for the issue of a licence must be made to the Commissioner for Labour in the prescribed form at least one month before the commencement of business.
- A licence is valid for 12 months from the date of issue and application for renewal has to be made not later than two months before its expiry.
- The maximum commission which may be received by an employment agency from a job-seeker should not exceed 10% of the job-seeker's first month's wages he received after he has been successfully placed in a job.
- Any agency failing to comply with the requirements of the law is liable to prosecution and revocation of licence.

EMPLOYMENT OF CHILDREN REGULATIONS

The Employment of Children Regulations made under the Employment Ordinance govern the employment of children in all economic sectors. A child means a person under the age of 15 years. Major provisions of the Regulations are:

- Children aged under 15 are prohibited from working in all industrial undertakings.
- Children aged 13 and 14 may be employed in non-industrial establishments, subject to the condition that they attend full-time schooling if they have not yet completed Form III of secondary education and to other conditions which aim at protecting their safety, health and welfare.
- Children aged under 13 are prohibited from taking up employment. However, for the purposes of art and training, the Commissioner for Labour may grant special permission for children to be employed as entertainers, subject to certain stringent conditions as the Commissioner may specify.

EMPLOYMENT OF YOUNG PERSONS (INDUSTRY) REGULATIONS

Employment of Young Persons (Industry) Regulations made under the Employment Ordinance regulate the hours of work and the general conditions of employment of young persons in industrial undertakings. A young person means a person of or over the age of 15 years but under the age of 18 years. Major provisions of the Regulations are:

- Working time restrictions for young persons employed in industrial undertakings:

Maximum working hours and working days	
Working hours a day	8 hours (between 7 a.m. and 7 p.m. only)
Working hours a week	48 hours
Working days a week	6 days
Maximum period of continuous work	5 hours followed by an interval of not less than half an hour for meal or rest

- A notice specifying the working hours and rest day arrangement of the young persons and vetted by the Labour Department should be posted up in a conspicuous place in the workplace
- Change of permissible working hours and rest days is not allowed unless prior notice has been served on the Commissioner for Labour 48 hours before the proposed change
- Overtime employment, night work and working on rest days and statutory holidays are prohibited
- Underground work in mines and quarries or in industrial undertakings involving tunnelling operations, and carrying loads unreasonably heavy for the young person's age and physical development are prohibited
- Employment of young persons in any dangerous trade is prohibited

[Source: Labour Department, The Government of Hong Kong Special Administrative Region, Labour Legislation, Overview of Major Labour Legislation) Review: 29/3/2005]

APPENDIX 3
EMPLOYEES' COMPENSATION ORDINANCE, CHAPTER 282

The Employees' Compensation Ordinance establishes a no-fault, non-contributory employee compensation system for work injuries. Major provisions of the Ordinance are:

Application
An employer is liable to pay compensation in respect of injuries sustained by his employees as a result of an accident arising out of and in the course of employment; or in respect of occupational diseases specified in the Ordinance suffered by the employees.

The Ordinance in general applies to employees who are employed under a contract of service or apprenticeship. Employees who are injured while working outside Hong Kong are also covered if they are employed in Hong Kong by local employers.

Assessment of Loss of Earning Capacity
A two-tier system - Employees' Compensation (Ordinary Assessment) Board and Employees' Compensation (Special Assessment) Board - is provided to assess the necessary period of absence from duty and the percentage of loss of earning capacity permanently caused to the employee as a result of the work injury.

Major Compensation Items
Compensation in fatal cases

Age of deceased employee	Amount of compensation
under 40	84 months* earnings or HK$303,000 whichever is higher
40 to under 56	60 months* earnings or HK$303,000 whichever is higher
56 or above	36 months* earnings or HK$303,000 whichever is higher

*   Monthly earnings is subject to a maximum of HK$21,000 for the purpose of calculating compensation in fatal cases.

Funeral and medical attendance expenses in fatal cases

Any person who has paid funeral of and/or medical attendance expenses on an employee who died in a work-related accident is entitled to claim reimbursement from the employer of the deceased employee of such expenses not exceeding $35,000.

(This is only applicable to accidents happened on or after 1 August 2000.)

Compensation in cases of permanent total incapacity

Age of injured employee	Amount of compensation
under 40	96 months* earnings or HK$344,000 whichever is higher
40 to under 56	72 months* earnings or HK$344,000 whichever is higher
56 or above	48 months* earnings or HK$344,000 whichever is higher

*   Monthly earnings is subject to a maximum of HK$21,000 for the purpose of calculating compensation in permanent incapacity.

Periodical Payment

An employee is entitled to receive periodical payments during the period of temporary incapacity (sick leave) up to 24 months. The payment should be calculated as follows:

$$\left(\text{Monthly earnings at the time of the accident} - \text{Monthly earnings after the accident} \right) \times 4/5$$

If the employee's temporary incapacity lasts more than 24 months, he may apply to the Court for an extension of his entitlement for the payment. The extended period shall not be longer than 12 months.

Medical Expenses
An employer is liable to pay the medical expenses for medical treatment which his injured employees receive, subject to a daily maximum as follows:
either in-patient treatment or out-patient treatment: $200;
both in-patient and out-patient treatment on the same day: $280

Settlement of Claims
Depending on the nature of the case, a claim for employees' compensation can be settled in the following ways:
Direct Payment
Direct Settlement
Settlement by Certificate
Settlement by Court

Compulsory Insurance
An employer must be in possession of a valid insurance policy to cover his liabilities both under the Employees' Compensation Ordinance and at common law for the work injuries for his employees.

[Source: Labour Department, The Government of Hong Kong Special Administrative Region, Labour Legislation, Overview of Major Labour Legislation)   Review: 27/7/2005]

APPENDIX 4

The following is a sample agreement for the Employer and Domestic Worker in **Singapore** *(as suggested and laid out, by Chew Kim Whatt in his book* Foreign Maids, The Complete Handbook for Employers and Maid Agencies*):*

This AGREEMENT is made this day _____ between _____, NRIC/passport number _____ of _____, of Singapore _____ (hereinafter called the 'Employer' of the first part and _____, passport number _____ (hereinafter called the 'Domestic Worker' of the other part).

NOW IT IS HEREBY AGREED AND DECLARED AS FOLLOWS:

1. **NATURE OF WORK, REST, TRAINING AND ACCOMMODATION:** The employee shall be employed as a Domestic Worker and her major duties and responsibilities shall include all aspects of housekeeping, babysitting, taking care of children and household chores including sweeping, cooking, washing of clothes, the general cleaning of the entire house, as scheduled by the Employer in the appendix.

    1.1. As the Domestic Worker is new, the Employer will give her time to adjust and learn and will train her to meet the Employer's expectations. The Employer shall ensure that the Domestic Worker has adequate rest hours at night and breaks during the day.

    1.2. The Employer must provide minimum welfare benefits for

the Domestic Worker including free meals and comfortable accommodation.

1.3   The Domestic Worker agrees that there is one day off per week to be scheduled by the Employer.

2.   **DURATION OF EMPLOYMENT**: The Domestic Worker shall serve for the duration of two years, from _____ to _____, as stipulated in the Singapore Government Ministry of Manpower work permit card.

3.   **SALARY**: The Domestic Worker shall be paid a salary of S$_____ per month at the end of each calendar month. The salary shall be paid in cash or into a bank account.

4.   **SALARY INCREMENT**: Annual increment to the salary shall be made on the anniversary date. The amount is at the discretion of the Employer and based strictly on performance.

5.   **SALARY DEDUCTIONS**: There will be six months' salary deduction of S$_____ per month from the Domestic Worker for the recovery of loans.

6.   **REPATRIATION**: The Employer shall repatriate the Domestic Worker to her country of origin in the event that the Domestic Worker prematurely terminates/breaches this agreement or her services are terminated by the Employer for negligence in the performance of her duties. The cost of the air ticket to _____ shall be borne by the defaulting party.

7.   **MEDICAL EXAMINATIONS**: The Domestic Worker shall be rquired to pass a full medical examination conducted by an appointed doctor upon her arrival in Singapore and shall be employed subject to her passsing the medical examination. She shall be required to pass a medical examination at six-monthly intervals thereafter.

8. **MEDICAL BENEFITS**: The Domestic Worker shall be allowed to consult a doctor and shall be provided with reasonable free medical treatment and medicines as recommended by the Employer's appointed doctor or any recognised medical practitioner.

   8.1. The Employer must ensure that the Domestic Worker has adequate rest during her illness.

   8.2. The Employer shall pay for medical expenses incurred by the Domestic Worker for all compulsory six-monthly medical examinations.

   8.3. The Employer shall cover the Domestic Worker under a personal accident insurance of not more than S$10,000.00 for the duration of her employment.

9. **TERMINATION OF EMPLOYMENT**: The Domestic Worker's employment may be terminated without any reasons assigned thereof as follows:

   9.1. By either party giving one week's notice in writing or verbally.

   9.2. No notice is required from the Employer in the case of the Domestic Worker's gross misconduct, indiscipline, insubordination, pregnancy confirmed by a medical test, or negligence in carrying out her duties and responsibilities.

   9.3. No notice is required from the Domestic Worker on the grounds of physical abuse or threats by the Employer.

10. **RESTRICTIONS**: The Domestic Worker shall not be allowed to change employment or work for any other party during her employment with the Employer. The Domestic Worker shall not be allowed to marry a Singapore citizen or permanent resident while working in Singapore.

11. **REPATRIATION UPON COMPLETION OF CONTRACT**: Upon completion of the contract, the Employer shall bear the cost of repatriating the Domestic Worker to her country of origin. In the event that the Domestic Worker initiates the termination of contract, she shall bear her own repatriation costs.

12. **DISPUTE SETTLEMENT**: Both parties must first try to resolve any dispute themselves, failing which the assistance of the agent of the Ministry of Manpower and finally, the Embassy may be sought to settle the dispute amicably.

13. **UNDERTAKING BY DOMESTIC WORKER**: The Domestic Worker hereby gives her undertaking willingly that she shall abide by the following rules and regulations during her employment in Singapore.

    13.1. That her presence in Singapore is strictly for the purpose of employment as a Domestic Worker.
    13.2. That she shall not indulge or be involved in any illegal or immoral activity during her stay in Singapore.
    13.3. That she shall not cohabit or marry a Singapore citizen or permanent resident.
    13.4. That she agrees to be medically examined by a doctor as and when required.
    13.5. That she shall pay her own return passage to her country of origin should she decide to return home under any circumstances before completion of her contract of employment. In the event that she does not have the necessary funds to pay for her passage home, she must work with the Employer until she has earned sufficient money to pay for the return passage.
    13.6. That upon the termination of her employment under any circumstances, she shall return to her country of origin immediately after cancellation of her work permit and visit pass by the Employer.

I,_____, passport number _____, hereby offer employment according to the above terms and conditions.

_____

Signature of Employer/ Date

Employer's Name: _____

I, _____, passport number_____, fully understand the contents of this agreement and hereby accept the offer of employment.

_____

Signature of Domestic Worker/Date

Domestic Worker's Name: _____

_____

Signature of Witness/Date

Witness's Name: _____

FOR FURTHER READING

Asia Pacific Mission for Migrants (year unknown), 'Perkembangan historis dan politik pemerintah dalam buruh migran Indonesia'

Chew Kim Whatt (2004) *Foreign maids, The complete handbook for employers and maid agencies*, SNP Editions, Singapore

Huang, Shirlena., Brenda S.A. Yeoh and Abdul Rahman, eds. (2005) *Asian Women as Transnational Domestic Workers*. Marshall Cavendish Academic, Singapore

Hull, Terence H, ed. (2005) *People, Population, and Policy in Indonesia*, Equinox Publishing, Jakarta

Kaur, A. (2004) *Wage Labour in Southeast Asia since 1840's: Globalization, the International Division of Labour and Labour Transformations*, Palgrave Macmillan, Basingstoke

— (2004) *Women Workers in Industrialising Asia: Costed, Not Valued*, Palgrave Macmillan, Basingstoke.

— (2004) 'Crossing Borders: Race, Migration and Borders in Southeast Asia'. In International Journal on Multicultural Societies (IJMS), Vol 6. No. 2 (December): 111-132; Special issue—Guest editors --Christine Inglis and Matthias Koenig 'Managing Migration and Diversity in the Asia Pacific Region and Europe'

— (2004) 'Mobility, Labour Mobilisation and Border Controls: Indonesian Labour Migration to Malaysia Since 1900'. Paper presented to the 15th Biennial Conference of the Asian Studies Association of Australia, Canberra, 29 June to 2 July 2004.

Rosenberg, Ruth, ed. (2003) *Trafficking of Women and Children in Indonesia*, ICMC & Solidarity Center, Geneva

INDEX

also from EQUINOX PUBLISHING

THE PEPPER TRADER:
True Tales of the German
East Asia Squadron and
the Man who Cast them
in Stone
Geoffrey Bennett
979-3780-26-6
2006, softcover, 392 pages

**SRIRO'S DESK REFERENCE
OF INDONESIAN LAW 2006**
Andrew I. Sriro
979-3780-20-7
2006, softcover, 592 pages

THE SECOND FRONT:
Inside Asia's Most Dangerous
Terrorist Network
Ken Conboy
979-3780-09-6
2006, softcover, 256 pages

WARS WITHIN:
The Story of *TEMPO*,
an Independent Magazine in
Soeharto's Indonesia
Janet Steele
979-3780-08-8
2005, softcover, 368 pages

SIDELINES:
Thought Pieces from
TEMPO Magazine
Goenawan Mohamad
979-3780-07-X
2005, softcover, 260 pages

AN ENDLESS JOURNEY:
Reflections of an
Indonesian Journalist
Herawati Diah
979-3780-06-1
2005, softcover, 304 pages

BULE GILA:
Tales of a Dutch Barman
in Jakarta
Bartele Santema
979-3780-04-5
2005, softcover, 160 pages

THE INVISIBLE PALACE:
The True Story of a
Journalist's Murder in Java
José Manuel Tesoro
979-97964-7-4
2004, softcover, 328 pages

**INTEL: Inside Indonesia's
Intelligence Service**
Ken Conboy
979-97964-4-X
2004, softcover, 264 pages

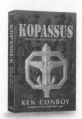

**KOPASSUS: Inside Indonesia's
Special Forces**
Ken Conboy
979-95898-8-6
2003, softcover, 352 pages

TIMOR: A Nation Reborn
Bill Nicol
979-95898-6-X
2002, softcover, 352 pages

GUS DUR:
The Authorized Biography of
Abdurrahman Wahid
Greg Barton
979-95898-5-1
2002, softcover, 436 pages

**NO REGRETS: Reflections
of a Presidential Spokesman**
Wimar Witoelar
979-95898-4-3
2002, softcover, 200 pages

ELLIPSIS
Laksmi Pamuntjak
979-3780-30-4
2006, softcover, 98 pages

SAMAN
Ayu Utami
979-3780-11-8
2005, softcover, 184 pages

THE SPICE GARDEN
Michael Vatikiotis
979-97964-2-3
2004, softcover, 256 pages

PT EQUINOX PUBLISHING INDONESIA

Menara Gracia, 6th floor • Jl. H.R. Rasuna Said Kav C-17 • Jakarta 12940 - Indonesia
T : +62 21 522 0875 • F : +62 21 522 0877 • E : info@equinoxpublishing.com • www.equinoxpublishing.com

THE KING, THE WITCH AND THE PRIEST
Pramoedya Ananta Toer
979-95898-3-5
2001, softcover, 128 pages

IT'S NOT AN ALL NIGHT FAIR
Pramoedya Ananta Toer
979-95898-2-7
2001, softcover, 120 pages

TALES FROM DJAKARTA
Pramoedya Ananta Toer
979-95898-1-9
2000, softcover, 288 pages

ILLUSTRATED

**MADE IN INDONESIA:
A Tribute to the Country's Craftspeople**
Warwick Purser
979-3780-13-4
2005, hardcover, 160 pages

BANGKOK INSIDE OUT
Daniel Ziv & Guy Sharett
979-97964-6-6
2005, softcover, 176 pages

A CUP OF JAVA
Gabriella Teggia & Mark Hanusz
979-95898-9-4
2003, softcover, 144 pages

JAKARTA INSIDE OUT
Daniel Ziv
979-95898-7-8
2002, softcover, 184 pages

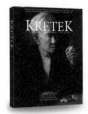

**KRETEK:
The Culture and Heritage of Indonesia's Clove Cigarettes**
Mark Hanusz
979-95898-0-0
2000, hardcover, 224 pages

ACADEMIC

SOCIAL SCIENCE AND POWER IN INDONESIA
Vedi R. Hadiz & Daniel Dhakidae
979-3780-01-0
2005, hardcover, 304 pages

PEOPLE, POPULATION, AND POLICY IN INDONESIA
Terence H. Hull
979-3780-02-9
2005, hardcover, 208 pages

COMMISSIONED

**TWENTY YEARS OF WELCOMING THE WORLD
Meliá Bali Villas & Spa Resort**
2005, hardcover, 160 pages

**CELEBRATING INDONESIA:
Fifty Years with the Ford Foundation 1953-2003**
Goenawan Mohamad
979-97964-1-5
2004, hardcover, 240 pages

CLASSIC INDONESIA

**INDONESIAN COMMUNISM UNDER SUKARNO:
Ideology and Politics 1959-1965**
Rex Mortimer
979-3780-29-0 (sc)
979-3780-27-4 (hc)
2006, softcover & hardcover, 464 pages

**JAVA IN A TIME OF REVOLUTION:
Occupation and Resistance 1944-1946**
Benedict R.O'G. Anderson
979-3780-14-2
2006, softcover, 516 pages

TRAVEL

THE NATURAL GUIDE TO BALI
Anne Gouyon
979-3780-00-2
2005, softcover, 448 pages